AF378624

PERFORMANCE SALOONS

HAMLYN
London
New York
Sydney
Toronto

PERFORMANCE SALOONS

Julian McNamara

CONTENTS

Published by the
Hamlyn Publishing Group Limited
Bridge House, Twickenham
Middlesex, England

Designer: Nicholas David Harris
Production consultant: ALMAC (Book Production Services) Ltd.

Filmset by: Colset Private Ltd, Singapore
Reproduction by: Anglia Reproductions, Witham, Essex.
Printed in Italy.

ISBN 0 600 50103 5

This book was designed and produced by Campbell Rawkins Limited, 2 Barbon Close, London, WC1.

Copyright © 1985 Campbell Rawkins
All rights reserved. No part of this publication may be reproduced, stored in a retrieval system, or transmitted in any form or by any means, electronic, mechanical, photocopying, recording or otherwise, without the permission of the Hamlyn Publishing Group Limited and the copyright holder.

1 An urge for performance

The urge to wring extra performance from standard saloon cars is a phenomenon almost as old as the motor car itself. The great names of motoring, names such as Bugatti, Porsche, Lancia and Rolls Royce, all in one way or another built their reputations by offering above average performance to the motoring enthusiasts of their early days. Indeed, it is doubtful if the Rolls Royce company would have got off the ground unless Sir Henry Royce had brought his engineering abilities to bear on improving the performance of the little two cylinder Decauville he had bought to take his mind off his electrical engineering business.

Indeed the early road races were dominated by cars which were little more than a standard production chassis with an enlarged engine and the smallest, lightest body that the regulations would allow. As the races became more specialised so the major companies turned to producing specially tuned versions of standard cars for events such as the Alpine Trials and the Prince Henry Trials. These trials became as prestigious in their time as international rallying has become in ours. Lasting over several days and taking in all kinds of terrain, these trials assured the winner of international publicity plus the patronage of the arbiters of automotive taste, the royalty and nobility of the day.

Just as motoring itself was much much a privilege of the wealthy in those days before the First World War so was motor sport. So exclusively did the sporting elite regard

themselves that when the pragmatic Mercedes company sought to enter a team of five 90 hp cars in the Gordon Bennett trophy of 1903 driven by factory test drivers and mechanics, the German Automobile Club overruled them insisting that Germany be represented by gentlemen. To capture this upper class sporting market almost every manufacturer from Austro-Daimler to Vauxhall maintained at least one model in their range named after some trial. Even Rolls Royce were not above this practice for, having won the RAC Tourist Trophy in 1906 and shown well in the Alpine Trials, both a TT model and the famous 'Alpine Eagle' appeared in their catalogue aimed firmly at this sector of the market.

The coming of mass production and the First World War ended this golden age. The motor car became the normal mode of transport for almost the whole of the American working population and spread down to the lower middle classes in Europe before the great depression of the late twenties. At first the great drive was to motorise everyone. Companies such as Ford, General Motors, Austin and Citroën mushroomed as they brought out cars for the war rich and the returning war weary.

The philosophy was simple. Give the people wheels and to hell with sophistication. A side valve engine was easy to build in large numbers, so also were pressed steel bodies and semi-elliptic springs. To someone who less than a decade before had never dreamed of owning more than a bicycle, cars built on these principles were more than acceptable.

The Citroën Cloverleaf and the Austin Seven, for all their charm, had cramped accommodation, appalling suspension and maximum speeds in the forty miles per hour bracket. The Model T Ford started life with two foot-changed gears and a choice of one colour. Heaters were non-existent, windscreen wipers were frequently a hand operated extra and front wheel brakes were considered an expensive and unnecessary complication, yet the cars sold. They offered convenience and the freedom of the roads. Moreover they allowed the levelling of class barriers and gave the socially ambitious a means of emulating the wealthy. They also disseminated mechanical education through a generation among whom were certain enthusiasts dying to apply their new found skills to wringing extra speed out of whatever was to hand.

Almost as soon as Herbert Austin's people's car appeared in 1922, owners discov-

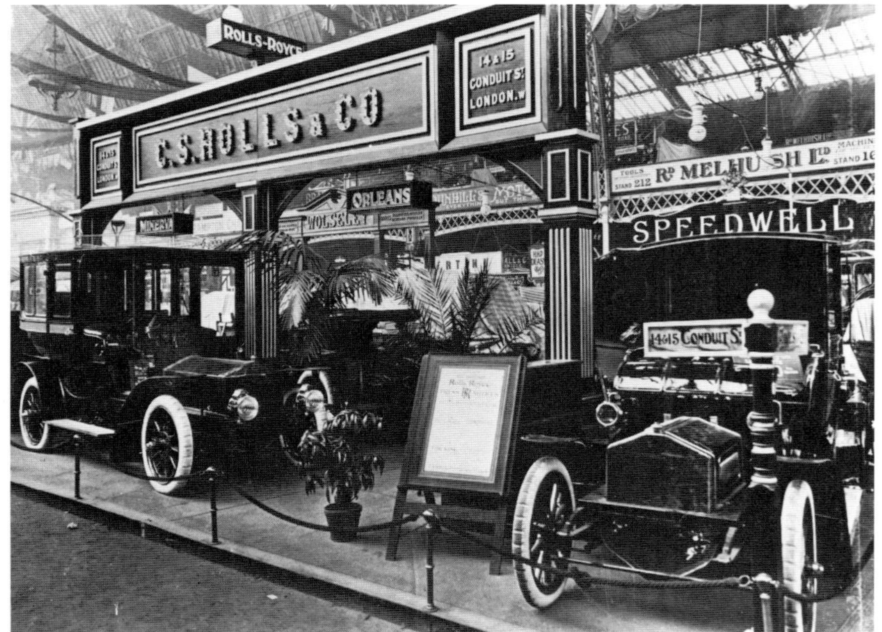

The Rolls-Royce stand at the 1905 Olympia Motor Show. Royce's engineering skill produced a car, the power and silence of which no contemporary competitor could match

ered that by advancing the timing slightly the speed was increased and by removing the bulky steel body and clothing the engine and chassis in aluminium, a reasonable power to weight ratio could be achieved. For those who already raced motorcycles the maintenance of the new baby cars was small problem especially in comparison to the often atrocious cycle cars which had been the only reasonably priced alternative to the motorcycle before the Austin Seven. The man in the street had found a way into motor sport.

Soon the 750cc class was the most heavily subscribed in any form of motor sport whether it was hill climbs, cross country trials or circuit racing. This success reflected well on the Austin company whose previous attempt to create a racing image had foundered dismally at the 1908 French Grand Prix. Specialist coachbuilders began to create stylish bodies for the little car and production was licensed worldwide. Austin themselves made attempts to capitalise on the racing success of the Seven — they offered a replica of the factory's Ulster TT team cars in detuned form unsurprisingly called the Ulster, but it was as the basis for slightly tuned, rakish looking confections from people such as Avon and Swallow Sidecars that they really found a way into the performance saloon bracket although 'performance' was still only seen very much in comparison with the standard product.

If mass production and cut price enthusiast motor sport were good news for Herbert Austin, the inability to adapt to them caused problems for a multitude of other car manufacturers. Throughout Europe and the USA, companies who had built small batches of cars before the First World War and commenced trading again in 1918/19 with the old production techniques, found themselves under pressure.

Only two factors seemed to influence the buyers of the 1920s; the first was price and the second prestige. Just as the pre-war trials had influenced the upper middle class, so they now looked towards the speed trials and Grand Prix type racing for their inspiration. Although Rolls Royce had long since abandoned active motor sport the immediate post-war years saw their only really serious European competitor Hispano-Suiza involved in all types of motor sport from hill climbs to the Boulogne Speed Trials of the early twenties.

These trials were a continuation of the pre-war festivals which had caused Emile Jellinek to demand faster and faster cars from the Cannstadt-Daimler company which had eventually led to the creation of the 1901 Mercedes. In Jellinek's day the premier event had been the Nice Speed Week and, as a Nice resident and the Daimler agent for most central European territories, Jellinek had been keen for his car, named after his ten-year-old daughter, to show well. The Hispano-Suiza company was determined to monopolise the post-war Boulogne Trials in the way in which Mercedes had dominated Nice and a fabulous line of machines from $4\frac{1}{2}$ to 8 litres duly stunned the assembled crowds. The 8 litre model in particular was almost universally known as the Boulogne whether or not it carried the lightweight bodywork so designated by the factory.

During the war the Sunbeam company had built a line of V12 aero engines and with the coming of peace utilised the expertise it had gained in doing so to begin a programme of world land speed record cars. At the same time they produced a series of Grand Prix cars, the most successful of which were the heavily Fiat-influenced cars of 1923. To capitalise on the sporting reputation these superb cars gave them, the company introduced a range of mechanically sophisticated ohv and twin ohc engine sports cars and tourers which, for the duration of the twenties, gave them a solid foothold in the performance market.

Ettore Bugatti had begun building neat and mechanically advanced small cars in his Molsheim factory in 1910. The 2 litre formula for Grand Prix racing which

A Bugatti Brescia shows its paces at the 1923 Amersham Hill Climb

replaced the internationally recognised 3 litre formula in 1922 suited his products extremely well as did the international 1½ litre voiturette class. Indeed, the first of his products to really make an impression internationally was the 1496cc Type 13. A team of these cars taken directly from the production line dominated the Brescia Coupe des Voiturettes in 1921 and established Brescia as the model name. These cars were four seaters as demanded by the racing regulations of the time for even Bugatti's road going cars offered extremely rapid performance, their 62 mph top speed being thought more than reasonable for any 1500cc in those days. Later in the decade Bugatti was to build a fine line of both straight eights and fours with two, three and four valves per cylinder which delighted motorists then and still retain a loyal following.

Perhaps foremost among Bugatti's rivals in the light, high performance market in France were Delage and Talbot-Darracq. The former ran his company into near bankruptcy in the early years of the depression by over spending a fortune on the development of the 1½ litre Grand Prix cars. However, he did have the satisfaction of watching his cars win every major European Grand Prix in 1927.

Talbot had produced a fine car in the guise of the 25/50 of 1912. It continued slightly modified after the the First World

Below: Prince Henry Vauxhall — last of the sporting Vauxhalls until the 1970s

War until the amalgamation with the Darracq concern in 1920. Subsequently both companies came under the control of Sunbeam. Darracq also built a team of extremely fast cars for the 1½ litre formula but had difficulty keeping them in one piece over race distance.

Without doubt the most beautiful and eccentric performance cars to emerge from France in these first post-war years were those of Gabriel Voisin. Although Voisin chose to persevere with the sleeve valve when almost every other world manufacturer had dropped it, his cars often showed a fine turn of speed. They were also extremely well built for Voisin had been a pre-eminent early aviator who had already lost one fortune building racing aircraft far in advance of their time, in the years immediately before the war. Like Delage he also entered cars under the 1½ litre Grand Prix formula but unlike Delage he managed to retain his company and keep it in sound running order. In the early thirties he was to amaze the racing world with the first ever front wheel drive V12 racing cars.

Of smaller car builders in Great Britain several worthy names gained prominence in the immediate post-war years. In 1918 Lionel Martin with an engineer named Bamford built the first ever Aston Martin. With engines of 1100 and 1500cc these cars were the light and nimble progenitors of a mighty line. The name derived from the Aston Clinton hill climb venue, Lionel Martin's favourite event. In 1924 one of these cars was to lend its chassis to one of the most advanced racing ventures of its day when one Major Frank Halford fitted the first viable turbocharged 1½ litre engine and renamed the car the Halford Special.

Although by today's standards these first Aston Martins would be classed as sports racing cars, an anomaly in the Le Mans rules dictated that all cars running there must be full four seaters. This effectively meant that any manufacturer coveting this most prized of trophies must perforce be prepared to equip his cars with a light four seat tonneau body. Only Grand Prix racing and the sort of chummy club and very amateur handicap races at Brooklands really merited a stripped two seater. Indeed until 1924 even Grand Prix cars still carried riding mechanics, brave lunatics who pumped Castrol R through plunger valves and often suffered serious injury as the pathetically inadequate tyres of the time threw the cars from the road.

Other small performance car builders in the UK included Alvis and Riley whilst the honorable Wolseley company who had already built up a solid reputation with their pre-war tourers were beginning to examine the performance model with some idea of capturing the market on quality rather than price.

Just as Sunbeam had established a reputation as suppliers of five sporting cars before the war, so too had Vauxhall with the Prince Henry model. Like Sunbeam they slipped easily back into this market at the close of hostilities with the 30/98. This magnificent 4525cc car produced almost 100 bhp at 3000 rpm from a side valve engine. It was flexible and vice free but most of all it offered built-in reliability, a very rare commodity in the early post-war days.

The 30/98 had become available in 1914, a development of the Prince Henry Vauxhall which had distinguished itself in the 1910 Prince Henry Trials. In detuned form it had been a well respected staff car for British staff officers and its post-war years were to give it cult status. Just why it bore the nomenclature 30/98 is a matter for conjecture but it was widely held that its designer, Laurence Pomeroy, was either gently mocking the pretentiousness of the 39/90 Mercedes or had decided to emulate it, in the process demonstrating that his machine had a higher top end power output, the latter figure in both cases being the available bhp. In 1922 realising the need for extra performance the car was fitted with an overhead valve engine of 4224cc and became the OE model. Unfortunately the takeover by General Motors of Vauxhall in 1925 sounded the death knell for these beautiful thoroughbreds; the last left the production line in 1927 and with it died all Vauxhall's genuine sporting pretensions until the 1970s.

Just as Hispano-Suiza, Rolls Royce, Benz, Austro-Daimler, Sunbeam, Fiat and Mercedes had successfully produced aircraft engines during the war, two aero engine manufacturers began automotive production at its end and both were to become first rank sporting names. In Germany the Bayerische Motoren Werke decided to get into motorcycle production and started development of the flat twin machine launched in 1923. In Britain, W.O. Bentley, after building the best rotary engine of the war, announced in 1919 that he was building an extremely advanced 3 litre motor car.

By the mid twenties the battle for the performance market was well established.

Far Left: The Halford Special joins the line up including Talbots, a Bugatti and an Alvis at a 1920s Brooklands meet. The Halford Special was the world's first turbocharged car

There had already been casualties in small numbers and triumphs on grand scales. In 1923 the twenty-four hours of Le Mans had begun and quickly became the premier road race of its day for touring cars. A win at Le Mans generally heralded a boom in sales be it in the index of performance which decided the overall winner, the overall race distance or the biennial Rudge Whitworth cup. At first all the cars were deemed to be road going tourers. They were driven to and from the circuit and at the race they were fully loaded with all the spare parts needed for the race and, with the fall of the flag, the first job of the driver was to fold the hood.

It was here that an ever more powerful team of Bentleys did battle with their lookalike French adversaries Lorraine-Dietrich for the overall honours, while Singers fought Rileys, Amilcars, Bugattis and the like in the intermediate classes leaving the eccentric index of performance category which computed capacity against time to finish largely to a host of long forgotten miniature French cars. Occasionally an Austin Seven derivative or one of their great rivals, Morris Garages (MG), would show well whilst both Frazer Nash and Aston Martin were to name road going replicas after successes in the 1500cc class in classic races.

These were the 'sports cars' of the twenties. They had to have four seats but most were available with beautiful coupé saloon bodies. Even Bentley supplied heavy town carriages on his 4½, 6 and 8 litre chassis as did Lorraine-Dietrich on their sport derived chassis. Bugatti too offered his sports cars with four seats and enclosed bodywork, doing well not only at Le Mans, but in all distance racing by the very weight of numbers of the private entrants.

Meanwhile the jazz age had awoken the American middle classes to the stylish world of the sports car. Companies such as Stutz with their Bearcats and Blackhawks vied with Duesenberg who had won the French Grand Prix in 1921. Auburn and Cord began to be recognised by discriminating motorists as pioneers in the design of fast roadsters and tourers. Packard genuinely represented quality equalling Hispano-Suiza and Rolls Royce while the mid twenties Cadillac provided powerful luxury at a price no European manufacturer could hope to match in terms of quality for money.

Alas the twenties were to slide into economic depression which would wipe out several of the major suppliers of sporting and luxury motor cars. Lanchester fell into the clutches of Daimler in 1931. Bentley's massive 8 litre cars could not avert financial disaster and the company was swallowed by Rolls Royce in the same year. Sunbeam-Talbot-Darracq, burdened by massive debts from tooling for new and technologically advanced models, tried desperately to survive in a world where fewer customers awaited each new model until with the recession over they became a bargain purchase for Lord Rootes.

In Germany with financial ruin stalking both companies, Mercedes (the original Cannstadt-Daimler Company) and Benz settled their differences and brought the two oldest names in the manufacture of motor cars into one group in 1927. Similarly the luxury car makers Horch amalgamated with Audi, Wanderer and DKW to form the Auto Union in 1932 in a move as much designed to pre-empt foreign purchase of any of the four as to rationalise to meet the straitened circumstances of the market.

In France the magnificent Citroën company was declared bankrupt and fell into the control of the Michelin family in 1934 just as the truly advanced and trend setting Traction Avant appeared to astonish the world. Delage gave up the fight and sold out to the Delahaye company in 1937 after the worst of the recession. Delahaye had traditionally built trucks but in the thirties, under the influence of two wealthy Franco-American racing enthusiasts, Laury and Lucy Schell, the owner of Delahaye, who rejoiced in the unlikely name of Charles Weiffenbach, was persuaded to build a superb line of grand tourers, sports and luxury cars culminating in both Formula One and long distance racing machinery.

Renault, who had maintained a superb record of wins in the major races prior to 1910 and had rallied successfully from 1925, felt the changing climate and in 1930 began the negotiations which were to lead the company into full state ownership after the Second World War.

In Italy Isotta Fraschini gave up the car market in 1927. Fiat gained control of OM and Itala, both companies with proud racing traditions dating from the turn of the century. Alfa Romeo's bank folded in 1926 and to survive this calamity the company had to sell one of its railway rolling stock factories, the underwriters of the car division. For a short while it looked as if the company which was then at the forefront of every major international racing formula would follow its bankers into liquidation. The fact that it did not rested solely on the reputation the products had gained in international competition for the export market was to prop up the company until Mussolini's government saved them with state orders for military aero engines.

In the USA Eliot Cord gained control of Duesenberg in 1926 and introduced their J series cars which would make the occasional visit as competitors to Le Mans. Cord also built cars under his own name and had taken control of Auburn just prior to the depression. Meanwhile Stutz cut its workforce and rode out the depression as best it could while other ailing firms became easy meat for the larger corporations to add to their production rolls. Dodge, who had dominated stock car racing in the twenties, were bought by Chrysler.

In Austria the Steyr company was taken over by Austro-Daimler in 1930. Ferdinand Porsche, who had recently joined the company from Mercedes having seen his position as head of design and development eroded by the influx of Benz staff, chose to leave and begin his own company in Stuttgart rather than rejoin Austro-Daimler for whom he had designed the Prince Henry cars and the highly successful line of Sacha 1½ litre sports cars in 1919.

While at Mercedes he had designed not only the company's Grand Prix cars but had given them the huge 500 series saloons and the 500S, SS, SSK and SSKL cars which kept them competitive in the market for large sports cars throughout the late twenties and into the mid thirties. His Parthian shot was the Steyr Austria. This was a magnificent straight eight engined car offering performance which even the best cars from Stuttgart would have been hard pressed to match.

The thirties were to redefine the image of the 'sports car'. Hitherto a sports car was almost anything which fitted into competition in one form or another. The majority of larger engined cars followed the pattern set by the Prince Henry Trials' cars in offering four seats. Weight was the only reason to neglect this configuration and fairly soon the specialist manufacturers, the Salmsons, Amilcars, Rileys and MGs, were beginning to realise that what had started as a means of reducing all up weight for serious competition was becoming a fad among the sporting car buyers. These well off young people actually wanted a car with only two seats and the bare minimum of weather protection.

As the depression cleared and men found themselves working again, their demands were once more for basic and simple cars, which was where the products of most manufacturers were suitably aimed. In a crass rationalisation Morris killed off the delightful small four and six cylinder overhead cam engines which he had acquired when he bought the Wolseley company, replacing them with mundane cooking machines with pushrod operated valves.

Unfortunately the Morris rationalisation rendered the 1936 T series of MG Midgets, which were to capture the hearts of thousands of motoring enthusiasts, rather agricultural. On the other hand it did mean that with only minimal work the engines could be kept in tune by any mildly skilled owner thus giving the car a far wider appeal than if a more sophisticated power plant had been used. By 1936 when the T type was introduced MG had already become the arbiter of sports car taste for the young Englishman.

From the first modified Morris Chummy, the company MG under Cecil Kimber, had managed to combine sporting flair with economy. His series of MG Midgets, Magnas and Magnettes fitted well into the motor sport of the period which was heavily influenced by haphazard handicapping methods which tended to favour smaller cars to the detriment of anyone who wanted to spend more in the hope of outright winning performance. Nonetheless it was MG who gave Britain her only real success in a major international event once the Bentley team had broken up in 1931 when a team of 1100cc MGK3 Magnettes took first and second in their class, plus the team prize in the 1933 Mille Miglia. Not until the magnificent Lagondas and the fine 1½ litre ERA voiturettes with their Riley based engines was Britain to have any real racing competition for the continental car makers.

1933, as well as giving Britain some hope for future overseas competition success, also saw the British sporting saloon line-up crowned by a new star — the first Rolls Royce-built Bentley, a stunningly attractive saloon with bodywork by Park Ward, dubbed by the advertising campaign 'The Silent Sports Car'.

This 3½ litre overhead valve machine was universally condemned by the purists and enthusiasts of the earlier Cricklewood-built cars of W.O. Bentley, mainly because of its silent and, in comparison to the overhead cam Bentley engines, only moderately powered engine. Be that as it may, the car's

1932 Swallow Austin 7. A luxury car in miniature from William Lyons' Swallow Sidecar stable

English style and French elan — W O Bentley offered a wide range of laundalette and saloon bodies on his cars right up to the magnificent '8's (**right**). Ettore Bugatti's son Jean was responsible for some of the most startling and stylish bodies to emerge from France in the 1920s (**below**)

looks, made a lasting and distinct impression on all the contemporary stylists and within months copies were pouring from every second rank performance manufacturer. Chief among them was one from Swallow Sidecars.

Swallow had moved to the larger engined chassis in 1920 to make the cars acceptable to the type of person they wanted to attract, which was the *nouveau riche* of the day. The first cars were almost a pastiche of the contemporary Magnette K salonettes yet Swallow's founder William Lyons' shrewd eye for style and flair for production economy made it a genuinely worthwhile contender in the sporting market. This was well in keeping with all Lyons' 'packages', for although the re-bodied Austin Seven had only come onto the market in 1927 it had stood the rigours of the depression well.

The stylish 'pen nib' paintwork and such niceties as a 'Lady's companion' built into the passenger cubby hole had added to the feeling that the Swallow Austin was a real luxury car in miniature. The theme had been carried intact through to a few Morris Oxfords and the stodgy but reliable Fiat 509A. Lyons had also offered a stylish body for the sports specification Swift of 1930 but the Swift company joined the mass of makers who disappeared in the last years of depression. Thus it was the so-called Standard Flying Nine which was to provide Lyons with the basis for what soon became rather aptly described as 'The Bentley of Wardour Street'*, although another Morris product, the Wolseley Hornet featuring the same 1100cc overhead cam engine which Cecil Kimber had so successfully used in his racing Magnas and Magnettes also featured in the Swallow catalogue. So successful was the Standard based Swallow that in May 1931 the 16 hp 'Ensign' chassis was utilised with ostensibly the same type of bodywork as the Nine. From the moment this car emerged, the link between Swallow and Standard which was to last right through until 1948 was assured.

In October 1931 the first SS had appeared. It utilised the 2054cc Standard side valve six cylinder engine which allowed a fair degree of tuning due to its stiff seven bearing crank. The gearbox was also a Standard unit but whereas Standard usually supplied this with a top gear ratio of 5·11:1 the SS adopted the optional 4·66:1 in the interests of less fussy high speed cruising. To improve the balance of the SS, Lyons set the engine some seven inches further back in the chassis than the equivalent Standard and

had managed to persuade Standard to modify their chassis allowing it to be underslung at the rear. The overall effect was a startlingly handsome motor car, the influence of MG and the Alvis Speed Twenty notwithstanding. The most interesting facet of the car, however, was that it sold for just £325 in saloon form.

This was at a time when the Morris Six based MG 18/80 saloon sold for £545 and the classic Lea Francis overhead cam six cylinder 'Ace Of Spades' for £495. True, both cars could match or exceed the SS on overall performance but Lyons had served notice of his intentions and with the introduction of the face-lifted cars in 1933 with their alloy heads and improved carburation the company could well claim to have provided the finest sporting value available in the United Kingdom at that time. The influence of the Bentley transformed the overall look of the cars as Lyons smoothed the lines and widened the radiator shell while reducing the windscreen height.

While the SS could honestly be described as imitative, Lyons' success in turn bred its own imitators. The New Avon Body Co built at their Warwick factory pretty Standard based sports cars designed by two talented brothers, Alan and Richard Jensen. These cars entered the market in 1930 and by 1934 the Jensen brothers had gathered enough confidence to start their own factory.

By and large the products of the Avon company were even cheaper than those of Swallow for they had no access to the modified chassis which as a Lyons design was supplied only to Swallow for the SS. The Avon tourer was sold for only £280 but their saloon cost exactly the same as the SS at £325. In 1935 they were offering a coupé with a dickey seat for £305 while the comparable SS was some £40 more expensive. By this time Lyons was beyond the point of worrying over competitors for the highly tuned SS sports four seater was selling well enough for him to consider taking a giant leap into limited mass production.

While Lyons was finding success in the sporting market another well known British manufacturer was fighting a losing battle to remain solvent. Just why the Triumph Car Company (as it was to become after its separation from the more famous motorcycle division in 1934) should have made such heavy weather of the thirties is open to debate. The company had started car production in 1923 with a side valve 832cc car which was aimed at the buyer who needed

*Wardour Street was then, as it still is, the capital of the British film industry. Old money resented this new, brash set ostensibly from outside the upper middle class establishment with whom the SS was extremely popular, especially in Jaguar form. In the 1950s the expression was revived for the Jaguar Mark VI.

more room and comfort than was available from the current Austin Seven. It was well engineered and reliable but lost out to its two major rivals in the British market, the Morris Minor and the Austin Seven, both in performance and price. Nonetheless Donald Healey, who was to become technical director of the company in 1933, managed to win his class in the 1930 Monte Carlo Rally driving one of these cars.

Triumph had pioneered hydraulic four wheel braking in the small car market as early as 1925 and all subsequent Triumph cars carried this feature. They were also to become the first manufacturers in the world to fit screen washers at the factory in 1935. The destroked 747cc Super Sports model of 1930 with a Cozette supercharger offered genuine 70 mph performance but at £250 it was almost thirty pounds more expensive than the equivalent MG Midget. The main markets for Triumph were the rough roads of Africa and Australia.

In an attempt to break out of the very competitive small car market the company decided to go up market and lure performance buyers with an equivalent range of cars to Riley. In 1923 the company introduced an interim model in the shape of the Super Nine. This broke with established Triumph procedure by using a bought in power plant, in this case the Coventry Climax 1081cc inlet over exhaust valve unit. The gearbox from the Seven was used offering four forward speeds and a sporting version named the Southern Cross model was available. These attractive little cars sold moderately well but they were to be only a prelude to the sporting cars which Healey was to develop under the managing directorship of Claude Holbrook after 1933.

The first of these were shown at that year's Olympia Motor Show. Billed as 'the car that is different', the Gloria brought the company into the sporting market and in its many different body options and engine sizes it was to soldier on until the company went into receivership in 1939. The cars were available with the four cylinder 1100cc Coventry Climax unit or the Gloria Six which boasted a four bearing six cylinder Coventry Climax unit of 1476cc. Both models were available in two stages of tune, with a choice of single or twin carburettors and all the Climax engines were heavily modified at the Triumph factory to the extent of changing the bore dimensions and lightening the moving masses.

The cars certainly bore a marked resemblance to the products of Victor Riley and often in the past have been unfairly accused of copying various features, especially in the styling department. By the mid thirties three separate chassis configurations were on sale: standard, short and 'Monte Carlo'. Onto these chassis went so many body and styling variations that it is little wonder the company showed a virtually constant lack of profitability.

To further cement the reputation of Triumph as 'almost sports cars' the original straight eight Dolomite with its supercharged 1750cc engine was so close a copy of the contemporary classic Alfa Romeo that the Italian company lodged a vehement protest with the company and threatened prosecution if the engine were not withdrawn. As the engine was hardly the outright winner which Triumph had expected it was quietly dropped in 1935. The Dolomite name lived on however and in 1½ litre guise became one of the fastest cars in its class. The gem of pre-war years was yet another Dolomite. The straight six engined 2 litre with overhead valves was a complete Triumph product. If it had come just two years earlier it could have had a dramatic effect upon the company fortunes but as it was it lost out heavily by costing as much as a 3½ litre Jaguar or the 2½ litre MG SA introduced within months of its announcement.

Whilst Triumph struggled on and Swallow under Lyons prospered another famous British sporting name nearly disappeared for ever in the mid 1930s — Lagonda.

The Lagonda company was started by an American perfectionist named Wilbur Adams Gunn and named after his birthplace on the Ohio river. Gunn had arrived in England seeking to further a possible career as an opera singer and stayed to make use of the fine mechanical training he had received as an apprentice at the Singer sewing machine company. Wilbur Gunn was a dedicated craftsman and so disliked the idea of buying components that he felt he could produce more suitably himself. He must also have been something of a visionary for his 1100cc light car of 1914 could probably be accredited as the world's first metal monocoque construction car. Although economical to produce the car failed to find the market which the ingenuity of its design should have assured it and the engine found its way into the more normal chassis assembly of the times.

Gunn died in 1920 leaving the firm leaderless and the company was administered by a trust which appointed a certain

General Metcalf to restructure and run the firm more along the lines of a normal business than the benevolent dictatorship which the founder had left behind. Metcalf was obviously a sportsman for under his leadership the factory prepared one of the later 1100cc cars to give 86 mph at Brooklands in 1925. The General must also have realised something of the way in which car development was progressing at this time for he sanctioned a 2 litre car with an engine designed by one Anthony Davidson as the flagship of the range when the 1100 had been replaced by a rather pedestrian 2 litre model type named 12/24.

The engine for the Two Litre featured hemispherical combustion chambers and although the carburation was poor even for 1925, they allowed a high degree of tuning and good overall flexibility. A speed model was produced which competed well at Le Mans in 1928. The two cars so entered were leading their class when they collided but the second placed car, driven by Baron d'Erlanger, struggled through to finish eleventh overall with a twisted front axle and no front brakes.

Three years later Lord de Clifford survived a six car pile up in Norway to take a supercharged Two Litre to fourth place overall in the Monte Carlo rally of 1931. That year also saw the introduction of a six cylinder 3 litre car based on the 1926 2½ litre six. It featured a Maybach semi-automatic gearbox and failed to find many customers due to its heavy weight and over complication. It was the culmination of a number of unspectacular stablemates for the Two Litre which had itself been heavily revised in the chassis department in 1928.

Not until 1933 did the company have a true successor to the almost legendary Two Litre and then in one year it produced two highly sophisticated and exciting machines at different ends of the performance spectrum. The most famous was the ageless, classically sleek M45 which benefitted from the demise of the Invicta company in 1932 by being able to take up the Meadows overhead valve engine which had powered those graceful cars.

Further down the scale, at the level of the contemporary Rileys and Alvis competition, the 1½ litre Rapier was a finely crafted twin overhead cam powered machine with a safe revving limit of 6000 rpm. To further make the point that both these cars were designed to be driven the M45 was named the Rapide.

The Rapide was to provide Lagonda with its biggest competition triumph for a team had been specially prepared for the Le Mans race of 1935. Even as the liquidators moved into the factory the Lagonda agents Fox and Nicholl managed to enter one of

Dripping with glamour, the superb Model J Deusenberg was the epitome of the pre-war US performance saloon with an engine displacing almost seven litres

them in the French classic and, as the supercharged Alfa Romeo team succumbed to various maladies, the car ran reliably home to win by over a lap.

This victory saved the company for it was bought by a wealthy enthusiast named Alan Good who sold the Rapier design and then liberated W.O. Bentley from the restricting influence of the Rolls Royce organisation to come and take charge of development at Lagonda.

Bentley took a fine machine and made it into a brilliant one through a process of logical evolution. His first act was to modify the suspension geometry of the car and uprate the specification in such a way that, as the LG45, it could take on the finest cars in the market for the rich and pampered sportsman. In 1938 he improved the car further by adding independent front suspension and hydraulic brakes so turning it into the LG6 but his real masterpiece for the Lagonda company was the 4½ litre V12 which first appeared at the 1936 London Motor Show and went on sale in late 1937. These cars were to have been known as the Lagonda Bentley or even the Bentley-Lagonda but a sharp reminder from Rolls Royce that they had acquired the rights to his name as well as his business deterred W.O. Bentley from this course of action. Even so the customers who queued to buy the best were well aware that the new breed of Lagonda was from the pen of the man who had won Le Mans more than any other designer of the time.

The mid thirties saw the final dying glories of Eliot Cord's car concern just at a time when the USA seemed to have recovered from the worst of the great depression. The superb Bentley-influenced Model J Duesenberg with its magnificent four valve per cylinder twin overhead cam engine of 6882cc had failed to find enough customers among the cream of American society to make it profitable and, although Cord owned Lycoming who supplied all his engines, and some extremely fine aero engines besides, his financial empire could no longer stand the losses incurred by the luxury and sporting car division.

The 1936 Model 852 Supercharged Speedster from Auburn was to be the last fling of this truly flamboyant group. It delivered some 265 bhp from its Lycoming straight eight side valve engine. It was available with saloon, speedster and closed coupé bodywork yet it was the racy boat-tailed speedster that caught the imagination of the public and brought the make classic status.

Even the darling of thirties automophiles, the front wheel drive Cord 810 with its pop-up headlamps and eye catching coffin-nosed bonnet, failed to bring in customers even when heavily discounted from an originally low price. Auburn's best year had been 1929 with a total sale of some 22,000 cars. The 810 Cord is recorded as having sold some 2320 units over its entire production run while the grand Duesenbergs never sold in anything but tiny numbers. Thus in 1936 died the most exciting line of independently produced sporting saloons ever built in the USA.

Gone they might have been but the influence of the Auburns and Cords lived on in the cars of Chrysler and General Motors through the rest of the decade and beyond. Buick, Chrysler, Plymouth, De Soto and Dodge all carried styling traits originated from Cord's products while Packard carried on with its magnificent V12 finding fewer customers as the years passed but owing a deep and unacknowledged debt to these fine machines.

Meanwhile in Germany the Mercedes-Benz company had returned to profitability and regained both its prestige and its sporting persona while quietly reinforcing its reputation for superb quality with an almost unflawed line of successful cars.

The decade began in an innovative mood for the combine for, with the 170, they had moved firmly into the lower middle class market against such traditional stalwarts as the General Motors controlled Opel organisation. In many ways the 170 was just a good quality compendium of current design practice enhanced by the addition of Mercedes-Benz attention to detail and quality. It carried a box section chassis frame and was powered by a 32 bhp side valve four cylinder engine. It did, however, offer something more than many of its rivals in the shape of independent rear suspension by swing-axle and a sort of independent front suspension from a transverse leaf spring. In effect the car could fairly be described as incorporating many of the ideas Ferdinand Porsche had been advocating for a 'people's car' before he left to join Steyr.

Other features of the car included four wheel hydraulic brakes, one shot chassis lubrication and pressed steel wheels as standard fitments. The success of this small car astounded the rather staid and status conscious board of Mercedes, so much so that it was joined by the 2 litre, six cylinder 200 model in 1932 which offered reasonable performance from an unstressed 40 bhp and in 1933 by the 290 with an enlarged side valve six cylinder engine. This offered genuine 70 mph performance in comfort with gear selection eased by an all synchromesh box.

So pleased were Mercedes with their foray down market that they overreacted to the success and built a car which was almost entirely modelled around the philosophy of Porsche and his Czechoslovakian contemporary Ledwinka in the shape of the 130H. This was an intriguing little 1300cc device with a rear engine and the same type of suspension as the 170. Both the 130H (H for Heckmotor or rear engine) and the 170H which followed it as the company realised that even at that level the market expected some performance from the house of the three pointed star, sold in small numbers and were rather underpowered thus alleviating the worst effects of the combination of rear weight bias and the swinging arm suspension which on a wet road in windy conditions became almost uncontrollable.

One interesting spin off of the H cars was a sports car based on the 130. This was known as the the 150H and the engine was mounted in front of the rear wheels. The power unit was an overhead cam 1½ litre unit which gave a genuine 55 bhp and scintillating performance. A combination of expense and market distrust killed this project which could well lay claim to being the first modern mid engined sports car.

In 1935 the company was well enough established in the middle class sector to risk a massive investment in completely new production techniques to cater for it. Instead of the traditional box section chassis the company introduced a whole new range based around tubular backbone chassis units.

At the lower end of the range the side valve 1700cc engine was retained but the attention given to the styling of the car added both desirability and performance to this somewhat lacklustre unit. The new car was known as the 170V and before production was halted in 1942 some 90,000 had been manufactured in a variety of different body-styles.

The 200 was retained as the next step up the range with a 230 which boasted slightly roomier passenger accommodation from a longer wheelbase. Finally the range was completed in 1937 with the 320. As with all cars in the range the figures were the first three digits of the overall cubic capacity.

At the top of the range the flamboyance of the legendary Porsche-designed SSK was carried forward by a superb, new overhead cam, V8-engined range of sports cars and tourers. These were automotive realisations of all the aggression and brashness of National Socialist Germany. Their flowing lines and outrageous performance in supercharged form made them the very finest of the larger sports cars to emerge from Stuttgart, even surpassing the superb Horch straight eights for outright performance.

These cars were the 540 series which had begun life as the 380K at the 1933 Frankfurt Autoshow. This had been turned very swiftly into the 500K and then, in 1936, it grew to the fullness of its size with the 540 at 5·4 litres. Although too big and cumbersome to be classed as anything other than a fast road car these Sindelfingen factory-built machines have become the most sought after classics in the world. In their time, and even after it, they appealed very much to the man who wanted the outrageous but backed by the oldest names in the motor industry. With 100 mph easily attainable with the supercharger turned on they were probably the fastest cars in production when introduced in 1936 although the factory was quick to warn that the supercharger was certainly not for anything more than the occasional high speed flurry along the Autobahn.

The early thirties also saw another famous name in performance saloons enter the lists — BMW. The company was already well established in the motorcycle field, and so rapid had been their progress that in 1928 when the board of directors mooted the intention of building a range of cars, it was decided to buy an extant company rather than try to develop all the necessary skills within the Munich based headquarters. The company chosen was the Dixi company of Eisenach who had been building motor cars from 1896 under the names of Fahrzeugfabrik-Eisenach and since 1918 as Gothaer Waggonfabrik.

In 1928 Dixi signed an agreement with Austin to build the Seven under licence and this had some influence in the decision by BMW to acquire the company. The vehicle which resulted from the takeover was strongly Austin-based but an altogether more substantial machine. It was immediately successful in the impoverished Germany of the time and, to add to the appeal, BMW built a very stylish sports version with a lengthened scuttle and pointed curved tail known as the Wartburg Sports. Like the Swallow Austin Seven the 'sport' was more imagined than real but it opened the possibilities of the sporting market to the South German manufacturer and the next models were aimed squarely into the small six cylinder sector.

The late Michael Frostick wryly suggested in his book on *BMW* that 'square boxy European saloons of no great performance but with exemplary roadholding, had a special place in the minds of enthusiasts; and save possibly for Lancia, BMW were pre-eminent.' The first small sixes which the company offered were also anything but sporty. They suffered from too much weight and an 1173cc engine with overhead valves but with only 30 bhp to motivate the solid saloon and tourer bodies with which the works supplied it.

Later the same year the 315 was offered with 1490cc engine although this car did not go into production until 1934 when a specially tuned team entry took the team prize in the Alpine Trial. The next development came in 1935 in the shape of the 1911cc type 319. By this time BMW were shipping cars throughout Europe and in Britain Frazer-Nash, the importers, had begun fitting them with extremely smart sporting coachwork both open and closed. The 319 was to develop almost, it seemed, organically into the rounded two door 320 and 321 saloons. In these machines the first distinctive flowing lines of the later cars could just be discerned but it was not until the advent of the 326 with its smooth and flexible 1971cc

engine with overhead valves operated by short cross over pushrods that the make began to set trends rather than follow them.

With the BMW 326 in its various configurations the Bavarian company moved into direct competition with the side valve Mercedes of up to 2·9 litres. In every way, with the possible exception of build and finish quality, they outshone them. It was an auspicious sign and one which they were quick to exploit with the sporty 327 and 328 versions that followed. While Auto Union and Mercedes had a monopoly of the German government's subsidy to Grand Prix

Below: 1939 BMW 319 at a pre-war British hill climb. BMW saloons were bodied under license by the UK importers, Frazer-Nash

Left: BMW 326 four door drophead tourer. With the 326 the Bavarian company launched their sales attack on the smaller Mercedes

racing, BMW concentrated on sports car racing and, both on the continent and in Great Britain, they soon secured themselves a name for providing competitive and reliable machinery in the 2 litre class.

Meanwhile the Auto Union was building some of the greatest sporting tourers in the world in the shape of the flamboyant straight eight Horch and mechanically sophisticated Wanderer cars. The amalgamation of the four companies had allowed them to rival Mercedes in offering cars across the full market spectrum and, as well as in Grand Prix racing, their cars were seen in contemporary rallies and sports car events.

While these cars kept Germany at the fore the Italian motor industry was capitalising on low local labour rates to attack world markets with some superb sporting cars.

Lancia, founded by an ex-Fiat Grand Prix driver named Vincenzo Lancia, built its first car in 1907. With it began the long company tradition of naming models after the letters Greek of the alphabet. The Alpha, as the car was called, boasted an L head side valve engine of 2534cc driving through a four speed gearbox which was sufficient to give 60 mph with sporting bodywork. The cars, however, were not meant to be sporting and by the time the Alpha reached the market it was burdened with heavy and luxurious Edwardian style bodywork.

This was to be the style of the company for many years to come. The ex-racing driver knew just how much it had cost Fiat to maintain its successful racing team and he knew how much prospective customers demanded of a product which had been successfully sold upon a racing reputation. He was to institute a rule in the company that no works car should ever overtake a customer on the public highway, no matter how urgent the errand, to reassure the buyer that his car was as quick and reliable as those of the works.

True, Lancia did enter cars for a few selected events in 1910. Notable among them was the American Grand Prix. Yet the effort was half hearted and seems merely to have been a advertising exercise to keep the name in the public eye.

During the First World War Lancia joined the likes of Napier, Vauxhall and Crossley as suppliers of allied military staff cars. The most popular model in this application was the 4940cc Theta which was later to feature in Lancia publicity as the first European car to carry full electrical equipment. A direct descendant of this car was the company's first post-war offering in the form of the monobloc straight four Kappa which in turn made way for the Dikappa with an engine of 4950cc featuring overhead valves operated by pushrods, and subsequently the Trikappa with an overhead cam engine of some 4594cc.

At this time Lancia also built a 6 litre V12 which saw the light of day at the 1919 Paris motor show but was quickly dropped for want of worthwhile interest. From this car Lancia is said to have evolved the techniques which allowed him to open a new chapter in the company's history by developing his extremely narrow V configuration engines. These were revolutionary in their own right, but when added onto the full package of Vincenzo Lancia's idea of what a middle class car should be, they just added cream to an already superb concoction.

While Wilbur Gunn had abandoned his monocoque Lagonda in favour of the simpler-to-build chassis and body formula of the day, Lancia sank his future into what was effectively the first ever unitary construction car.

The Lambda as the car was known was tested in 1921/22 and introduced in 1923. As well as unitary construction the front suspension was the independent sliding pillar type and with its 2 litre 22° V4 engine with one camshaft for each bank of two cylinders it was a revolutionary package. Performance for the long wheelbase car was never startling yet the road holding was exemplary.

The styling was stark, but the long, low lines gave the car a lean and fast look. This was accentuated when the detachable hard top was removed and this feature too was unique to Lancia even though specialist coachbuilders had been in a position to create such bodies for as long as the motor car chassis had been available. In short the Lambda was a triumph and an arbiter of performance for its day for while not as powerful as some of its rivals (even though the engine was later expanded to 2·4 litres and eventually 2·6) its advanced specification added to an early adoption of four wheel brakes gave it magnificent cross country speeds which were to help it find its way into competition in private hands, and also when the works campaigned them in long distance events in the mid twenties.

By 1930, however, Lancia had reverted to a normal chassis configuration under pressure from both customers and coachbuilders. In its production life the model had been through nine evolutionary stages which involved the engine changes plus in the eighth and ninth series the adoption of separate chassis and from the fifth series the change from a three to a four speed gearbox.

From 1928 the Dilambda with its narrow V8 and more powerful 3960cc engine replaced it as the top model in the Lancia range and, as Vincenzo Lancia had decided that the development of the original model was over, the Lambda was dropped from the catalogue in 1931 after a production run of over 13,000. Not only did the Lambda disappear but the Dilambda was replaced by what many among the Lancia following considered a retrograde step, the Astura.

The Dilambda was joined by a new model called the Astura but so marked was the distaste of traditional Lancia custom for the new car that the Dilambda was allowed to plod on in production until early 1936 by which time the Astura had gained ground enough to fully replace it. In 1934 the Astura engine size was increased to 2972cc and with suitable coachwork it became the *de rigeur* transport for the proliferating officials of the new government of Italy.

Meanwhile Lancia was creating the first of a new breed of small cars. It was to have a full monocoque body, all round independent suspension, an engine to give it sports car performance and still be affordable to the newer generation of lower middle class Italian car buyers. In 1937 the car was ready. It was small and, by the standards of the day, considered rather ugly. But it was all that its creator could have wished as his last major design. In keeping with the company's revised policy of pandering to Italian nationalist fervour by invoking Roman deities in its naming policies, the car was named Aprilia and it offered performance and handling undreamt of from so small an engine mounted in a 'people's car'.

While the Aprilia was pointing at new directions in car design for the likes of Porsche and Citroën to follow in later years, perhaps the most important performance car in terms of long term influence which Great Britain was to produce in the thirties was unveiled at the 1936 London Motor Show.

William Lyons of Swallow Coachbuilding had been steadily gaining market credibility with his range of SS cars. All except the 1935 SS Airline, a rather badly executed variation on the Kamm inspired craze for fast back styling of the day, had sold in greater numbers than anyone but Lyons

Pininfarina bodied Lancia Aprilia of 1940

would have been prepared to predict. In this atmosphere of buoyant confidence the company had expanded to cope with the future.

Lyons had bought out his original sidecar building partner, William Walmsley, sold off the various parts of the business concerned with anything other than building complete cars and floated SS Cars Ltd in 1935. Reasoning that a cheap but powerful sports saloon on traditional lines would find a ready market if the dual requirements of reliability and elegance could be met, Lyons hired an ex-Humber engineer named William Heynes to oversee the development work and approached specialist engine designer Harry Weslake.

The first fruit of the association between Lyons and Weslake was a high compression head for the Standard 16 and 20 hp engines he was then using. Within a year the major prize was a complete new overhead valve cylinder head which, when fitted to the 2½ litre Standard side valve, increased power from 70 bhp to some 104 bhp while the use of light alloy pushrods allowed the engine to be safely revved to 4700 rpm in normal usage. By further lengthening his already well proven chassis, Lyons was able to produce a body which resembled at a glance both the Alvis Speed Twenty and the 3½ litre Bentley.

This 100 mph car was the supreme product of Lyon's philosophy and it was a complete manufacturing project even though the engines and the chassis were still being provided by the Standard Motor Company. As such it deserved a new name and after checking with the Armstrong Siddeley Company, who had used the proposed name for one of their famous radial aero engines, it was duly given to the new car. A campaign of teaser ads which extolled the virtues of the forthcoming new machine followed (and which were later to be repeated almost verbatim in the road test reports of the motoring press) before the car was proudly displayed upon the SS Cars Ltd stand at the Motor Show. The car which had been introduced to the press at a special lunch at the Mayfair Hotel some two weeks previously was the SS Jaguar. The world's finest range of sporting saloons had seen the light of day.

Below: The Barnato Hassan Bentley with which its owner Wolf Barnato beat the Blue Train

Bottom: A 1936 SS II saloon meets a Standard Flying Twelve. Until 1946 all Jaguars had Standard engines

2 Post war doldrums

With the Second World War over, car production proved almost impossible to get restarted. Throughout Europe shortages of coal, steel, rubber and machine tools inhibited attempts to re-open the production lines for civilian consumer production before the beginning of 1946. In the USA, although industry had been spared the bombing and looting which crippled Germany and France, even the mighty General Motors was unable to introduce any new models until the end of 1946.

Only France and Great Britain were in any position to offer the grand tourers and smaller sporty cars of before the war. As then they were still very much the province of the few customers who had the money. As companies such as Delage, Delahaye, Talbot and Hotchkiss slowly resumed their normal business it seemed natural for them to return to the *Grands Routiers* of the immediate pre-war years which had seen France produce some of the most elegant cars in the world.

As for Voisin, his attempts to re-start were abruptly halted by a workers' commune which had seized his factory and branded him a collaborator. The same fate awaited Louis Renault, whose factory at Billancourt had provided the Wehrmacht with some fourteen thousand trucks per year. He died awaiting trial in an unheated prison cell in the winter of 1944. Ettore Bugatti found his factories in Alsace had been impounded by the French government in a move to gain reparations. The factory had formerly been impounded by the Germans and given to Trippelwerke for the purpose of developing an amphibious infantry vehicle. The ensuing legal wrangle was to prevent the resumption of any further worthwhile production and in the opinion of most of Bugatti's friends and family to shorten his life.

True, a few Bugatti Type 101s were destined to leave the factory but they were in effect merely pre-war Type 57s brought up to date by the addition of superior equip-

Last of a great line — the 1951 Bugatti Type 101

ment, such as hydraulic brakes which had made their marque debut in 1938, and full width Detroit inspired bodies, yet to all realistic intents the car production company had ceased to function by 1950.

The Talbot company had been bought in 1935 by an Englishman named Antony Lago and thus been saved from the fate of Sunbeam which had become a marketing tool for the Rootes Group, producing badge engineered Humbers. From the end of the war Lago struggled to keep alive the greatness of the name with a series of cars based upon the pre-war 4 litre unit which was overbored to 4482cc. These were reliable and at one time in the late forties and early fifties Talbot-Lago, as the company had become known, were using the engine to power both Grand Prix and extremely successful Le Mans machinery. Even so the company was in the hands of the receiver by 1951 although it recovered and struggled on through to 1960 using Ford and BMW engines in place of its own units.

1951 also saw the end of the big 4½ litre Delahaye as Weiffenbach took to building a four wheel drive reconnaissance vehicle for the French army. Weiffenbach's last performance fling was the magnificent Model 235 of 1952 but demand had vanished and in 1953 after producing just three cars the combined Delage-Delahaye company was to merge with Hotchkiss.

Hotchkiss themselves, realising that the era of the great cars was dead in France, had a brief and costly flirtation with an advanced design by Gregoire which featured all independent suspension and a superb flat four light alloy engine of 2186cc. Unfortunately it failed to attract a viable amount of custom and the company foundered as a car manufacturer in 1956.

Salmson had produced cycle cars and lightweight sports cars before the war and had instituted a range of beautifully made twin overhead cam engines in 1929. They were to fare slightly better than most French specialists with their 2300 sports using this engine in its final incarnation. Although more a genuine sports car than a *Grand Routier* the car was available in coupé form which gave minimal accommodation for rear seat passengers. This single model with its various body options and updates was to keep the company in some sort of production until the end of the fifties when Renault, hungry for production space, acquired the Billancourt factory and submerged the name for ever.

The demise of the great French marques and especially the flamboyant and powerful *Grand Routier* was not only a result of stagnant markets and production shortages. The major contributory factor was the death of the home market due to the swingeing 'tax of envy' levelled on all large capacity cars by the immediate post-war government. In effect this gave separate classifications against arbitrary fiscal horsepower ratings. To favour the smaller mass produced cars the system rose in graduated stages until it reached 16CV which was set at about 2·9 litres. After this the rate increased by two hundred per cent over the 12 to 15CV category. Even this latter category was almost unbelievably expensive at the then equivalent of twenty-three pounds so the effect can be easily imagined when related to the larger classes.

These same taxes were to bring about one of the largest revolutions in the evolution of the performance saloon. While the glamour slowly departed at the top of the French market the middle sector had to learn to live

Italian automotive flair quickly re-emerged post war. This is the 1951 Alfa Romeo 1900 Berlina

with conditions imposed upon it. A combination of good fast *Route Nationale* type roads, the most expensive petrol in Europe and the tax ratings made the likes of Citroën, Simca and Renault learn that, although parsimonious, the average French driver expected something more from his everyday transport than the side valve plodding box typical of the thirties.

Small cars were fine but they were expected to cruise all day *pied au plancher* on the good roads without undue mechanical problems and without incurring penalties in the amount of fuel used. Each of the major manufacturers was to find a way to offer something extra to the average motorist during the fifties and performance was to be the key to the market even though at the beginning of the fifties the smaller Renaults, Peugeots and Simcas had as little in common with the *Grand Routiers* as had the Model T with the Duesenberg or the standard Austin Seven with the 3 litre Bentley at the end of the previous war.

In Germany the problems facing the motor industry were little short of catastrophic. The once proud Mercedes-Benz factories in Stuttgart had received the full attention of the RAF to the extent that very little remained usable except the rubble of the walls. The Berlin factories had paid the price of liberation by the Russians with the whole of their salvageable tooling departing eastwards while BMW lost its Eisenach factory in the partition of the country and most of its product rights to the Bristol Aircraft Company as war reparations.

Volkswagen had fared relatively well in comparison, for although its factory had been bombed most of the damage sustained had been to the structure of the buildings, while Opel was still part of the powerful General Motors organisation and although some plants were in communist hands, production of the Kadett was started with very little delay. Of all the manufacturers the Auto Union was the worst hit; one of its major plants was given to Poland while all its major manufacturing centres except Igolstadt and Neckarsulm were in East Germany and these had suffered the attentions both of Bomber Command and the reparations committees.

Even had there been the ability to produce the glorious cars of the late thirties, like France, Germany lacked anyone wealthy enough to buy them. Only in the few European countries which had profited from the conflagration such as Switzerland and Sweden were there enough potential customers to make a fast tourer a real possibility and even here that market was severely limited by various shortages.

Thus the industry hauled itself shakily onto its feet, fighting shortages of crucial material and capital, producing the utility cars and trucks which the market could readily absorb. Nonetheless the love of motor sport which had fired that nation in the thirties was never quite extinguished and, in a country whose talented engineers had invented the motor car, even a Volkswagen engine could be made into a tool of the chase.

Italy was spared the grasping hands of the reparations bodies. The only impediment to the resumption of production apart from workers committees and general shortages was the unstable and undersubscribed market. Lancia could, of course, trade upon a reputation which had been as much enhanced in the Second World War as it had in the First by staff car popularity, but the rest of the industry had been badly shaken by Il Duce's war. Having produced some of the finest chassis in the world the Alfa Romeo company was held in thrall by a combination of tyre shortages and government ineptitude. No matter that the 158/9 Alfetta could sweep the circuits of Europe in formula racing, no matter that the greatest coachbuilders in Europe were creating *the* bodystyles of the fifties and the sixties, luxury car production was as much inhibited here as anywhere in Europe.

In Britain government ineptitude reached heights hardly understandable by rational man. The Labour government hobbled Britain's car industry by allowing only the largest and most commonplace manufacturers access to steel supplies. Luckily for the car buying public this policy was tempered with reason to extent when the allocation for steel was made conditional upon the percentage of exports any company could achieve. Another loophole was discovered when some companies found that various non-ferrous metals were not rationed. MG and Jaguar, who because of lack of investment could do nothing but offer models designed before the war, found ready export markets in the USA and to some extent avoided the steel embargos. Meanwhile specialist high performance builders, whether long established like Alvis or newly fledged like Healey, could use aluminium bodywork and so avoid the restrictions of steel rationing.

. . . . while British dignity continued unabashed, expressed here in a 1946 AC 2-Litre

Jaguar, MG and Alvis were not alone in exploiting a market for the high performance saloon in those grey days of austerity. The AC company began business in the early years of the century. After the First World War they built some most successful cyclecars, not to mention the first car to lap Brooklands at over 100 mph. Like Salmson the firm had put its credibility behind decent engine technology, although in the case of AC it was a single overhead cam engine with the cam driven from the rear of the block. It was extremely reliable, having been designed in time for the 1919 model year and subtly refined over the years. The company had also used it well in motor sport away from the febrile atmosphere of Brooklands, an almost unmodified example taking the overall honours in the Monte Carlo Rally

of 192- while the company was under the directorship of S.F. Edge, a man who had won one of the pre-1914 Gordon Bennett races on a Napier.

The 1946 AC 2 Litre was both beautiful and practical. In overall concept it was far nearer the traditional idiom than any of its close rivals but its impeccable finish and handling put it ahead of many similar saloons elsewhere in the world at the time. The six cylinder engine was mounted low in the chassis which relied on traditional beam axles front and rear for its exemplary ride and road holding. Full width bodywork coupled with the depth of glass in the stylish divided front windscreen made the car one of the most imposing (while at the same time traditionally British looking) cars of the period.

Leaving Britain and its weather behind and no doubt heading for France, just a short hop away by Silver City Air Ferry, this Bristol 403 would have made light work of the drive to the 'Med' in the early 1950s

As AC were demonstrating what a small company with imagination could produce, The Bristol Aeroplane Company were proving that a successful company with large resources could manufacture mediocrity from a brilliant pattern.

The BMW range of immediate pre-war years has been mentioned previously. With the cessation of hostilities the Bristol company decided with help from the pre-war BMW importer that a British BMW would be a fine idea. The design chosen for plagiarism was the elegant Autenreith coupé style. By raising the waist line and carefully moulding the contours of this car the original coachbuilder had produced a vehicle which belied its chassis type construction giving the impression of the sleekness only-monocoque or the better examples of unitary construction could bring about. Like the bogus British pasta of post-war years, the discerning customer refused to warm to this admittedly beautifully constructed half caste and Bristol soon replaced it with the 401 with a body which although showing no sign of originality at least only stole the grille and bonnet from its teutonic predecessor.

More in keeping with traditional British elegance was the car with which Alvis made their foray into the post-war market. Like the original Bentley and Sunbeam companies, Alvis could claim to be one of the few British car makers to stick with the quality-first principle of Rolls Royce. Like Rolls Royce they became much involved in the manufacture of aero and heavy duty fighting vehicle engines but unlike Rolls Royce they had never shied from innovation. The late twenties and early thirties had seen the company experimenting and successfully producing sleek front wheel drive cars while the immortal Speed Twenty and Speed Twenty-fives were ample recompense to a generation of drivers which had lost the glamorous big engined Bentleys and in all probability could not have handled them anyway.

The TA21 with which the company attacked the post-war market was merely a 3 litre variation upon a previously underpowered theme. It owed much in styling to the AC but the lightly stressed overhead valve 2993cc engine offering its paltry 85 bhp was very much a product of its time. Even so, the TA21 was to produce

The Bristol 405 of 1955 was in essence 403 mechanicals in a four door body with vestigial fins

Evolution of the big post-war Jaguars began with the interim Mk V of 1948 which retained pre war styling and power units with added independent front suspension

The continued acceptance of the cars both at home and abroad gave Lyons the breathing space he needed to make sure that any new model he might introduce would not be a rushed job. In 1948 he discontinued production of the 1½ litre, thus severing his final links with the Standard company who since 1945 had supplied this unit, and introduced the interim Mark V.

As with all his previous new models the styling of the new car was designed to preserve the better features of the earlier cars while incorporating some of the better innovations of prevailing fashion. The car appeared somewhat nose heavy when viewed from the side as a result of a new deep box section chassis plus the use of independent front suspension by wishbones and torsion bars. Very little had altered in the engine department with the faithful 2½ and 3 litre pushrod engines retained but the car proved a very successful means of bridging the gap between the 1937 models and those of the 1950s.

While the Mark V collected even more friends for the marque around the world, Lyons' plans for his own engine production facilities were bearing fruit. The XK engine, with its hemispherical combustion chambers and twin overhead cams, had been conceived by the management at Jaguar during nights spent 'firewatching' during the war. Again Lyons' rationale was simple and straightforward. He knew he would need an engine tractable enough to power medium to large saloons yet flexible enough to allow tuning to combat the best which the continent could put against it in the sporting field. A V8 was rejected for reasons of both cost and development complexity; thus a straight four or six ohc engine which could be produced upon the same machinery seemed ideal. In the event the few four cylinder units which were produced proved both disappointing and unrewarded by public demand. With the one exception of a successful record gathering programme by Major Goldie Gardner in his XJ four cylinder engined MG Magnette K3 based EX135, it was allowed to quietly drop from the company plans.

The first production car to give the public some idea of the new engine's potential was the immortal XK120. This superb sports car borrowed its overall lines from the 1940 racing versions of the BMW 328 yet miraculously smoothed and blended them into a delightfully harmonious recipe for one of the all time great street cars.

the timelessly elegant and respectably fast TC21 Grey Lady saloon. One hundred bhp and a reputed 100 mph were on offer, but the greatest virtue of the car was its scaled down Lagonda looks. The Grey Lady was doomed to disappear in 1954 as the bodywork sources dried up, but the chassis lingered on offering itself up to the graceful Graber bodied confections which saw the company through to the TF series of the mid sixties.

Jaguar greeted the peace with a re-packaged version of the car which had established the name. Gone for ever were the initials SS which would in any case have been totally out of character in Wardour Street.

A 1½, 2½ and 3 litre version of the Jaguar were on offer and although the company was beset by the same shortages as the rest of Britain's motor industry, they were rolling off the lines by October 1945. So popular were these cars that by the early months of 1947 rumours were circulating that Jaguar were accepting no further orders for an indefinite period. The main market for the larger cars was rather surprisingly the USA where, although the cars were undoubtedly quaint in comparison with post-war Detroit styling, the wealthy fondly embraced the flowing pre-war lines as being more sophisticated than the products of their own industry. This state of affairs was to protect Lyons from much of the government meddling which dogged other makers.

Such was the success of this car that it all but threatened to overshadow Lyons' next masterpiece which followed it onto the market exactly one year later. Introduced at the 1950 London Motor Show, the Mark VII was Lyons' first genuine 100 mph mass production saloon. Like the XK120, it featured the XK series engine in 3½ litre giving 160 bhp at 5200 rpm. Suspension was once more independent by torsion bar and wishbone at the front while the familiar semi-elliptic set up was retained at the rear. Servo assisted brakes helped tame the 34 cwt beast and, although re-circulating ball steering was retained from the Mark V, much thought had gone into reducing the vagueness asso-ciated with this system.

Some twenty-seven million dollars' worth of US orders greeted the car in its first two months on the American market and as befitted such a currency earner the car was reserved as an export only model for another year while the home market received an improved and updated Mark V to satisfy burgeoning demand. It was to be the basis of all the Jaguar company's flagships for the next ten years, evolving through Mark VIII and Mark IX versions to eventually make way for the unitary construction Mark X in 1960; by which time it had been long since joined by a whole family of cars bearing the stamp of William Lyons' genius.

Below: The Mk VIII and Mk IX Jaguars (**bottom**) of the late 1950s were outwardly almost indistinguishable but mechanically the Mk IX introduced features that were to be further developed in later cars

The beautiful Alfa Romeo 6C 2500 of 1939, a typically stylish product from the Milan company

Meanwhile, having seen the success of Jaguar in the overseas market, the Austin company tried their own recipe for performance upon the world and particularly in the USA in the shape of the radically avant-garde Atlantic. This used an engine from their small truck range in tuned form in a controversially styled but fairly light and aerodynamic body. The car was extremely successful in several major record attempts, including several US stock car categories, yet it failed to achieve the required level of custom and was later superseded in the Austin range by the phenomenally successful Austin Healey of 1953 which although using the same 2660cc pushrod engine was a car of totally different character.

Alone among the famous makes which had been swallowed by the major combines Riley carried forward the tradition of sporting saloons they had pioneered before the war with the little fabric-bodied Nines with the RM series. This retained the traditional graceful radiator shell and the unique engine configuration with its twin cams mounted high in the block operating the overhead valves through short pushrods. Available almost immediately after the war in 1½ litre form the much revered 2½ litre was re-introduced at the end of 1946 and was warmly welcomed back.

The steering, as befitted the illustrious sporting history of the marque, was rack and pinion (although this meant that the 2½ litre car was heavy to park), and the pre-war practice of using hydromechanical brakes was continued. Unfortunately these delightful and still sought after cars were to disappear in 1953, replaced by the boring and bulbous Austin A90-derived Pathfinder, but the engine soldiered on until the end of the fifties by which time it had found itself way into that other much devalued marque, Wolseley.

The Sunbeam name was revived by the Rootes corporation with the post-war Sunbeam-Talbot 10. This rather pleasant looking machine owed most of its mechanical components to the truly appalling Hillman Minx of the late thirties and lacked performance to an extent which would have caused ridicule in the old independent company. The pleasant looking but mechanically archaic 80s and 90s which made their debut in 1948 offered lively performance for their day. Regardless of a rather imprecise steering column-mounted gear shift and beam front axle, the 90 with its 80 bhp overhead valve engine acquitted

itself extremely well in rallies of the day. The old order had definitely gone, however, and the succession of Sunbeam Rapiers which followed these cars were purely badge engineered Hillmans — although by a process of continued refinement they had become extremely pleasant and vice free tourers by the time of their demise in 1966.

Performance was still in demand at the top of the market even though the customer's choice was becoming more and more restricted. Rolls Royce were one of the few

companies to read the needs of the post-war market accurately and in adopting a single model policy with a standard steel body they expanded upon the already high reputation of the classic marque with their famous overhead inlet/side exhaust straight six engined cars.

For a time the identity of the Bentley name was completely submerged in this traditionally styled thoroughbred but it was to rise again dramatically with the introduction in 1951 of the first of the breathtakingly elegant R type Continentals. These cars carried all the bravura of the marque in their quietly arrogant fastback styling and although the power output, claimed by Rolls Royce, as always, to be 'adequate', was only in the region of 178 bhp they showed a fair turn of speed and acceleration for such a heavy car.

These cars had their roots in the immortal Embiricos Bentley of 1935- which was a specially bodied chassis using the standard 5·3 engine and independent front suspension of

The Lancia Ardea of 1939 was the world's first mass production small car with independent suspension all round. The model was re-introduced post-war and run on until 1952

the day. Attention was paid to cleaning up the lines of the car to provide better airflow and improved engine cooling, which had proved the Achilles' heel of many pre-war grand tourers. The resulting car managed a top speed (which was also its cruising speed) of some 112 mph — enough to embarrass any comparable luxury tourer from anywhere else in the world. The same designer who had created the slippery body, Paulin, and the coachbuilder responsible for realising his design, Van Vooren of Paris, were commissioned by Rolls Royce to translate this one-off machine into a production car capable of carrying four people in Rolls Royce type sumptuousness. The resulting machine was named the Corniche and had little of the traditional Bentley or Rolls Royce about it. The engine was the inlet over exhaust unit which was not to become available until 1945, while the radiator and grille were replaced by two vertical air intakes in the smoothly stream-lined nose.

It fully vindicated the design philosophy of all concerned during continental long distance running trials and was left for further testing in France with at least a hint of the possibility of some record breaking being considered. Unfortunately it was trapped by the collapse of France in 1940 and destroyed by a German bomb whilst awaiting shipment at Calais, yet the idea of the Corniche never quite left the minds of the men at Derby.

In 1950 H.I.F. Everndean who, had worked upon the original Corniche project, obtained the go-ahead to create a successor. His brief was to use only the available mechanical

1947 Healey 2.4-litre Elliot saloon closely pursued by a 2-litre Riley at the 1953 International Trophy run at Silverstone

components of the standard steel-bodied Bentley Mark 6 saloon currently in production, yet to build something really special. The resulting car could achieve 120 mph without undue fuss and possessed a 0–60 mph capability of 13·5 seconds, in those days a tremendous achievement for a car weighing 33½ cwt. The car was to stay in the catalogue until the S Series replaced the shorter wheel based R Types. Even so the

The superb Bentley Continental, perhaps the pinnacle of the 1950s performance saloon ethos. This particular car is the prototype which survived the usual RR practise of testing to destruction and is now in private ownership

body soldiered resolutely on becoming the S Type Continental and giving lesser manufacturers a lesson in the aesthetics of vehicle design.

W.O. Bentley himself meanwhile was still directing the technical fortunes of the Lagonda company. Seeing undue difficulty in re-establishing a market for the thirsty and complex V12, he had spent some of his spare time during the war years designing an engine which was to rival the Jaguar XK unit both on the tracks and in the showrooms. Like the far sighted Lyons, the great W.O. feared the resurgence of the great continental houses and like Lyons adopted the twin overhead cam route in developing his engine. The 2580cc unit was to grace a fast tourer with extremely advanced independent suspension by coil and wishbone at the front and torsion bars at the rear. In the

interests of driving ease he retained the Cotal electrically operated four speed transmission he had favoured in the thirties and rounded off the package with inboard rear brakes and rack and pinion steering.

Unfortunately Bentley's dream car fell foul of the political climate prevailing in 1946 and, having been denied the materials to produce the car by a government which could not be mollified by luxury performance cars unless they were earning dollars, the company went into liquidation in 1947. The remains of the company and the superb engine were acquired by tractor manufacturer David Brown. He lost no time in incorporating the unit in his brand new Aston Martin DB2 sports car but also revived the Lagonda concept with a substantially re-styled and rationalised version of the car in 1948. With subsequent repackaging the car was to stay available until 1958 having found some very up market and discerning customers indeed.

As the upper end of the British market geared itself for the future, traditional rivals were at last coming out of the shock

The gathering pace of reconstruction in the German motor industry was marked by the appearance of a completely new model range from Mercedes in 1951. This is a 1956 model 220S

of war on the continent. By 1950 Mercedes had reclaimed enough of their factory to be able to manufacture a new vehicle which was to be its flagship in the head to head fight with the Jaguar Mark VII in world markets. The Jaguar was destined to outsell it by a ratio of some ten to one but the Mercedes 300 was a pointer for the Stuttgart maker to its post-war recovery.

The 300 went on sale in 1951 at the same time as Mercedes launched their post-war range of overhead cam six cylinder engines. Although lighter than the Mark VII, it was inferior both in the power available and in its road manners. Nonetheless a short chassis version known as the 300S which made its debut in 1952 could well be accounted the first of the post-war Mercedes performance cars.

The 300S, seen with the benefit of hindsight, was the true descendant of the magnificent 500 and 540K pre-war tourers. It weighed in at a massive 3832 lb but in its later incarnations with Bosch fuel injection it could top 110 mph and was reputed to handle fairly well. Its main problem was that it was a car of such limited appeal and high expense that there was no real market for it.

This was certainly not true of the 220 series which began to find its way into the world market in 1954. For the first time Daimler-Benz adopted the slab sided styles which had been gaining popularity since the late forties and in doing so produced a neat and elegant car which was to remain current until early in 1960. The first car seen was the 220A, introduced at the 1954 Geneva show to mark the beginning of an all conquering return to the Grand Prix circuits for two seasons by the Stuttgart manufacturer.

The range also included a smaller version of the body, known originally as the 180 and featuring either a four cylinder 1800cc side valve engine or a choice of two diesel motors for the taxi market where Mercedes had found great popularity with their earlier diesel engines. This led to an interesting hybrid for the 1955 season when the 220 unit was incorporated in the smaller body to become the 219.

Trading on the company's return to Grand Prix racing plus the interest generated by the confrontation with Jaguar in the endurance races of the day, the 220 sold in vast numbers both to wealthy German burghers and in the jaded export markets where its genuine 95 mph and 11·9 second 0–50 acceleration combined with the all round independent suspension and comfortably appointed cabin confounded most cars aimed at the same market.

By 1955 the 220A had been joined in the medium range by the 220S. This offered a genuine 100 mph capability from 100 bhp attained by using twin Solex side draught carburettors. The brakes had also been improved with servo assistance coming as standard and alloy drums for improved cooling. It was a car unique within a section of the market which had been almost exclusively dominated by British vehicles since 1945 and for the first time it demonstrated that a well engineered and fast car could hold its own against cheaper rivals in the middle market sector. It was a principle that the company were to build on remorselessly.

The late 1950s Mercedes model line up also included the 180 range with a four cylinder engine on a slightly shorter wheelbase

In 1952 BMW brought forth their first post-war offering in the shape of the 2 litre 501. Here the high price and the failure on the company's part to properly evaluate the needs of the market were to work against the Bavarian manufacturers. With its overhead valve six cylinder 326-derived engine it was certainly no match for the swifter and more frugal 220S although the introduction of the 502 with its 2·6 litre V8 evened the score as far as top speed was concerned. For some reason, however, the potential buyers never seemed quite at ease with the single body-shell style of the cars. As BMW lacked the financial resources to re-tool before the beginning of the 1960s the cars proved something of an albatross to the company even though the 3·2 litre version of the V8 was to sell more than the rival Mercedes 300.

Italy meanwhile was busy recovering her position in the bespoke world of the truly wealthy with magnificent cars from Ferrari and Maserati. Alfa Romeo had also launched firmly into this market with their first post-war offering, an elegant 2½ litre factory-

Shades of the Sunbeam Rapier in the pretty Pininfarina bodied Alfa Romeo 1900 Berlina of 1956

built saloon named the *Freccia d'Oro*. Under the skin, however, it was basically the 1939 car with improved suspension and brakes. By 1951 when the model was dropped, some 1900 had found customers in three separate bodystyles — the factory-bodied two door saloon, a convertible by Pininfarina and an extremely elegant closed coupé bodied by Touring.

In 1950 Alfa offered the first of its true post-war saloon designs with the 1900. Although the interior of this car was spartan to the point of masochism the mechanical specification was every bit as advanced as anything else in production anywhere in the world. The engine followed traditional Alfa practice with twin overhead cams and hemispherical combustion chambers with five main bearings. All round independent suspension was by coil and wishbone at the front and live axle with coil at the rear. To stop the car the company chose the newly evolved Girling twin leading shoe hydraulic brakes and, with an optional twin choke Weber carburettor, the 1900 would cheerfully exceed the 100 mph figure.

In slightly tuned form the car was a natural front runner in contemporary rallies and one example survived the gruelling pace of the 1954 Tour of Sicily to take second place behind a 3300cc Lancia and ahead of the international sports car fraternity with their purpose built racing machinery. Besides the interior only the gear change came in for adverse press comment, the column shift being rather imprecise and slow. Development eliminated some of these problems yet not until 1955 was a floor mounted change standardised.

By the end of 1952 the 1900 had forged a new niche for Alfa both at home and abroad. It became the standard by which other 2 litre saloons were judged and as

such the factory sought to keep it at the forefront with a constant development programme. To this end it acquired radial ply tyres as standard by 1952 and in 1953 the initials TI made their debut with an uprated engine with twin Weber carburettors and twin exhausts. This gave the car 110 bhp without undue increase in fuel consumption and pointed the way to further model development policies across a product range which from 1955 was to feature the delightful Giulietta family of small saloons and sports cars.

Originally intended as a competitor to the Lancia Appia which had survived the war in almost unmodified form, the Giulietta was seen first in coupé guise at the 1954 Turin show. The sensation which the car created seemed out of all proportion to its economic importance to the company. The traditional twin overhead cam layout had been retained but in the place of the heavy cast iron block was an all alloy unit which in single carburettor form gave a useful 65 bhp from 1290cc. In 1955 when the pleasing but boxy Berlina saloon made its appearance it was to prove by far the fastest standard 1300 on sale with a genuine maximum speed in excess of 90 mph coupled with first rate economy and good overall reliability.

By 1956 some 90 bhp was being extracted from the Sprint variant and this was in turn translated into road performance by the TI model which made its appearance that year. Some 39,055 of these little boxy saloons in the original 1290cc were to leave the Portello factory before the model was discontinued and the engine was to power a host of delightful saloons and coupés as it gradually grew from its 1300cc through

1600, 1750 and 2 litre incarnations. To say that this series of Alfas were 'mass produced craftsmanship' may sound a contradiction but it conveys some of the elan of the cars. The one Achilles' heel was rust yet, in an age where most of the world's major makers saw corrosion as a legitimate way of shortening product life and boosting replacement sales, this was perhaps to be expected.

While Alfa achieved resounding international acclaim with its new generation Lancia were busily preparing the generation of cars to replace the evergreen Aprilia and Ardea. In 1950 the B10 arrived bearing the name Aurelia. Originally introduced in saloon form with pleasing but somewhat pedestrian four door styling, the B10 was ace designer Vittorio Jano's first effort for the Lancia company. The narrow V configuration was retained for the six cylinder pushrod 1754cc engine. The sliding pillar independent front suspension was also retained but a novel feature was the use of a rear axle mounted gearbox.

Corporate feeling that the original engine lacked punch saw it enlarged to 1991cc in 1951 and a trickle of specialist bodies on the basic floor pan began to emerge from the coachbuilders. It was one such body upon a shortened floor pan which provided the motoring world with what was to become the definitive GT shape. The B20 Aurelia looked good and proved competitive in any number of contemporary rallies and production car races. In 1953 the engine size was once more increased to 2660cc and the car became one of the few of its day which could offer four seater 120 mph performance. It was, however, extremely expensive and maintenance was never straightforward. The smaller Appia, which had been introduced as a replacement for the Ardea in 1953, while not exactly losing money for the company certainly did not make any. Only with the introduction in 1957 of the beautiful Pininfarina-inspired Flaminia, which drew on the Aurelia series for its main components, did the company have a viable money maker on the stocks and by that time a financially disastrous Grand Prix programme had denuded the company of the capital to exploit this beauty.

By now the only sector in the middle fine performance bracket still not covered by Jaguar was a compact sub 3 litre. At the Earl's Court motor Show in 1955 this gap was filled with the introduction of the 2·4.

The new car marked a radical departure from established Lyons methods insofar as

Alfa stylists had little trouble in grafting the traditional three piece grille layout to a three box, four door saloon. The Giulietta Berlina of 1955 was genuinely sporting with a top speed of over 90 mph from a 1300 cc engine

it was the first Jaguar without a separate chassis. Like the Mark VII it featured re-circulating ball steering and the seven bearing six cylinder engine was yet another derivative of the by now well proven double overhead cam XK unit, but the new 'compact' Jaguar featured an all new suspension system with coil and wishbones at the front and trailing link located by Panhard rod at the rear. Twin leading shoe Girling drum brakes were used and these proved adequate for the road testers of the day.

As with all other new Jaguars, the production was largely to head westwards across the Atlantic and with this in mind the suspension allowed more roll than would otherwise have been acceptable to British buyers, but all things considered, Jaguar had produced a smallish saloon with enough power and elegance to finally see off the last few British manufacturers who still tried to compete.

A year later with Jaguars having won Le Mans, Rheims and the Monte Carlo Rally rumours began to circulate to the effect that the 3½ litre engine from the XK140 was destined to find its way into the 'compact'. After a disastrous fire at Jaguar's Browns Lane Assembly plant the big-engined car finally made its debut in 1957. Apart from stiffer front suspension the new car differed only in detail from the 2·4. A new grille was used with a larger radiator while two SU HD 6 carburettors replaced the Solexes of the 2·4. The trusty XK unit was now giving 210 bhp in its 'B' configuration and the car was rapturously greeted by the motoring press as a true sports saloon in the grand touring tradition.

The 3·4 and the later 3·8 were to keep Jaguar at the forefront of saloon car racing until the early sixties when the big American Galaxie 500 made its track debut, but its real contribution both to the Jaguar company and the UK was to provide a viable alternative to the compact sized Mercedes-Benz which had by now acquired the added advantage of Bosch fuel injection.

While all the companies so far mentioned offered performance for the saloon driver it can easily be seen that it was at a specific price. That expense coupled with the general shortage of cars in most European countries conspired to create a grass roots movement which was to rebound and shake the marketing policy of every major car maker. That phenomenon was the number of small companies who took mundane machinery and tried to add the missing excitement. These men could best be collectively described as the 'Tuners'.

The various factors which allowed the cut price performance generators to flourish differed slightly from country to country. In post-war Germany the complete lack of any but the most mundane cars brought forth such companies as Porsche and Veritas. The latter started by rebuilding pre-war BMW 328s. They progressed to building competition cars by 1946 and by the end of 1949 had moved from the original factory in Bavaria to Messkirch in the French occupation zone. Hitherto the company had been offering its wares against the dictates of the US forces which had specifically banned the construction of cars with a capacity exceeding 1 litre.

Realising that the supply of pre-war BMW units was drying up, in 1949 also saw the small company commissioned its own 2 litre engine from the Heinkel company. This used three Solex carburettors and in touring form was reputed to give 140 bhp. It

Top: For over a decade the 'compact' Jaguar saloons first introduced in 1955 set the tone of the British sporting saloon, as beloved in the stockbroker belt as in the flasher parts of London's East End. This is the 3.4-litre engined Mk II of 1963

Above: While Mercedes and Jaguar battled for sales, Ferrari found a following right at the top of the market. The Testarossa sports car of gave its lines to a range of superb Pininfarina styled grand touring cars

followed BMW practice by being a seven bearing six-cylinder and featured hemispherical combustion chambers and a single overhead cam. Plans for a long chassis saloon using the engine eventually came to nothing due to a general lack of customers wealthy enough to afford the proposed car but a neat closed coupé and a roadster which was little more than a track car with the bare minimum of road equipment, saw the company through to 1952.

Ferry Porsche chose his father's VW as his base vehicle when he commenced production in Gmund, Austria, in 1946. Taking the engine from the stillborn Berlin-Rome racing coupé he had helped develop in 1939, he dropped it into a hand built aluminium space frame chassis in front of the rear wheels. This mid-engined car was to be the first of the whole Porsche genus although by the time regular deliveries were instituted in 1948, the engine had been moved to the back of the rear axle.

Soon Porsche were supplying equipment to other tuning specialists notably Denzel of Austria, who built a similar looking car, and Glockler in Frankfurt who created the first of the immortal Spyders of the company. Unlike Veritas, Porsche had enough business contacts to see his company through the immediate post-war period and in the

early fifties a fine series of agricultural tractors kept the company healthy. Although by the time of the introduction of the 356B the engine shared only the configuration with the original VW engine, the early flat four cars were always liable to dismissal by the more traditional sports car snob as 'hotted up Volkswagens'.

Unlike Porsche, Denzel concentrated upon the VW engine until the firm ceased trading in 1961. As well as producing sports cars the company supplied various tuning devices such as twin carburettor manifolds for standard Beetles while a full engine conversion with high lift cams and a reprofiled crank was available from the mid fifties.

In Britain the tuning fraternity was almost indistinguishable from the 'specials brigade'. Unlike in other countries rising production was also accompanied by rising taxation. To circumvent the purchase tax which almost doubled the cost of any new car, a plethora of small British manufacturers offered kits of parts which when assembled on a proprietary chassis or engine and gearbox combination gave a cheap alternative to the mass produced cars of the era.

One of the first and most successful of these specials was the Dellow. First marketed in 1949 this rather crude looking device was a derivative of a successful

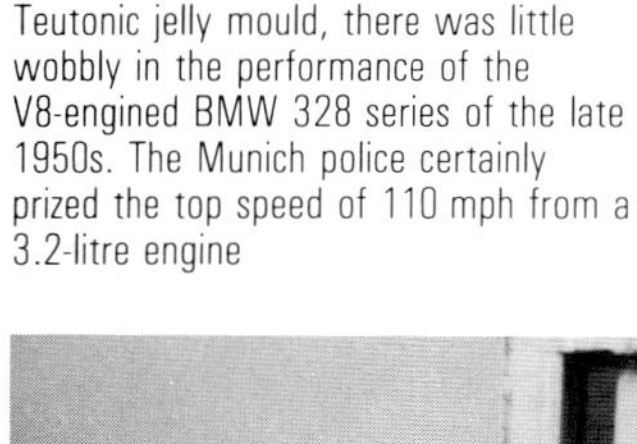

Although looking somewhat of a Teutonic jelly mould, there was little wobbly in the performance of the V8-engined BMW 328 series of the late 1950s. The Munich police certainly prized the top speed of 110 mph from a 3.2-litre engine

trials car. Like many of the other kit cars and specials of its day it used the side valve Ford 10 engine and running gear although various states of tune were offered including a supercharged version. Although the car never really achieved the enthusiast status of a contemporary Morgan or MG TD, it sold fairly well until 1956 when an attempt was made to update it by furnishing it with full width glassfibre bodywork. By this time the beam front axle had been replaced by transverse leaf independent but the car had established a pattern for a whole new sector of a British motor industry and many similar offerings of various degrees of sophistication were to follow its lead.

The trials which had spawned the Dellow and many similar devices can really be thought of as the birth of cut price motor sport in post-war Britain. While other countries allowed motor sport to take place on open roads, Britain had been bound by laws enacted in the early years of the century against any form of racing on public roads. For the motor sport enthusiast this meant that unless he had the money to participate in the type of racing carried out at Brooklands or Donington Park in the inter-war period, he was forced to look to hill climbs which took place on specially designated private roads or perhaps the sand races which where held on beaches and mud flats. True, there were other sports such as rallying but in the post-war climate with its shortages of petrol and tyres, long events were rare and participants usually confined to works teams.

In this atmosphere the off road trials, which soon came to be known as 'mud plugging', offered the would-be competition driver an almost unrestricted form of competition where the low revving side valve engine was in its element. Many of the drivers who were to grace the newly emerging racing circuits which Britain's unique wealth of disused airfields later provided started in the post-war trials and the low cost specials based upon Austin Seven and Ford chassis were to provide many with the tuning knowledge which led to the club racing boom on these circuits in the fifties.

Indeed, when the newly fledged circuits did start offering regular motor racing in Britain it was largely the special builders and the garages who specialised in tuning who provided the cars for would-be competitors. Names such as HWM, Cooper, Kieft and Allard began to attain wider fame, first for the little 500cc Formula Three cars

and Bristol powered Formula Two machinery, later for full scale Grand Prix cars or as in Allard's case, Monte Carlo Rally and Le Mans standard machinery using Cadillac and Ford V8s at first and Jaguar engines later.

Other new companies were due to join them in the early fifties such as Colin Chapman's Lotus Specials and clubmen sports cars, TVR with their competition cars and Eric Broadley with his Lolas. All of these cars at some time or another used the redoubtable 1172cc side valve Ford engine as well as the BMC pushrod A and B series engines which powered such machinery as the Morris Minor, the Austin A30 and the grossly underpowered but very pretty ZA and ZB MG Magnettes which were that company's offerings once the pre-war Y type ended its long production run in 1954.

Where the sports car and single seater drivers ventured, the saloon pilots were destined to follow and by the late fifties saloon car racing had taken on all the cut and thrust of the more glamorous formulas. Established stars such as Stirling Moss and Mike Hawthorne, who were more usually associated with Monaco and Le Mans, thought nothing of jumping into a highly tuned 'tin top' when not driving more exotic machinery and the works cars soon sported the kind of performance parts which the specialist tuners had pioneered. By the end of the fifties any number of companies were available who would sell almost any uprated part that the would-be saloon car racer might need. Where the homologation regulations allowed, often the only standard part left on an engine was the cylinder block and even these could be lightened, strengthened, dowelled or have the cam moved upstairs if necessary.

In Italy too the tuners had their day and the number of garages which offered special coachwork and engine modifications upon standard Fiat machinery were prolific in the extreme. Some offered sports car conversions which took the Italian giant back to the great races of the world with contenders in the 1100 and other sub 1500cc classes. Others offered pretty four seater coachwork upon the floorpan of the ubiquitous Topolino although in these cases the racy lines flattered only to deceive for the tiny four 500cc engine could never really offer anything but mediocre road performance.

Perhaps the best known in the immediate post-war years was Piero Dusio. His first and arguably his most successful racing cars were based upon Fiat mechanics and for his ill fated Grand Prix car attempt of 1948 he assembled a talented team including the elder and younger Porsche, Eberhan von Eberhorst and a young Austro-Italian engineer destined for more lasting fame, Carlo Abarth. With the demise of the project, Dusio was to find a home in Argentina as the Peron government desperately tried to recruit talent enough to allow full scale motor production.

The SIATA company, although primarily concerned with building cute sports car bodies on Fiat 500 chassis, adopted a policy of offering the customer just whatsoever he desired in the late forties and early fifties. This included cylinder head conversions from side to overhead valve for all of the current post-war Fiat side valve range plus a full range of other tuning equipment for the marque including twin carburettor manifolds and special cranks and cams. From 1956 they offered a neat high performance derivative of the Fiat 600 but faded from view at the end of the decade.

The much loathed horsepower tax made France almost a tuner's paradise. Almost as soon as the taxes were enforced anyone who could obtain more power without enlarging the basic tax classification had a potentially profitable business. Four speed conversions for the Citroën Traction were common as were twin carburettor conversions while to greet the advent of the 4CV the Renault company created SAPRAR as a means of making a further profit from customising its own cars.

While Italy had its battalions of Fiat fanciers, France produced the likes of DB who used basic Panhard Dyna and Citroën components in their street going sports cars and tuned the engines to make almost a clean sweep of the smaller international categories in the early fifties. Another company which began by tuning the ubiquitous 4CV Renault was Jean Rideles' Alpine which opened its international sporting career with a class win in the 1955 Mille Miglia. Even the humble Citroën 2CV had its avid performance tuners for the same Miglia saw a modified, but still recognisable, example running successfully in the smaller class entered by its progenitor M. Dagonet of Rheims. This pocket racing saloon had been extensively lightened by the use of glass fibre panels while the engine had been restroked using aluminium cylinders in cast iron jackets, twin carburettors and twin straight through exhausts.

One particular mid fifties venture did manage to combine the elements of the successful tuner and the grand tradition of the extinct *Grand Routier*: the Brasseur styled Facel Vega. Facel Metallon were a company who had specialised in providing high quality steel bodies to the defunct great names of the French motor industry. This led the company into difficulties but, rather than learn from them, the decision was made to build a fully updated grand tourer both to preserve the skills of the company and as a profitable exercise.

By utilising a Chrysler engine and gearbox the company hoped to offset some of the enormous development costs. By making the interior more luxurious than anything other than a custom built Rolls Royce they sought to woo the young rich for whom the Rolls was too staid and the DB4 too small. The result was a full four seater with ample power and style which reached the Salon in 1954. Hailed by the press as a return to the pre-war practice of specialists such as Railton, the Vega lit the way for a few even more auspicious followers.

The smaller Fiats had been built under licence in France by Simca since 1934. With the cessation of hostilities this company began a programme of product development

which was to take them to the forefront of French industry. Just as the products of the Renault and Citroën empires had their tuners and competition exponents so Simca had theirs.

The impact on the market by the French in the fifties was marked by two quite distinctly different vehicles, one from Renault and the other from Citroën. The DS19, although never intended as a product to tempt the performance buyer, marked an evolutionary leap forward for the whole of the motor industry.

While its 2 litre, long stroke, wet liner engine was a survivor of the 1934 Traction Avant, the superb hydraulic suspension plus the beautifully streamlined efficient shape of the 'Goddess' allowed it to cruise at speeds which only the most powerful multi-cylinder engines in the truly exotic Routiers had previously attained.

Not only was it sleek, and by the standards of the day fairly fast, the DS pioneered the philosophy of having the maximum wheelbase possible in the given length of the car for increased high speed stability and comfort. Its weight saving monocoque construction was also a pointer to the bravest of the world's manufacturers of the way that the industry was moving. The following twenty years were to see the car spread its unique influence worldwide, while successive power increases leading to the fuel injected DS23 kept the car competitive throughout its production life, both on the road and in the international rally scene, with the best that rivals could field against it.

The Renault Dauphine was the most successful small car to emerge from the nationalised *régie* in the decade. Introduced in 1956 the car was a direct lineal descendant of the 4CV which had seen the company regain the lost territory of the war years. An 845cc overhead valve four cylinder rear mounted engine gave the car 30 bhp at its introduction and its all round independent suspension, although open to criticism for rear end breakaway, endowed it with a ride quality unequalled by other small saloons of the day.

Amedée Gordini was, like Ettore Bugatti, a talented Italian engineer who preferred to live and work in France. He began his business naturally enough by tuning the Fiat derivatives which were produced under licence by Simca. This in turn led to small

As well as breaking many rules of traditional automotive design, the highly innovative Citroen DS series was a consistent rally winner. Here a DS 19 powers its way through the mud of the gruelling East Africa Safari Rally

run production sports cars bearing the name Simca-Gordini which did well enough in competition to encourage Gordini, who acquired the nickname 'Le Sorcier' for his tuning wizardry, to contemplate both international sports car and Grand Prix racing from his Paris based workshops.

Gordini racing cars were small and fragile but extremely fast and attractive. Somehow, although the team existed on a budget which at times became totally non-existent, the company managed to put together a major racing programme which lasted from 1948 to 1955. With the withdrawal of Talbot at the end of the 4½ litre unsupercharged Grand Prix formula, Gordini was the only man carrying on the tradition of France upon the race tracks and the country took him to their hearts in a way which almost bordered on reverence.

Shoestring budgets and unreliable cars however took their toll and in early 1956 Gordini gave up the unequal struggle. Renault, ever open to suggestions which would increase the marketability of their cars, took him in house and gave him an almost free hand to create performance versions of the current range. The result was the 1957 Dauphine-Gordini. 'Le Sorcier' had added the magic of his name to a tuned version of the car with a full four speed gearbox to replace the old three speed box (at a time when the more conservative European manufacturers thought four speeds to be confusing for the average driver) and an extra 8 bhp from improvements in the breathing of the engine.

The following year the Floride sports coupé appeared, again bearing the Gordini name, and the success of the co-operation was assured. Renault had touched upon the hitherto unknown fact that the man behind the wheel on his day out wanted to be associated, even by proxy, with the glamour of the racing and rallying world. They had found a way to exploit the hidden desire of the man in the street to take to the circuits and opened a new avenue of small cut price performance marketing which was destined to grow with the oncoming years.

The Gordini tuned Renault Dauphine of 1957 was one of the first of the combinations of standard saloon from a big manufacturer with race bred experience, the formula that was to prove such a marketing success in the 1960s

3 The sixties: Mass market performance

While the immediate post-war years saw an erosion of the more traditional performance names the affluence of the next decade was to turn round overall market trends and put performance back at the top of the salesman's pitch.

For Great Britain the early sixties were to prove both the most successful and the most innovative period for its motor industry. In France industry was quietly consolidating the rebuilding efforts of the fifties and beginning to make inroads into non-French speaking export territories. Italy was entering a new period of mass mobility while the economic miracle had taken off in Germany, spearheaded by burgeoning vehicle exports worldwide.

In the USA performance still meant cubic inches yet the movement of Ford and General Motors to adopt a more cosmopolitan model policy was already in train. The introduction in the mid fifties of the Thunderbird and the Chevrolet Corvette demonstrated that the marketing men in Detroit realised a need for lighter, more manoeuverable machinery, the sixties were to see the rise of the American compact in their wake.

In retrospect the most important single

model to emerge anywhere in the whole decade was a tiny car, built largely as a reaction to the fuel crisis of 1956 when Nasser closed the Suez canal and gave Europe its first oil shock. As with all great motoring innovations the resulting vehicle was the carefully considered fulfilment of a basic need, in this case the problem of transporting four adults in the most economic means possible while still providing the minimum standards of comfort and road holding without resorting to the engineering of desperation which had been responsible for the rise of the 'bubble car'.

The Mini, as the car came to be known, was the brainchild of Alec Issigonis. This extraordinary engineer had been responsible for the first all new post-war Morris car, the 1948 Morris Minor, a car designed from the outset as 'Britain's Volkswagen' and the 'Mini-Minor' (as the car was introduced) represented his thoughts on a logical successor to this trend setting machine.

Feeling that rear engined cars were inherently dangerous due to weight distribution, Issigonis opted for a front engined, front wheel drive package. In an effort to save weight and steel he placed the smallest

The Mini's impact on the market was given a tremendous boost with the launch of the Mini-Cooper. The remarkable performance of the tiny car was kept before the public's attention by a series of rally wins. This is the 1967 Monte-winning Mini-Cooper S

BMC engine available transversely above the front wheels and adapted the gearbox so that it sat in the sump where it was lubricated by the engine oil and drove the wheels through a central differential. To save further weight and complication the whole engine and drive train assembly was supported by a front sub-frame which also carried the rubber cone suspension whilst the rear also boasted a separate sub-frame assembly.

As originally planned the car was to feature BMC's hydraulic suspension, a simplified system inspired by that used in the Citroën DS, developed by another engineer named Alex Moulton, but failure to have the required number of units ready in time led to the adoption of the rubber cone system as the only viable alternative.

Interior space was maximised and costs were pared down by adopting sliding front widows and hinged rear ones. This in turn allowed capacious storage pockets in the doors to complement the storage shelf which replaced the more normal dashboard. The overall styling, although hinting at the bulbous fashion of the fifties, was largely dictated by the interior layout and its attractiveness was largely a by-product of its efficiency.

The road testers of 1960 adored the little car, even though several were caught out in heavy rain by the factory having fitted the rubber door seals incorrectly on the first few hundred cars allowing them to flood. The fashionable set of the day took to the car immediately yet the general public viewed it with the same sort of suspicion which had greeted the DS in 1955. Sales of both the Morris Mini-Minor and the later Austin Seven, its identical twin except for the badges, were disappointing in the first year. A new impetus was needed although the staid management of BMC were unable to see it.

The push, when it came, was from a most unlikely source. Formula Junior had been announced in 1959 as a proving ground for racing talent on its way to Formula One. The rules stated that a proprietary engine of not more than 1000cc must be used, although within the block a number of modifications were allowed. The BMC small overhead valve unit became a natural choice in this area for its strong uncomplicated block allowed basic tuning modifications to the

Ford of Britain also saw the potential of combining their already successful Cortina with a race proven name. The Lotus Cortina launched in 1963 more than fulfilled its promise both on the race-track and in boosting sales across the range

cam, valve timing and compression to take it up to 85 bhp. This engine was thus already in an advanced state of race development when the Mini was announced. It did not, therefore, take long for such companies as Downton Engineering, The Cooper Car Company and the late Graham Hill's Speedwell organisation to grasp the saloon racing potential of the little box with a wheel at each corner.

The writing was firmly on the wall for the future of the little car when Graham Hill surreptitiously filled the tank of one of the Speedwell cars with a methanol mixture, and proceeded to drive calmly away from the 3·8 Jaguars and Raymond May's Ford Zephyrs. Perhaps luckily for Hill the engine found the diet of dope too rich and expired before the end of the race thus saving Speedwell the embarrassment of discovery by the scrutineers; but the racegoing public had seen an early demonstration of the car which would become the young enthusiast's dream of the coming ten years, the competition modified Mini.

By the early months of 1961 even the BMC management had accepted the need for a more powerful Mini and began to examine the specialist markets with a view to mass production. Eventually the Cooper Car Company was selected as they already had a basic 55 bhp road going conversion and Cooper Formula One cars had taken their first world championship with Jack Brabham the previous year.

Where the standard car used the basic 848cc A series engine in single SU trim, the Cooper conversion used twin 1¼ inch SU carburettors and displaced 997cc from a longer stroke of 81·28 mm, as opposed to the standard engine's 68·26 mm, and a bore reduced from 62·94 mm to 62·43 mm. The recast crankshaft was supported by thicker webs and a re-profiled cam. Larger valves with stronger springs coupled with a three branch exhaust manifold completed the package.

Although the standard Mini drum brakes were sufficient for most road use the Cooper used seven inch discs. To facilitate more accurate gear selection a remote control was fitted which left the gear lever comfortably to hand between the front seats in a proper floor mounting. Revised exterior trim and two tone paintwork (although this latter feature was optional) differentiated the exterior of the new cars.

This version was to see the start of a dynasty of Mini variants which were destined to dominate the European circuits and rally-

ing. It was also to become the only profitable part of the Mini range for, in their unease about launching such a radically different car, the BMC management had misjudged the potential market and priced the car to compete with the bottom end of the Ford range. This horror, the side valve E93A Popular, was nothing more than a repackaged pre-war Ford 8 and still featured such delights as vacuum driven windscreen wipers and mechanical brakes. Thus the standard Mini, locked into a fixed price format as it was, made a loss for BMC throughout its heyday in the sixties.*

One month after the introduction of the Mini, Ford announced their own new contender for the small car market. Although this featured an overhead valve engine and independent front suspension by MacPherson struts it was still years behind the Mini in overall concept. Even so the Anglia in its 105E form was destined to prove extremely tractable in the hands of some of Britain's tuners.

Sidney Allard was quick to see the potential of the new car and by fitting it with a Shorrocks supercharger and strengthening the body and suspension he produced the interesting Allardette. Other companies offered full engine conversions to take the unit right up to Formula Three specification, while, seeing the success of the Mini-Cooper as a sales getter, Ford started to take an active interest in the possibilities of the car at a very senior level.

Cooper rivals Lotus were approached with a view to some form of partnership and for a time Lotus supremo Colin Chapman was seen to be driving an indecently quick version of the car. In his memoirs Jim Clark recalls with pleasure borrowing the car for a trip to Scotland and being able to race the current Mark II Jaguars with ease. This twin cam venture came to nothing in the end although Ford did use the Kent 1500cc pushrod engine in a GT badged car both for homologation purposes and to add some much needed gloss to the car in its last season of production.

The car chosen by Ford for the distinctive Lotus treatment was the Cortina. This represented Ford UK's major hope of salvaging the medium sized saloon car market after the disastrous failure of the mock Lincoln-styled Consul Classic of 1961. The Cortina made its debut in 1962 with a new 1198cc pushrod overhead valve engine. In 1963 the Cortina Super was announced with 1498cc Kent engine. It was avidly adopted by sales representatives and soon earned the nick-

*Even though the E93A was officially no longer available at the Mini launch date of August 1959, old stocks of the 100E were sold off as Populars at a similarly low price of £494 to the Mini price of £496.

name of 'the poor man's Aston Martin'.

So popular were the hot saloons that soon afterwards a GT version was introduced complete with a centre dashboard console with four extra gauges, improved suspension and brakes and an uprated engine fed by a side draught 28/36 Weber carburettor. Although this car was never to achieve the grass roots track and rally success of the tuned 105E Anglia variants, which were still competitive in the early seventies, the Cortina GT became the archetypal, upwardly mobile sales manager's car. The true high performance variant of the car had already appeared some months before.

In January 1963 the respected motoring weekly *Autocar* had previewed the car in an article which began with the words: 'In Great Britain the success of improved performance cars has been phenomenal; it is seldom appreciated that the suspension steering and brakes on the modern mass produced cars have such a degree of inherent safety that considerable increases in performance can be made with relatively minor changes.' It had then gone on to describe in some detail the changes made to all these areas in the new car. Ford had learned well from Renault and BMC the benefits of association with a glamorous Formula One team and, in the wake of Ford's final failure to buy out Enzo Ferrari in 1963, they had allied themselves with the most glamorous racing team then existing: thus was born the legendary Lotus-Cortina.

The engine had been seen already in the Lotus 23 sports car which had made its debut at the 1962 Nurburgring 1000 Kilometres. It was a product of the combined talents of Chapman and his two erstwhile engine wizards Keith Duckworth and Mike Costin of Cosworth. In essence it was based around the normal 1500 block with the bore increased to allow the engine to attain a capacity of 1558cc. An alloy head with twin chain-driven cams incorporating all Cosworth's accrued knowledge from building Formula Junior conversions of the Ford 997cc Anglia engine was its major attraction.

To provide the desired compression increase, slightly domed pistons were used with cut outs for the valves to allow a normal compression ratio of 9·5:1. Twin 40 DCOE Weber carbs fed the mixture and a four into one exhaust system was incorporated.

Transmission modifications included a close ratio gearbox, aluminium remote assembly, a larger diameter clutch and a strengthened prop shaft. Unlike the original Mini-Cooper which resolutely retained the wheels and tyres of the standard production car the Lotus-Cortina incorporated lightweight steel 5½ inch rims in place of the standard 4 inch items.

The ride height was lowered by as much as 3½ inches at the rear where the standard semi-elliptic springs had been replaced by coils over shocks with a live rear axle located by trailing links and Chapman's own variation upon the A bracket theme. At the front steel castings replaced the standard car's welded pressed channel track control arms and a stiffened anti-roll bar was used as the lower wishbone. Uprated springs and a higher ratio steering box completed the handling modifications here.

Where there is weight there is a performance penalty. With this in mind Chapman had fabricated the bonnet lid, boot and door panels from aluminium and even the full width bumpers were replaced by quarter units to save weight. The whole performance package was rounded off by 9½ inch discs at the front and 9 inch drums at the rear. The interior was neatened by the wood rimmed steering wheel and aluminium faced instrument binnacle while from the outside the cars were easily distinguished by the white paintwork with a green full length side flash.

Unlike BMC, who were keen to modify the Coopers in house, Ford left the main bulk of the work to Lotus, who opened a new extension to their Cheshunt factory to deal specifically with the car. They were also content to leave the competition preparation to Lotus and in the matter of the racing programme Team Lotus was solely responsible. To maximise the potential publicity value of the car Jim Clark, Peter Arundell and Trevor Taylor were co-opted as drivers, all seasoned single seater pilots, and Ford began a long saloon competition campaign which was to completely transform the somewhat staid European corporate image.

While the Lotus Cortina comfortably established Ford at the 1600cc competition level, BMC had not been idle. Almost from the moment it had appeared, the Mini Cooper had formed the basis for some hairy competition cars and by the middle of 1962 overbored cars were running in the 1300cc classes and acquitting themselves extremely well. A new larger engined car was clearly called for from the factory and in response to this need the 1071cc Mini-Cooper S was launched in the summer of 1963.

This was to mark the debut of the Mini as BMC's main competition machine until the end of the decade and as such it offered many of the features which the specialists had begun to incorporate. Larger main bearings, a tougher block and crank, Hidural valve guides with hardened valve stems and a larger clutch all helped in the search for more reliable peak performance. Larger disc brakes and wider wheels helped tame the extra power.

By June 1964 the S had become a family, a 970cc and the immortal 1275cc variants having appeared. Such was their impact upon international competition that by 1965 the organisers of the Monte Carlo Rally felt obliged to disqualify the overall winning 1275S and its sister cars on a fabricated technicality, handing the victor's laurels to the thoroughly outclassed and outdriven Citroën DS23 which followed them home. For that particular rally as in the previous years the rules were so loaded against the all conquering Mini that the team cars were actually running slower than the average production variant.

Inevitably the success of these cars and the Lotus-Cortinas was bringing about a revolution on the smaller saloon marketing front. An epidemic of GT badging broke out with local variations (in France the word *Rallye* was fairly commonly substituted) on the most unlikely vehicles. For the first time major car manufacturing companies were actively encouraging the client to seek performance after years of de-tuning production cars to the disgust of the enthusiasts.

In the UK Vauxhall Motors, who had yet to learn from Ford that an indifferently handling saloon based around outdated American styling was not the way to mass market sales, began a long haul to catch up with the market by adding a colour contrasted stripe to its 1962 Victor FB, increasing the power output from 48·5 to 71·3 bhp and dubbing it the VX 4/90 (four cylinders/90 mph).

In the previous year Renault had acknowledged the British predilection for uprated machinery by commencing production of a subtly anglicised version of the Gordini Dauphine at Acton while the new Renault 8 acquired the Gordini name along with an uprated 1100cc engine.

The Rootes group had been taken unawares by the overwhelming success of the Mini. Their answer was the Hillman Imp. This superb little car owed much to the current NSU Prinz in style but overcame many of the drawbacks of the rear engine configuration by carrying its weight more evenly divided front to rear. In this it was aided by the adoption of the revised and productionised Coventry Climax slant four, overhead cam, all alloy Formula Two engine.

Unfortunately the rush to put this fine car on the market meant that it arrived in the showrooms without a full development programme. This, coupled with a certain delicacy of the cylinder head, which was compounded by corrosion if the right coolant additives were not used, soon gave the car a bad name. Nonetheless it was an instant performer and in competition form, especially the later 998cc variants, was to

Constant development kept the ageing Citroen DS series at the forefront of international rallying. Here a DS 23 grapples with the mud of the Moroccan rally. With injection, the DS 23 was a considerable performer for its day

out-perform the Mini in small saloon car races and the smaller rally categories well into the mid seventies. Although never a major all round sales success for its makers the car stayed in production until the mid seventies becoming more and more refined, while the engine was to soldier on until 1984.

Further up the range from the Mini, BMC had adapted the transverse engine and gearbox layout for the Austin-Morris 1100. These cars represented a massive step forward both in safety and accommodation over the mass of rear engined rear wheel drive continentals which had hitherto dominated the class. The shortcomings, such as low corrosion resistance, aggravating engine mounting and universal joint failures plus irritating smaller problems, were not to become apparent for a few years and the cars set a trend which was to be almost universally copied in Europe and later Japan. To cash in this initial popularity BMC used a twin SU version with an MG grille and improved trim plus a luxuriously upholstered Riley version in the hope of convincing the young married man that here was a saloon replacement for his MG Midget or MGB. With 52 bhp available from the 1098cc engine performance never matched pedigree, although when the 1300 was introduced in 1967 a useful 90 mph cruising speed became available.

During the fifties VW had been content to refine their rear engined Beetle and let it find its own level with those who needed a well built economic small car. Specialists such as the coach builders Karmann were entrusted with the more glamourous convertible versions while the success of Porsche in the sports car field reflected well upon the factory. Some condescension toward the performance market occurred in the mid fifties when the factory adopted the Karmann-Ghia coupé as its official sports model. In 1960 the 1200 engine was deemed in need of extra power mainly to compete against the success of other rear engined rivals and the power was increased from 30 to 34 bhp.

Even this left much to be desired as a new generation of motorists watched the products of rival manufacturers cruise effortlessly past them and in 1961 a new bodystyle with a 45 bhp 1493cc flat four overhead valve engine was introduced. Although this model sold reasonably well it failed to replace the Beetle in the affections of the motoring public with the result that by 1966 the engine was made available in the

The BMW 1500 launched in 1962 staked the Bavarian company's claim to the youthful performance market which it would come to dominate

famous Porsche designed bodyshell while the smaller engine was expanded to 1285cc and 40 bhp at the end of 1964.

This desire for more performance was by now common to the whole German motor industry. It was a trend which had been well read by the directors of BMW and their middle class contender in the market was to prove the salvation of the company.

By the mid fifties the failure of the market to absorb the bulbous 500 series had made the company almost totally reliant upon sales of motorcycles. This in turn meant that when the bubble car boom began, BMW were ideally placed to exploit it. This they did, manufacturing the Isetta under licence from the Italian ISO company, using their own engines. In turn this gave way to the 700, a small car powered by the largest flat twin BMW motorcycle unit.

These micro-cars just about kept BMW afloat but a slump in the fortunes of the motorcycle division meant that another more successful model was needed and needed quickly. The company had already tried to beat Mercedes in the 2 to 3½ litre market and come a bad second. The new rationale was to build a car with similar quality and performance as the smaller Mercs and aim it firmly at the younger man who felt the products of the Stuttgart manufacturer were too middle aged for him.

Even as the tooling for the new model was being installed the board were forced into serious consideration of an offer for their Munich car factories by Mercedes, who

Aimed even more squarely at the 'executive' performance bracket was the BMW 1600 launched in 1966, a coupé derivative of the 1500 saloon

wanted more space to keep up with the worldwide demand for their fine trucks, yet the spirit of independence prevailed and in 1962 the BMW 1500 made its debut. The new car was conventional enough even by the standards of the day and the Michelotti-styled bodywork, although purposeful, had a bluff and boxy functionality about it which seemed only to verge upon attractiveness accidentally.

For the front suspension the company had opted for the precision of coils and struts while at the rear semi-trailing links were employed. The heart of the car, the beautifully detailed 1499cc overhead cam engine, used a new method of casting which offered high rigidity with low weight. The stroke was 71 mm and the bore 82 mm and this oversquare package gave a useable 80 bhp at 5700 rpm.

Public response to the cars was overwhelming and realising that the car they had was a winner the Bavarian company were not slow to exploit it. Discovering that they had created a new type of young persons' luxury express, the company first increased the power output to 90 bhp at the same 5700 rpm limit and concurrently introduced the 1800 version of the engine in the same body package. This gave 110 bhp in Titrim with fuel injection and allowed Autobahn cruising at over 100 mph but more importantly it demonstrated the fact that the rigid bodyshell could easily cope with even more power. This was forthcoming and by 1966 the company were ready to drop the 1500 engine in favour of an overbored 1600

unit which offered better torque and 83 bhp in single carburettor form plus a 2000 which in fuel injected Ti form gave 120 bhp.

The early sixties were also a formative time for the car production division of Mercedes-Benz for the opening of the decade saw them launch a new series of bodystyles across the whole range. These styles were a complete break with the graceful rounded shapes of the previous series. The glass area was increased with wraparound front and rear screens and slimmer A and B pillars while the rear of the cars sported ugly angular fins. Some thought had gone into the cars, however, especially to the frontal area where drag was reduced by glass fairings over the headlights and a general streamlining of the traditional Mercedes grille.

These were the first in a line of cars which with detail changes and much refinement were to take Mercedes into the 1980s. To introduce them Mercedes commenced a competition programme which was to bring them almost every international rally victory during the period from 1960 to 1963. By this time Mercedes had overcome many of the disadvantages inherent in the swing axle rear suspension and in the process they had introduced a degree of flexibility which they were quick to label 'camber compensation'. Even so the cars still exhibited some of the characteristics of the early swing axle designs especially in wet conditions. This aside the range was magnificent in its anticipation of the demands of a type of customer who required his high speed motoring complemented not only by comfort but by safety.

The Mercedes company had been experimenting with crushable rear and front zones since the early fifties and the W111/112 series cars of 1959 to 1960 were the first the public saw of them. Not until the arrival of the Rover 2000 in 1963 was Mercedes' supremacy in the field of safety development challenged and it still remains a highly promoted area in Mercedes marketing strategies.

The impact of the charmingly styled and proportioned Rover 2000 was at least as great as that of the BMW 1500. It had taken six years and a total commitment of resources at the Rover company to develop and although some British Rover purists scathingly dismissed it as a 'Solihull Citroën' the rest of the motoring world embraced it wholeheartedly.

The nucleus of the new small Rover was a 1978cc single overhead cam, five bearing, four cylinder engine. Power output was claimed as a relatively low 99 bhp at 5000 rpm yet the company had obviously brought this about intentionally by using a single SU rather than the more modern and efficient Weber carburetter variants then available. Handling was exemplary with a De Dion rear set-up including inboard rear disc brakes and Watts linkage while at the front coil and wishbone was used. The steering was a weak point for rather than rack and pinion the Rover engineers elected to stay with the worm and roller set-up from the 'Auntie' Rovers which had preceded it.

There was little doubt that the trend-setting Citroën DS had heavily influenced the design of the car — in fact one prototype looked extremely similar to the French product — yet the build quality of the new car was nearer in essence to Stuttgart than the Quai André Citroën. As well as a cellular protective cage and crumple zones, Rover had taken care that inside the car there were no protruding surfaces left unpadded to cause unnecessary injury in the event of a crash. The windscreen wipers parked in such a way that they were shrouded by the bonnet to minimise danger in the event of a pedestrian accident while a collapsible steering column was incorporated for driver safety. Under the bonnet the engine had been mounted in such a way that it would drop under the passenger compartment rather than enter it in a high speed frontal impact and the passenger cell was so arranged that in any but the most major shunts the doors would open. These are features taken for granted since the early seventies but never seen together on any one car before the small Rover.

In 1961 Standard-Triumph had been acquired by the truck manufacturer Leyland and a year later the newly buoyant company made an effort to re-introduce the concept of the 'small six'. The ingredients were the body and chassis assembly of the four cylinder Herald plus an all new 1596cc overhead valve engine. The new car was named the Vitesse and by the standards of the day fully justified its title. Unfortunately the company did little to modify the rear suspension from the standard Herald with the result that it was extremely suspect when camber changes intruded upon high speed cornering. Not until the live rear axle was changed in 1969 to a coil and wishbone system was the car fully sorted although in 1967 the company had installed the larger 1998cc engine from their 1963 Rover rival known, somewhat predictably, as the Triumph 2000.

The 2 litre class seemed to have some status throughout Europe in the early sixties probably due to the fact that manufacturers had always, either for taxation purposes or economy, tended to offer their middle class products at around the 1½ litre mark. The motoring trades of the day tended to refer to this new breed of 2 litre cars, which from 1966 also included the BMW, as the 'middle luxury class'.

This class was to prove difficult to define yet fairly easy to identify and from that date has become probably the most highly prized sector of the market. Irrespective of the top end, or even the mass market for under 1500cc cars, the market created by BMW, Rover and Triumph with their middle class expresses has thrived ever since and has seen the bulk of all technical motoring advance since the early sixties.

This market potential was certainly not without influence on the decision by Mercedes-Benz to acquire Auto Union in 1959. As an exercise Mercedes designers

Below: The Pininfarina styled 1973 Fiat 130 Coupe. With its Ferrari derived engine, this car is still one of the most attractive of the post war Fiats

Bottom: The 1975 Fiat 130 saloon offered full five seats and Ferrari-like performance but mechanical complexity dogged any greater success it might have had in world markets

were instructed to design a replacement for the delightful little two stroke DKW and from this grew a whole range of mid market saloons. In 1964 Volkswagen acquired an equal share of Auto Union having already made an agreement with Mercedes that each would refrain from entering the other manufacturer's established markets. This was later converted to a majority interest and by 1969 to outright ownership by Volkswagen.

In 1965 the first of the modern Audi family, reviving a famous pre-war name, reached the public in the shape of the 1·7 litre 80. This followed the lead taken in the medium saloon range by Ford with its Cortina and Taunus variants. The engine was a single overhead cam unit offering some 80 bhp, disc brakes and MacPherson struts were used at the front and a beam axle at the rear. Interestingly the car was designed from the outset for front wheel drive thus departing completely from both VW and Mercedes-Benz practice. Quality plus integrity of design were the dominant features highlighted in the marketing campaign but the ability of the car to outperform its nearest market rivals was carefully made apparent, a trend which was to remain constant as the range expanded.

In Italy the sixties were a high point for Alfa for their Giuliettas needed only updating and larger engines to stay competitive with anything the market might throw up. In 1962 a six cylinder 2600cc version of the twin cam was introduced and with it a larger and sleeker coupé with a full four seat capacity. This was never intended to sell in the same volume as the smaller cars but nonetheless proved extremely successful in the export market.

Lancia, on the other hand, saw the decade in with the revolutionary Flavia. Introduced first in coupé form in 1962 the Flavia marked an exciting new departure for the company. The engine was a flat four with a bore of 82 mm and a 71 mm stroke. It was designed under the direction of the man who had been responsible for the pre-war Fiat Topolino, Dr Fessia. Ninety bhp was available from the 1500cc unit at an easily attained 5800 rpm and this was later to rise to 102 bhp at the same revs for the 1800cc development of the engine. The bodywork chosen for the saloon was squared off and businesslike with a large glass area while both Pininfarina and Zagato offered coupé variants.

To take care of the buyer who wanted a respected turn of speed from a smaller engine the company then brought out the car which in coupé form was to become the staple product of the company into the early seventies. This was the Fulvia. Here the narrow V configuration was maintained but as introduced the 1100cc engine was capable of pushing the top of the range coupé to a maximum of 106 mph from 71 bhp at 600 rpm.

For the top end of the performance car market in Britain 1960 saw Jaguar taking over the ailing Daimler company. The main motivation for this move was the need to acquire more production capacity to meet the demand for the medium sized cars. An unexpected benefit was gained in the shape of Daimler's traditional limousine market for which the Majestic Major had been announced the previous year. Another spin off was the acquisition of the Daimler 2½

When first launched, the second generation Audi 100 series entered the performance market with a flourish. This is a 1977 model. In 200 turbo guise the car was for a time one of the fastest performance saloons in production

The Jaguar Mk X launched in 1961 was the first big Jag to employ all unitary construction. A 4.2-litre engine and independent rear suspension derived from the E-Type gave the somewhat ponderous looking car impressive speed and handling

litre V8. This had been used to power a glass fibre bodied sports car named the Dart but Lyons was quick to realise that if the engine were mated to the bodyshell of the 2·4 he would have a potential winner.

This car retained the traditional Daimler fluting at the top of the radiator and the plushness of the larger Daimlers in its walnut and leather interior. With the exception of the engine it was mechanically identical to the Mark II versions of the 2.4 and 3.4 Jaguars which had been introduced in 1960. These had been improved in all aspects with disc brakes all round, a wider track at the rear and transmission modifications. Trim alterations included thinner pillars, restyled grilles and faired in fog and spot lamps. To compete against the growing power of its US rivals the 3·8 litre version of the XK unit was also offered in this guise having been first seen in the XK150 sports car.

The 1961 Motor Show at Earl's Court announced the arrival of an all new large saloon to replace the Mark VII derived Mark IX. The separate chassis had finally disappeared from the Jaguar line-up as this car used to good effect the lessons learned on the smaller saloons. Disc brakes were standardised from the outset along with the independent rear suspension from the E type which comprised transverse links and coils. The 265 bhp delivered by the 3·8 unit with three SU HD8 carburettors gave the car a reasonable turn of speed by any standard and a choice of manual or automatic transmission with optional limited slip differential was available.

Regardless of the fact that the new car looked larger and heavier than its predecessor it could reach 60 mph from rest in 10·2 seconds and maximum speed was 120 mph. It was to be Jaguar's last really big car and their most successful. In 1964 the rear end treatment was incorporated into the Mark II range to originate the S types while in 1965 it received the 4·2 litre version of the XK unit with its smoother torque characteristics. In this form it was repackaged in 1967 as the 420G with improved trim. The floorpan was also used for the replacement of the Majestic Major limousine in 1967 and in this guise the Mark X lived on into 1985.

At the very top end of the market a new trend was manifesting itself in the shape of new cars from Jensen and Bristol. The Bristol 407, although as superbly built as the older cars which had used the BMW derived 2 litre mill, followed the Facel lead of using a large understressed American, or in this case Canadian, engine to achieve full GT performance without the punitive tooling costs. The engine chosen was the 5·2 litre Chrysler unit. The bodywork was a straightforward modification of the elegant coupé coachwork which had been introduced two years previously with the 406 and to make it an even more attractive businessman's carriage the Chrysler Torqueflyte box became available.

The Jensen brothers had been building small numbers of exclusive and powerful cars alongside the mass produced sports cars, they sub-contracted for Rootes and Austin-Healey, since 1946. Although the aim was to make a profit, the level of trim and finish which they incorporated meant

Jensen's Vignale bodied Interceptor combined brute power, good looks and British craftmanship in a highly desirable package

let V8 of 5·3 litres and the car was launched at the beginning of 1964. Alas, faulty pricing and production difficulties were to kill off the company by 1967 but the cars with their turtle motif badges have survived to become one of the most sought after rarities of the decade.

Late in 1959 the S series of Bentleys was announced. Powered by the new Rolls Royce 6230cc overhead valve V8, the standard saloon was indistinguishable from the SII Rolls Royce Silver Cloud except by the Bentley grille, engine plate and insignia. By 1961 the picture had changed slightly with the introduction of superbly proportioned Continental coupés from both Mulliner and James Young. In October 1962 these were joined by the graceful four door Flying Spur with its flowing sculptured lines hinting at the direction of later products. In these three models the features which were later to characterise the superb Corniche were already to be seen, but the days when the company could proudly and truthfully claim to be producing the fastest production car in the world had faded.

By the mid sixties the enhanced performance saloon had lost much of its novelty. To radically influence buying patterns something new was needed and whatever it was, BMW felt that they had the answer. The 1965 2000S coupé with the 120 bhp version of the original 1500 engine was proving popular in the extreme. In style it was reminiscent of the last fling with the V8, the 3200S, but the clean line was a direct development of the saloons. Its one serious market drawback was the price which because of the pillarless configuration was almost half as much again as the saloon.

To offer the same performance and yet keep the overall price at a level which would maintain the company's growing popularity with the younger professional and executive classes was a problem. The obvious solution was to drop the 2 litre engine into the 1600 coupé bodyshell. This was launched in 1967. Response was overwhelming. Not only was the car ideal for the young professional with sporting interests, it also attracted the newly emergent super rich, the rock musicians and the fashion designers, and with its rigid construction and fine power to weight ratio it found a ready niche in the affections of the continental competition motorist.

In the 2002 anyone could feel like a rally ace. It looked right and with its predictable 'lose it and catch it' type of handling it could be made to perform spectacularly in the

that they seldom did more than break even. During the fifties they had offered the beautiful and stylish 541 series which utilised Austin engines in a tubular chassis covered by a glassfibre shell. The lines of these cars were vaguely adapted to the bulbous and rather ugly CV8 saloon which followed the Bristol 407 into the market a year later in 1962.

Like Bristol, Jensen used the Chrysler V8 but they opted for the 5·9 litre unit which gave a healthy 305 bhp. With the Torqueflyte automatic transmission, which was standard, the car was reputed to be good for an exhilarating 135 mph maximum coupled with a 0–60 mph time in the region of 10 seconds. As if this was not enough, for 1964 the new 6.2 Chrysler Hemi was fitted giving 330 bhp. Even if it lacked the elegance of a Ferrari the Jensen certainly gave nothing away in performance.

Meanwhile at the tiny newly formed Gordon-Keeble company the idea was to produce a fibreglass car which would not only perform like a Ferrari but look like one. This dream was realised with the Bertone styled GK1. This was a full four seater with a two door body and, although leather was an extra, it offered a very comprehensively equipped interior in the luxury style of the time. The powerplant chosen was a Chevro-

hands of the less experienced weekend sportsman. Perhaps more importantly it gave the company a fine, all round sporting machine with which to begin re-establishing the reputation it had enjoyed in the years immediately prior to the war.

By this time the monetary problems which had beset the Bavarian manufacturer had long passed. The problem was to find more capacity, a need which had seen the company take over the smaller Glas concern in 1966. The capacity so gained allowed the expansion of the range and in 1968 the first all new post-war six cylinder engine made its debut. This was a seven bearing unit of 2494cc utilising the same overhead cam set up as the four cylinder units. On introduction it gave some 150 bhp at 6000 rpm and the company were happy to assure the press that there was plenty of scope for further development. With the engine a new larger range of saloons was introduced, comparable in size and capacity with the S class Mercedes-Benz. A direct rivalry in the market sector which the Stuttgart company felt was its own was on the cards; as if to confirm this the engine had been introduced in 170 bhp form using the capacity which Mercedes had made synonymous with the three pointed star: 2·8 litres.

While the whole German industry seemed set to steamroller any opposition into the ground, the mid sixties marked a distinct downturn in the fortunes of the British. While the industry was primarily orientated towards a seller's market in the post-war years both the low productivity of the British workforce and the appalling mistakes of the senior management in developing badly engineered, designed and finished cars could largely be ignored. Even a product line as mediocre as the Austin-Morris Farina range with their badge engineered upmarket derivatives could find some support due to an unsophisticated home market and a general world shortage.

With the industrial troubles which beset the industry in the mid sixties and were destined to last into the mid seventies, plus the total failure of certain designs (such as the larger Austins) added to the influx of competitively priced French and German cars with more durable ancillary equipment, market leadership began to escape from the majority of British companies.

True, the Mini-Cooper and the Lotus-Cortina were still competitive but a healthy performance saloon market was largely ignored by the new type of senior management who tended to listen only to the accountant rather than the marketing and engineering departments. In the face of threatened home markets, eroded overseas sales and the ever escalating costs of retooling for new models the late sixties saw mainly repackaged versions of the existing designs.

The new shape Lotus-Cortina when it arrived in the spring of 1967 was heavier than its predecessor necessitating uprating of the engine. The unit installed in the Mark II was claimed to deliver 108 bhp at 6000 rpm as opposed to the original 105 at 5500 rpm. The independent rear suspension was

The Cortina Mk 2 also got the Lotus treatment. Graham Hill is seen here at the wheel at a Brands Hatch meeting in the year of the car's debut, 1967

replaced by leaf springing and the trim was almost identical to that of the Cortina GT. Although in some respects this made the car more mundane, most road testers of the time felt that it was a superior road car to its predecessor offering more comfort, a quieter ride and similar road holding with more predictable rear end breakaway characteristics.

Although it showed well on the occasions that the factory entered it in competition, the car was destined to be used officially for only one season. During this time it suffered from competition on the tracks in the form of the Porsche 911 and the much improved Ford of America Galaxie 500, and on the forest rally trails from the hordes of Mini-Coopers which coupled a similar power to weight ratio with superior front wheel drive traction. At the end of 1967 the factory cars were sold and the next machine to carry the colours of Ford Motor Sport into action was probably the last truly significant performance saloon to emerge in Britain in the decade, the J25 Escort Twin Cam.

While the production-derived sector of the market was entering its most stormy phase the upper end of the market saw some of the cream of Britain's specialists introducing models designed for long term production, some to survive in modified form to this day.

Pace setters here were Jensen, who unveiled their superb Interceptor at the 1966 Earl's Court Motor Show. Based upon the proven chassis of the CV8 and carrying on the Jensen brothers' tradition of providing the most sumptuous of interior furnishings, the car was little short of a masterpiece. The supremely pleasing shape had been conceived by Touring of Milan and built by Vignale. It departed from previous Jensen practice insofar as it was constructed in metal, for the simple reason that Vignale only worked in metal, but otherwise was a perfect blend of Italian styling, American brute power and British craftsmanship.

Under the sleek fastback styling with its unique wraparound hatchback rear window there was ample room for four adults and their luggage. On the road the performance was shattering for such a large car. A maximum of 133 mph and a 0–60 time of 7·3 seconds from the first production cars remained remarkably constant during the production life span. Obviously this was achieved at some cost in fuel consumption, yet the man who could afford to buy the Jensen was not the type to be easily deterred by passing economic considerations. He could take comfort from the fact that the 20 gallon tank would normally carry him for about 300 miles of extremely quick and comfortable motoring.

For those who wanted the ultimate in sure footed high performance, the Interceptor had yet another facet. As a result of some fine experimental results from a modified CV8 an option adopted at the outset of the car's development was the Ferguson Four Wheel Drive system. Even today it is rare to encounter an ex-Jensen FF owner who will not extol the virtues of these magnificent vehicles. Unfortunately the car was only available until the 1970 season due to the

Below: Ford's marketing department brought out all the obligatory 'swinging London' props for the launch photography of the 1971 Escort RS 1600 at Brands Hatch

Bottom: Renault continued the Gordini connection into the 1970s with the performance model Gordini R8

cost, both in financial terms and skilled manpower, of modifying the basic chassis to take the Ferguson set-up.

The same show also saw the introduction of a new super luxury product from Jaguar in the guise of the Daimler Sovereign. This was the first Daimler to use the 4·2 XK engine and it shared the bodyshell of the S Type Jaguars. The Sovereign was aimed squarely at the middle aged man who would not buy or could not afford a Rolls Royce. To this end power steering and overdrive were standard fittings as was thermostatically controlled heating.

That same year saw the definitive shape of the next generation of truly luxurious Rolls Royce coupés with the two door version of the newly introduced Silver Shadow and Bentley T series. These were the first unitary cars to come from the world renowned maker. The V8 engine was retained but all else was new. Early examples, although offering the usual 'ample' supply of horsepower tended to roll excessively although the suspension, coil and wishbone front and semi-trailing link at the rear, featured a unique self-levelling system.

Of the bodystyles available without doubt the most enduringly beautiful was the Mulliner coupé which was also available in drop head form from 1967. Here the body-style was to progress to grace the wonderful and much sought after Rolls Royce Corniche upon its re-introduction but in the mid sixties it took up where the Flying Spur left off as *the* gentleman's sporting conveyance.

At the bottom of the market 1966 saw the introduction of the new 1100 family run-about from Vauxhall in the shape of the HB Viva. Although the standard car owed much to the Opel Kadett the specification was basically similar mechanically to the smaller HA series car it replaced. Interestingly this model marked the entry of Vauxhall into the performance game with a 'Brabham De Luxe 90' version. This, as the name suggested, was capable of 90 mph or more by virtue of the addition of an extra carburettor, a slightly hotter cam and attention to the spring rates and manifolding. It was never really given the chance of success on the scale of the Lotus-Cortina or the Mini-Cooper due to the moribund attitude at Vauxhall towards motor sport.

At the Russelsheim headquarters of Opel there was no such hesitation. In the Kadett the company had an international winner. To make it even more up to the minute and attractive to the small car performance customer the range was widened in 1968 by the addition of two fast back derivations plus the adoption of the overhead cam 1·7 and

Simca 1100 seen here in its final LX performance version. This car can lay claim to be the first of the new generation of 'hot hatchbacks'

1·9 litre engines of the medium sized Rekord. These cars were solidly built and extremely tractable and fully justified the *Rallye* tag which the company gave them by performing well at all levels from club rallies to full internationals.

By this time Vauxhall had developed their own potential rally winner in the form of the pretty but purposeful HBGT. This used the 1975cc overhead cam engine of the Victor in twin carburettor configuration giving a peak of 112 bhp at 5600 rpm. The disc brakes plus the lowered, uprated suspension from the Brabham were used and the whole package was neatly finished off with a matt black grille and alloy wheels, giving it a look reminiscent of a miniature Pontiac GTO.

This too was fated to remain a street cruiser for the well heeled boy racer who found the more established makes *passé* or whose father owned a Vauxhall dealership. It was of interest only as an early pointer to some of the developments which would emerge from the British branch of GM in the seventies and eighties.

An interesting anomaly in the Vauxhall range at this time was the 1967 Vauxhall Ventora. This was the medium sized Victor bodyshell carrying the engine of the top of the range Viscount. This six cylinder pushrod lump gave an extremely torquey 140 bhp with the result that the Ventora became a favourite Q car with many police forces. The interior specification on these cars was higher than the Victor's and the modifications to the suspension made it a reasonable proposition handling wise. Its weakness lay in the price for it encroached on the territory of the Rover 2000 and the Jaguar 2·4, both cars which could nearly match it in performance but offered superior cachet to the middle luxury buyer.

By 1968 both Rover the Triumph were well aware that their 2 litre saloons needed more vigour to keep pace with market demand. Rover solved the problem neatly and efficiently by shoe-horning the ex-Buick 3½ litre V8 from their larger cars into the engine bay of the 2000. Apart from modifications to the front bodywork to accommodate the larger radiator and wider section tyres very little was needed besides the obvious engine bay changes to cope with the increased power. The result was the car the police had been praying for, fast enough and manoeuvrable enough to catch speeding offenders while at the same time offering good overall economy and (until Rover was integrated with British Leyland) excellent reliability.

Triumph chose to approach the problem from a different angle and their power increase came from expanding the 2 litre six to 2½ litres and using the Lucas fuel injection from the TR5PI sports car. To rid the car of its foreshortened appearance, Michelloti were commissioned to redesign the front and rear and the result was an extremely pleasing package which fitted well into the company's plans to venture into the executive area.

The decade however still had more to offer to the performance market.

Ford Escort Mexico 1600 GT

4 The muscle cars: Performance USA

Throughout the forties and fifties, American car manufacturers had been offering larger and larger engines, partly to keep up with the ever burgeoning bodywork dripping with chrome and fins, seemingly always larger and heavier each year. Despite the larger cubic capacity, the cars were not performers because of 'lazy', under-stressed engines producing lower power outputs and because of all the weight which had to be hauled along. However, by 1960 the first rumblings of the 'muscle car' era could be felt in Detroit — people were actually thinking about shoe-horning large V8s into small to medium sized bodies. The first efforts were not quite right, either too puny like Ford's first 352 Special, or too large and heavy, like the large Chevrolet saloons of the early sixties. But the idea was there, and it was not long before the car which most recognise as the first true American muscle car came along — the Pontiac GTO of 1964.

The GTO was basically a Pontiac Tempest saloon, but with a 6·4 litre V8 in the front producing up to 360 bhp, depending on the engine tune specified, and with just enough steering, braking and suspension modifications to enable it to stay on the road under the onslaught of all this power. The GTO was noisy, fearsome and as fast in a straight line as the car from which it had rather pretentiously stolen its name — the Ferrari 250 Grand Turismo Omologato. The two cars were entirely different in character, pedigree and price — the Pontiac costing a quarter of the price of the Ferrari and quite rightly so. Nevertheless it was this unashamedly cheap, honestly brutal performance which attracted so many buyers, leaving the other manufacturers without immediate competitors. A car which would smoke the rear tyres, drag its one and three quarter tons over the standing quarter in less than 16 seconds, then go on to around 130 mph must have seemed very good value for around three thousand dollars.

So, Ford, General Motors and Chrysler had to do something fast to stop this runaway sales success, or at least cash in on it. Ford took their first step after the 352 Special with the Mustang introduced in

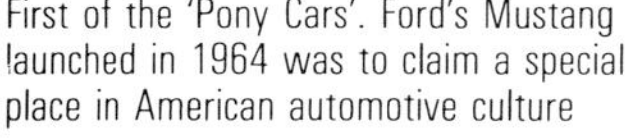

First of the 'Pony Cars'. Ford's Mustang launched in 1964 was to claim a special place in American automotive culture

1964 and with it a legend was born.

The Mustang followed a slightly different concept to the GTO. Although the Mustang was available with huge, powerful engines, many were fitted with lower powered engines and obviously sold to those who just wanted some borrowed style afforded by the 'Pony Car'.

Several engines were offered from a small six to the 289 cu in and 390 cu in V8s and 302 cu in and 429 cu in 'Boss' engines. When the Mustang evolved into the restyled Mach 1 in the early 1970s, it was offered with the 428 cu in 'Cobra Jet'. The ultimate versions of the Mustang were the Shelby GT 350 and GT500. Carroll Shelby, of AC Cobra fame, helped to modify the Mustangs quite extensively, extracting up to 350 and 400 bhp from the two models. The car's other modifications such as body bracing and stronger brakes and transmissions were done at Ford before it was transferred to Shelby for the engine modifications, some cars even being fitted with superchargers.

General Motors had the Chevrolet Impala with the 425 bhp 409 cu in engine in pro-duction in the early sixties, but this was largely eclipsed by the fabulous success of the GTO.

The next large muscle car that Chevrolet produced was the Chevelle SS396. This was smaller than the Impala and handled better, and eventually grew into the SS454. However, perhaps the best known and most popular American muscle car is the Chevrolet Camaro — a very emasculated form of the same name is still on sale today.

The Camaro was GM's answer to the Ford Mustang. The first Camaro of 1966 was cleanly styled with a semi-monocoque body from the windscreen back while the front structure was given strength by its sub-frame. Engines ranged up to the 283 cu in and 350 cu in V8s, with a large number of sport and cosmetic option packs being offered. The hot models were the SS350, SS396 and Z28, and with an option pack which put the headlights behind the black mesh grille, the Camaro looked very purposeful indeed.

In 1969, the Camaro was restyled but not launched until 1970. The method of con-

The ultimate muscle car from the Chrysler stable was the extraordinary Plymouth Superbird of 1969 distinguished by a tail mounted spoiler that would not shame an executive jet and a pointed fibreglass nose with pop-up headlights. Such baroque creations marked the end of the muscle car era

struction and many of the mechanics remained the same, but the bodystyle took on a much more European flavour, being strongly reminiscent in the front-end treatment of Jaguar's XJ6. The number of option packs did not alter much however and the Z28 was the one to go for. The classic Camaro continued in unadulterated form until mid 1970, when it was toned down to meet the emission regulations. The best Z28s developed about 360 bhp which was sufficient to push the car to 60 mph in about 6·5 seconds and on to 120 mph top speed.

Chrysler had also been in on the game from the early sixties with their medium sized (by American standards) Dodge and Plymouth saloons. The Dodge Charger and Plymouth Road Runner were cars which, although not always looking very exciting, could turn in very respectable quarter mile times. The cars were powered by 413 or 426 cu in V8 engines which pushed out between 340 and 400 bhp, depending on capacity and specification, and which drove through three or four speed manual gearboxes or a three speed automatic, the latter being a popular option.

The Chargers and Road Runners continued throughout the sixties in much the same guise, but the 426 cu in engine was developed into one of the most famous V8s ever — the Hemi. This engine, with its very strong bottom end and efficient hemispherical combustion chambers, developed around 490 lb/ft of torque and was able to push the 1¾ ton car to 100 mph in less than thirteen seconds.

Although Chargers and Road Runners had pure muscle, they were also reasonably civilised. However lacking in creature comforts in standard trim, they did handle and brake very well by the standards of the day, even if the engine was rather noisy when extended.

A later development was the Dodge Super Bee. This popular car was introduced in 1968 and was fitted with the 383 cu in Chrysler V8, producing 335 bhp at 5200 rpm. Even though the car was not quite as fast as the Road Runner it would still sprint through fourteen-second quarter miles and had a good ride combined with handling which was also considered good for the day. Even the brakes did their job of retarding the one and a half ton car well.

But the ultimate Chrysler muscle car had to be the Plymouth Superbird. Built in 1969 specifically for NASCAR racing, a certain number had to be sold for it be homologated — that is, to qualify as a stock car for racing. The most striking features of the car were the very high tail-mounted wing spoiler and the extended streamlined nose with faired in headlights. With similar running gear to the Hemi-charger (heavy duty suspension and brakes, a manual gearbox and the 426 cu in engine) but faster, it was a winner.

The last car which needs a mention is the Chevrolet Corvette, America's only real sports car of the fifties and sixties. Introduced by GM in 1953, the first versions were not very muscular with straight six engines and two speed automatic transmissions, poor performance, accommodation and braking, but then came the small block 265 and 283 cu in engines. In 1957 the car's looks changed slightly — no really big alterations to the glassfibre, but with detail changes front and rear and four headlights deemed necessary to complement the newly found power.

In 1963 the car was restyled as the Stingray, with independent suspension, distinctive round tail lights and the 327 cu in engine which had become available only a short time before. Disc brakes appeared and then in 1969 the completely new, shark-like body came out, still in glassfibre and with round tail lights, but with much meaner looks and fashionable pop-up headlights. Engines of up to 454 cu in were offered, power outputs grew and performance increased, with 0–60 mph times dropping down to the seven-second region. But by 1972, power outputs had dropped and continued to do so throughout the 1970s. The Corvette was not the only car to be reined in like this — the decline was universal.

After ten performance packed years, the muscle car era just had to end. Such an uneconomic and selfish way of transporting people simply could not be justified in the face of the fuel crisis of the early seventies, the pollution caused by so many cars burning so much fuel and the insurance companies' reaction to performance overkill, however much fun it happened to be. Perhaps that was one of the problems.

Whatever the reasons, never again will we see an abundance of cut price performance — big heavy cars able to overcome their weight and poor aerodynamics with sheer muscle and turn fourteen-second quarter miles straight off the showroom floor. Never again will the burbling of a marginally silenced, large capacity V8 noisily sucking through drainpipe sized carburettors be the music of American roads.

5 Sixties survivors

By the end of the sixties 'performance' had settled into a well defined and recognised feature of the mass market. Even the boy racer image was beginning to die off as manufacturers grudgingly acknowledged that a high performance derivative of a standard production saloon need not have 'go faster' stripes.

The advertising men were quick to exploit the new urge required by their customers. Hitherto, where elegance and low maintenance had been prime selling points, these themes were replaced with the 'getaway' feeling, the car not only as a splendid means of escape but also a mandatory aid to the Martini lifestyle of the beautiful people.

Accessory shops which had been back street affairs in the preceding decade were suddenly to be found in the very best shopping areas as well as almost every garage forecourt. True, the red velvet steering wheel cover and the nodding dog for the rear parcel shelf still featured heavily but they had also been joined by a whole host of performance products for almost every make imaginable.

Twin carb conversions, special exhausts and reprofiled cam shafts, not to mention uprated valve spring kits and suspension tuning equipment were available over the counter. Special rally type seats could be bought already equipped with the necessary mounting kit for most standard saloon cars and the alloy steering wheel with a leather rim became the badge of a worldwide breed of weekend customisers.

The manufacturers behind this new breed of competition-linked hardware bore such names as Janspeed, Moto-Lita, Momo and Recaro. They tended to be small specialists who had turned the flexibility of their size to good effect in meeting demands which the major makers by virtue of mass purchasing and mass market production economy could never quite match.

Some of these tuning concerns were destined to become part of the greater picture in terms of factory adoption, others were content to remain small and carry on providing services that the manufacturers

Stylish transport for 'sixties getaway people, the 1969 Ford Capri

could or would not. In many cases among the performance equipment makers the products on sale to the public were merely a means of subsidising the racing activities of the company. Indeed, most of the engine tuning kits were directly developed from successful competition modifications.

Even in areas as hitherto unexciting as shock absorbers the demands of the performance driver began to bring new names to the fore. Realising that an indifferently handling car could be transformed by the use of uprated dampers, the customisers started fitting the products of such companies as Bilstein and Koni, or for the really advanced there was the Adjustaride range from Armstrong. Not only did these shocks improve handling but the quality of improvement meant that whereas most standard shock absorbers were expected to last only some 30,000 miles the competition favourites could exceed 100,000 over rougher terrain and driven harder.

When Colin Chapman fitted modified aircraft wheels to his single seater racing cars in the fifties he could hardly have foreseen the impact that this was to have on overall car styling a decade later. The late sixties were to see the birth of the specialist wheelmaker as well as a belated spurt by the established suppliers to catch up. Alloy wheels of just about every imaginable configuration were to feature heavily on the accessory shopping lists of the late sixties and the general leap forward in tyre design as Michelin's patent on radial ply tyres expired was there to help achieve the fashionable low and squat look that the performance exponent wanted.

Into this background of ever more personalised cars Ford launched its Capri range. Partly born of the stateside success of the Mustang and partly to meet the requirements of the normal saloon car user who wanted extra style for little extra cost, it was designed from the outset as an attempt to be all things to all men.

At its introduction in 1969 the sleek styling with its full four seat capacity was the first attempt by a major European manufacturer to adapt the lines of the exclusive GT car to the floorpan of a production saloon. The mechanical components were common to the whole Mark II Cortina range with the exception that at the top of the range the 3 litre pushrod V6 of the Zodiac was offered. Thus in its basic variation the car offered the pushrod 1300 and 1600 units of the Cortina while at the 2000 level it used the V4 of the contemporary Corsair.

These 'cooking' versions were merely a Cortina in a sports jacket and as such ideal for the family of business users who could enjoy the sleeker lines without the penalty of an increased insurance premium. For those who wanted extra power, a GT version at each capacity level was available with uprated suspension, Weber carburation and more overtly sporting trim inside and out.

For its time the handling of the car was excellent. Rack and pinion steering had been adopted from the Escort while Ford had become so adept at setting up their favoured live axle and semi-elliptic rear suspension that road testers were hard put to induce either over or understeering characteristics.

Like the other British built Fords of the day three 'option packages' were available. They comprised the X, L and R. The X pack was concerned mainly with interior appointments and offered such extras as dipping mirror, moulded rear seats, reclining front seats and reversing lamps. The L pack offered a locking fuel cap, overriders, bright metal side flashes and dummy air scoops. The R stood for rally and added Rostyle wheels with 5½ inch rims and Pirrelli Cinturato radials, a rally type leather rimmed steering wheel, a map reading light, fog and spot lamps mounted below the front bumper and, if one really craved it, matt black bonnet and boot panels.

On all except the 1300 models disc brakes at the front and drums at the rear stopped the car, aided on the performance derivatives by a Girling vacuum servo. The excellent Cortina gearbox was used for the smaller engined versions with synchromesh on all four forward gears.

Ford advertising made much of the car with reference especially to the number of variations available due to the engine, colour, trim and equipment options. The campaign was squarely aimed at the man who had never before been able to afford a sports car and even if he had, would not have been able to fit the family inside it.

In Germany, where the car received the mechanical components of the Taunus range, the car was greeted by being named car of the year. It was an auspicious debut and one which the competition department at Cologne were both ready and eager to capitalise on. For the first time Cologne felt that they had a potential challenger to the reputation of BMW in the prestigious European Touring Car Championship and by 1970, with the aid of a 3100cc version of

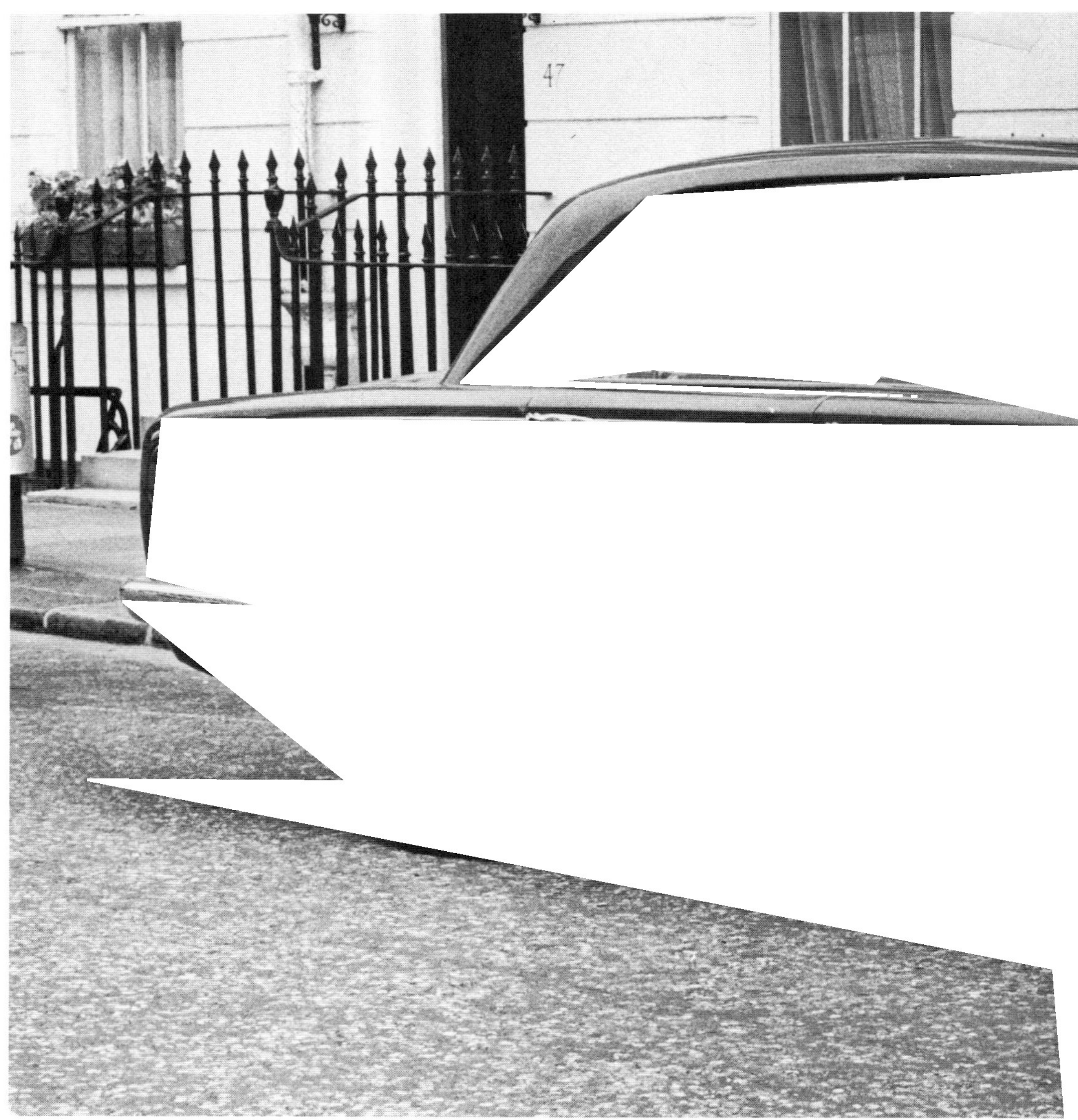

The T-series Bentley, a superb performance saloon of the '60s and '70s in its own right, provided the basis for the Mulliner bodied Corniche which remains in production

the Dagenham built V6, they decided to go racing in style.

Throughout the early seventies the big Capris were to reflect on the race tracks the success that the Escort was to find in international rallies. While the evergreen Mini fought it out with the Simca 1000s, Renault Gordinis, Abarth Fiats and Steyr-Puch derivatives in the smaller class events, the BDA engined Escorts did battle with the 2002 Ti on and off the racetrack leaving the bigger engined Capris to fight it out with the BMW CSLs in the major league.

The CLS was a straightforward development of the original 2000CS derived from the 3·0 CSi introduced in 1970. This desirable and tractable car provided smooth, elegant transport for the man who wanted something expensive and different. In competition guise when bored out to its 3½ litre maximum with its wide wheels and fins, aerofoils and spoilers it gave a useful 430 bhp. In the hands of such stars as the late Ronnie Peterson, Jackie Ickx and Niki Lauda it proved a fine match for the RS3100. Often both the Ford and the BMW would show the way to the flag with success in such gruelling classics as the Le Mans and Daytona twenty four hour races.

The original RS3100 Capri is now very much a collector's item yet so successful was the car that it has survived in much modified form to this day. Interestingly, the development which has seen the Capri evolve into the sleek 2·8i model of today has been almost a microcosm of the develop-

ment of the production-derived performance saloon throughout its years of production.

From 1970 the cars acquired a single overhead cam engine in 1600 and 2000 guise while 1973 saw a restyling of the bodyshell to incorporate the fashionable hatchback. Just as the up market versions of competing manufacturers adopted fuel injection for increased efficiency, so too the Capri has been equipped with it on the top of the range version. The four speed gearbox made way for the five speed unit in 1976 while low profile tyres and heavily revised suspension geometry follow the patterns set by more expensive machinery. Overall, however, the car is still in essence the same vehicle which the Ford marketing depart-

ment originated in the mid 1960s. The sports saloon for the family man, the car which he always promised himself and that has always been excellent value for money.

The Ford V6 3 litre engine was used to power yet another sports proposition which has survived since 1968 in the shapely guise of the Reliant Scimitar. This was an attempt by the small manufacturer from Tamworth to finally break away from the image of suppliers of tacky three wheeled fibre-glass bodied economy cars and vans. It worked.

The original design for the Scimitar was commissioned by the Daimler Motor Co in the year that was to see them admit defeat. The designer, David Ogle, was left with the prototype and Reliant were delighted to

Sales of the fibreglass-bodied Reliant Scimitar did not sparkle in its original 2+2 coupe form but took off with royal patronage for the GTE 'performance estate' version. The formula remained successful into the 1980s

step in when Daimler bowed out and launched the car with a straight six Ford 2·5 litre engine in 1965. In 1966 with the launch of the Dagenham built V6 the coupé was redesigned almost back to its prototype configuration (it had been designed around the Daimler 2½ litre V8) and offered with the new engine.

As a replacement for the none too spectacular Reliant Sabre the car was ideal, yet it still lacked overall market appeal for in its original GT configuration the rear bench seat was unuseable except for extremely small children or parcels. This left the car in competition with every other small powerful glassfibre bodied sports car, a market which although healthy was destined to see almost all the companies who participated in it finish their trading careers in the bankruptcy courts. The distinguishing factor for the Scimitar came about as a direct result of a publicity exercise by the Triplex Glass Company.

To introduce their range of tinted safety glass they approached the Ogle concern to design a radically different estate version of the car using large expanses of curved glass. As a publicity exercise it was totally successful but it also gave the directors of Reliant food for thought due to the increase in the amount of rear accommodation and luggage space.

The Triplex Special had never been intended as a production vehicle with the result that the Ogle stylists had to completely rethink the rear styling and engineering of the car. The result was an extension rearwards of the cabin roofline and the substantial box section chassis. This allowed the mounting of a rear frame to take the weight of the lifting rear door as well as an extended wheelbase to give room for two rear passengers. The rear suspension, an advanced coil system using parallel trailing arms and lateral Watts linkage, was revised and the rear track widened. By the end of 1968 all was ready and the new car was introduced as the Scimitar GTE. So popular was it that by 1970 the original GT had been dropped as the company tried to meet demand.

Like the Capri the Scimitar has seen changes in its long production history although in concept it is still very much the same practical and exhilarating package which emerged in 1968. Long a favourite with the sporting fraternity the car has grown in luxury and refinement both inside and out. In 1979 a convertible version was developed and this together with the GTE marked the change from the Dagenham built Ford V6 to the lighter and more powerful Cologne built 2·8 V6 found in the Capri 2·8i.

6 The big three: Jaguar, BMW, Mercedes

Previous page: BMW 745i

Right: Hidden beneath the spoilers, flared wheel arches and garish completion trim is one of the most elegant of all Jaguars, the V12 XJC coupe. Jag's re-entry to the race-track in 1976 proved to be an heroic failure due to problems with the homologation rulings

Below: Somewhat more staid in tone — the top of the range Daimler Double Six, a present day evocation of the great Royal Daimlers of the 1930s

1968 ushered in new cars from Mercedes-Benz. The ugly squared rear line was smoothed and the improvements incorporated into the cars brought them to a point of development which the company was justifiably confident would see them well into the next decade. Most important among these new cars from Mercedes' standpoint was the new 280 series. This featured new 2778cc overhead cam power plant available in two stages of tune.

By now the confusing typology of the various cars of the marque had settled into a routine. On the saloon cars the S designated that the car was of the more luxurious range, E indicated fuel injection and the letter L meant the longer wheelbase was incorporated. Thus while the 280S used twin Zenith carburettors the 280SE and SEL offered the Bosch fuel injection system.

Although the 280SEL offered a top speed of over 110 mph and delivered a satisfactory 146 bhp at 5000 rpm the greatest innovation on these cars was the abandonment of the swing axle rear suspension in favour of a semi-trailing wishbone. Here the company had obviously taken note of the superb handling of both BMW and Jaguar for the system was mounted in its own sub-frame with a view to minimising road shock noise and preventing undue intrusion into the luggage carrying area.

For those who still wanted extra urge the 300SEL was continued, having been introduced in the early sixties and subsequently much refined in 1966, with the 6·3 litre engine from the top of the range 600 limousine. This car was to become the standard by which succeeding Mercedes saloons were judged for it was quite simply the most effortless way to travel quickly from one point to another that the market had yet encountered. Unfortunately attempts in the long distance saloon events to utilise this abundance of power proved abortive, due to transmission and minor structural component failure, but the philosophy of a large unstressed V8 in a precision engineered chassis was the opening chapter of a new era in Mercedes production.

Fine machines as these cars were, the limelight was to be taken from them by Sir William Lyons. Although Jaguar production was only perhaps one tenth of the output of that of the three pointed star the image of the marque was still just that much glossier. Perhaps because Jaguar did not build agriculturally crude diesel taxis in the same bodyshells as it offered to its luxury customers, or perhaps because although Jaguar had never enjoyed the reputation of Mercedes on the racetracks of the thirties they had proved the equal of the Stuttgart company in the long distance sports car races of the fifties and early sixties, the world still loved Jaguars.

The 1968 offering from the Coventry company was to prove the epitome of the stylish high performance saloon both to the commentators of the time and to the truly discerning customers of the next decade and a half. Sleek, beautifully finished and magnificently equipped, the XJ6 was the last major styling exercise over which Sir William Lyons retained control.

Perhaps in the depth of the radiator there was some little imbalance in the overall sweep of the line. It was an area which was to be remodelled in 1974. Perhaps in offering the XK unit, which was beginning its nineteenth year of uninterrupted production and development, Lyons could be accused of putting 'old wine in new bottles', but nonetheless the company had produced its major masterpiece.

The new saloon was very much in the classic Lyons mould. Proven components from predecessors complimented new development in a way which ensured continuity of quality alongside modernity. From the E type series II came the servo assisted all round discs and rear suspension while the transmission options were merely uprated from the previous model catalogue.

The XK was available in two sizes, the well proven 4·2 with 245 bhp at 5500 rpm and a new 2·8 derivative designed expressly for those countries which still clung to a horsepower tax. This latter unit was credited with some 180 bhp at 6000 rpm and was in fact an enlarged version of the familiar 2·4 litre unit. It was never to prove satisfactory when judged by the standards of the smaller engine however and was destined to be replaced in the overall line-up by an 'economy' 3·4 version in 1975.

The design of the front suspension broke with the previous range of saloons by adopting a coil and wishbone configuration which, when complemented by rack and pinion steering with power assistance optionally available, gave the car the precision of handling previously attained only by nimble sports cars. This coupled with a maximum of 120 mph for the 4·2, plus excellent road holding, a 0–100 mph time of only thirty seconds and a tested 0–60 mph time of around eleven seconds, put it well ahead in performance terms of all but the most exotic of the two seaters available.

Jaguar XJ6

JAGUAR XJ6 3·4
Country of origin: *Great Britain*
Engine: *2 × ohc S6*
Capacity: *3422cc*
Bore and stroke: *83·0 × 106·0 mm*
Power output: *162 bhp*
  @ 5250 rpm
Carburation: *2 × SU HIF 7*
Number of gears: *5*

PERFORMANCE
Top speed: *190 km/h*
Acceleration (0–100 km/h): *11·0 sec*

DIMENSIONS
Length: *4·959 m*
Width: *1·770 m*
Height: *1·370 m*
Wheelbase: *2·865 m*
Doors: *4*
Seats: *5*
Fuel Capacity: *91 litres*

Just as with every other major new Jaguar Lyons had spotted a trend and fitted the vehicle to it. Not only that, he had rationalised a product range which had grown unbelievably clumsy. In 1968 the press department of Jaguar had proudly announced that the amount of options available over the combined Jaguar-Daimler range added up to a hefty 189,024 possible variants. The XJ6's introduction was yet another major worldwide triumph which left the majority of customers having to wait for up to two years to become the proud owner of the latest big cat.

Even a star like the XJ6 needs time to wear itself into the market. Very few cars have ever been offered for sale without the months following initial launch throwing up the type of teething troubles which cannot be spotted until the new model has been maltreated by everyday motoring. Usually these would have been quickly dealt with by Jaguar at Browns Lane but in the gathering climate of even worse industrial relations throughout Britain, Lyons was forced by an inept government into merging with the newly constructed British Leyland organisation.

Because of the loss of sovereignty over policymaking, teething troubles such as overheating and poor electrical equipment were to remain with the XJ for far longer than the type of customer the car was aimed at would tolerate. Morale at all levels in the company began to suffer and in the years following the model's introduction it was made worse by the break up of the management team which Sir William Lyons had so carefully built.

So starved was Jaguar of investment, as its profits were siphoned off to prop up the appalling mass market offerings of the group, that the mechanically identical XJC coupé derivative of the car, which had been scheduled to appear two years after the saloon, was not available until the early months of 1975. Nevertheless Jaguars continued to roll from the production lines and in 1972, just prior to the massive energy crisis brought on by the middle East war, the ultimate performance saloon appeared.

The XJ12 was the pinnacle of Sir William Lyons' long career in the motor industry. The engine had grown from a stillborn racing project, the XJ13, which had been conceived to redress the balance when international sports car racing grew too far from the road going product for the Jaguar D types to compete.

The original V12 had been of twin over-

head cam per bank configuration with the capacity set at 4994cc to render it eligible for the prototype class of the late sixties. For production purposes this was altered to a single overhead cam per bank driven by chains and the capacity was raised to 5343cc. To save weight the block and crankcase were integral and cast in alloy as were the heads and, when first seen on the Series III E Type, the induction was by way of four twin choke downdraught Zenith carburettors.

The new engine offered 272 bhp at 5850 rpm and at this level the torque characteristics made a torque converter not only desirable but almost a necessity. Thus although the V12 E type was available with a five speed ZF box and twin plate clutch the saloon when it arrived offered no alternative to the Borg-Warner automatic box.

As the top of the range model it would have been logical to expect Jaguar to offer the XJ12 with the latest in fuel injection

1984 model Jaguar XJ6. A rigorous shakeout in the early 1980s cured quality control problems at Jaguar and re-established the marque's reputation in the vital US market

yet surprisingly the 175CDSE Zeniths were retained. The higher efficiency cooling system of the new car was to finally solve the overheating problem of the earlier XJ6 yet complaints were soon heard from XJ12 users in hot climes that the system was not up to coping with the heat from the twelve cylinders plus traffic conditions in desert cities.

Inside the car new dash layout common to both 6s and 12s made the dials easier for the driver to read while, somewhat belatedly, Jaguar followed Mercedes in offering an L option with four inches extra legroom in the autumn of 1972. The reaction of the motoring press was one of incredulous adulation, even though by this time the quality control systems and central purchasing policies of BL were beginning to compromise the reputation of the make for reliability. One respected US glamour magazine even advised its readers to start sleeping with the wife of the local Jaguar agent to obtain one of these rare beasts.

The XJ12 and the coupé version of the XJ series were the last manifestation of Lyons' rule however for in 1973 he retired from the company which he had brought into the very highest ranks of the world's prestige manufacturers. The lack of direction and aesthetic control which were to succeed him were easily apparent in the shape of the 1975 XJS. Perhaps in this unhappy ugly duckling the death of Malcolm Sayer, the man largely responsible for translating Lyons' ideas into practical style, was most keenly felt. The overall looks of the car were and are uniformly hideous with the result that the car, which technically is far superior to almost anything from Stuttgart, Munich or even Modena, has to sell on the fact that its competitors outprice it. Even so the XJS will probably never approach the sales totals of the BMW 635, the Mercedes 500SEC and only Ferrari policy keeps it ahead of the low volume Ferrari 400i.

However as Jaguar suffered, both Mercedes and BMW were going from strength to strength. While Jaguar management were blaming the fuel crisis and the rampant inflation which followed it for bad sales, the two German companies were busting sales targets. While the big cat licked its wounds and top BL management planned ever more horrendous Austins and Rovers, the Germans calmly carried forward a well structured programme of investment in an effort to monopolise the luxury and middle luxury markets Europe-wide while establishing an even bigger bridgehead in the United States.

The 1972 crop of S class saloons from Mercedes were complemented by an angular yet elegant coupé. Based upon the floorpan of the 280S the 280CE offered pillarless looks, a fair turn of speed and exceptional handling and economy for its class. The power plant was the twin overhead cam 2746cc six cylinder unit which had appeared to bridge a gap left in the engine range with the demise of the older single cam engine.

This engine also powered the smallest of the S class saloons. As was common practice by this time the engine was offered in the two stages of tune designated by the S and SE letters. In SE form it developed 185 bhp while meeting US anti-pollution regulations for that time while the Solex carburettor-equipped alternative managed a reasonable 160 bhp.

For those who needed more power, cast-iron block single overhead cam V8 engines of 3½ and 4½ litres were available. To house these robust and reliable engines, both of which featured Bosch fuel injection, the S class body was another subtle refinement of the preceding bodystyle yet, as well as making the style more strikingly

BMW 525i

elegant, the designers had incorporated all the latest developments in safety equipment that their fertile technical division could supply.

While other performance orientated manufacturers worried about the new US safety and emission controls, Mercedes had driven their cars straight through them, and done it with much less loss in output and efficiency than Detroit. The safety car had come into its own and from within the moribund fool's paradise which was British Leyland the marketing men at Rover could only watch in disgust as their own projects had long since been cancelled to make way for Leyland's idea of a middle luxury car.

In Munich BMW also took a route of consolidation. The exception was the 5 series which cleverly offered middle luxury motoring to the man who would otherwise have been left without an alternative to Ford or Audi with the demise of the Rover 2000 and the gradual price increases which lifted the smaller Mercs into a new price zone.

The BMW 5 series was a logical progression insofar as the dimensions were very little larger than the 2000 model which it replaced, being 3 inches longer with a wheelbase increased by 4 inches and an overall width increase of some 1½ inches. The clean, neat lines showed the on-going influence of Michelotti while the MacPherson strut front and semi-trailing rear suspension was almost identical in configuration to the larger 2½ and 3 saloons.

The newer, larger body and the increased equipment incorporated in the 5 obviously gave it a weight penalty over the earlier 2000 saloon but to overcome this the Tilux engine from the older model had been further developed to give an extra 10 bhp. In injection form the 520i developed a respect-

BMW 323i

able 130 bhp at 5800 rpm and although expensive outside its home territory immediately started to gain ground against all of its competitors.

In the following year it was offered with the 2500 engine in carburettor and injection form as the 525 while further engine options allowed the 5 series to become one of the most comprehensive ranges on offer with the adoption of the 1800 (518), 2800 (528) and in 1981 the magnificent 3½ litre engine was installed taking it right up into the highest league of performance with a top speed of over 150 mph. From 1980 the body was re-styled yet the 5 still represents a quality saloon which has its own special niche in the international market among those who really like to drive the 'wolf in sheep's clothing' type of car.

The phenomenal success of the 5 obviously influenced the Bavarian company in their choice of a successor to the superb 2002. It was to be some three years however before the public were allowed to view this car. Through the early seventies the charisma of the 2002 and the smaller 1602 were enough to assure them of an extremely healthy following in world markets. To add to the basic range the 2002Ti had been introduced in 1971 with an engine offering a peak output of 130 bhp at 5800 rpm from basically the same unit which was to power the 520i in the following year.

The same engine was also offered to special order when BMW joined the hatchback craze with their Touring model in 1971 and, for those who wanted motoring tinged with fresh air, a cabriolet joined the range from 1973. In right hand drive countries the tilt of the engine combined with the location of the steering column made the fitting of injection on the small coupé a problem. This was overcome by offering an uprated twin carburettor version of the standard 2002Ti engine which produced the same output. This car was known as the Tii. Meanwhile at the upper end of the small performance saloon scale a special homologation effort was made by offering a limited number of 2002 Turbos in 1974 and 1975.

Obviously BMW were prepared to fight at all levels of the performance market and the seventies were to prove that the world was more than willing to absorb the type of good quality product that the Munich company was capable of producing.

Thus, the 3 series when it finally arrived in 1975 found a rapturous welcome from both customers and press. True, it was not the same type of basic rigid coupé as the 2002 and as such it was never an easy proposition to prepare for the race-tracks. What it offered was the same type of crisp upmarket styling of the 5 series in a package which could be made as luxurious as the customers whim dictated.

At its introduction the car came in three engine sizes plus the top of the range unit was available in the fuel injected derivation as the 320i. The suspension from the 5 series had been adapted for the new cars and all shared the same basic bodyshell. The bottom of the range was the 316 which used the engine from the 1602 slightly uprated to give 90 bhp at 6000 rpm. For those who needed extra power there was an interim model between this and the 320 in the form of the 318 which used an engine of 1766cc giving 98 bhp at 5800 rpm while the 320 in carburated form delivered 109 bhp at 5800 rpm.

Far from being a 'Mercedes in miniature', which was the marketing strategy of the original 1500 range, the new cars reinforced the conceptual image of a company committed to following its own path. There was a distinctiveness about the style and the quality which was unrivalled anywhere else in the world at that time. As well as performance, economy had been a prime consideration in the design of the new cars and the simple and conventional lines were shaped with a view to a production run as long as the preceding styles.

The marketing strategy reflected this and advertisements stressed that the quality control levels applied to the top of the range coupés were the same as those applied on the production line of the 316. Trouble was taken to assure the buyer that in buying a small BMW he was still in essence drawing upon the skill which had dominated the European Championships for both touring cars and Formula Two. 'Beautiful BMW' became the copy line in BMW ads and, as the new small cars began to proliferate on the streets of the world, the only problem the company seemed to have was that of producing enough to satisfy the demand.

With the exception of the introduction by Mercedes of a five cylinder diesel engine which subsequently achieved some semblance of performance when it sprouted a turbocharger, the rest of the decade for the Stuttgart company was one of gradual refinement of what was already an extremely desirable product line rather than radical innovation.

In Coventry lack of real investment produced a similar policy, although by 1972 the

BMW 323i

Country of origin: *Germany*
Engine: *sohc S6*
Capacity: *2316cc*
Bore and stroke: *80·0 × 76·8 mm*
Power output: *150 bhp
 @ 6000 rpm*
Carburation: *LE-Jetronic*
Number of gears: *5*

PERFORMANCE

Top speed: *204 km/h*
Acceleration (0–100 km/h): *9·0 sec*

DIMENSIONS

Length: *4·325 m*
Width: *1·645 m*
Height: *2·570 m*
Wheelbase: *2·570 m*
Doors: *2 or 4*
Seats: *5*
Fuel Capacity: *55 litres*

M·DW 3805

BMW 635 CSi

total production at Jaguar had dropped below ten per cent of the output of Mercedes-Benz. The 1975 introduction of the XJS was a move by the company both to recapture the top end of the sports car market which the E type had dominated while at the same time giving the company a rival for the exotics from Italy and coupés from Stuttgart and Munich.

The fact that the world did not like the styling merely compounded the sorry reputation the corporate mentality of British Leyland had managed to endow the Jaguars with. A further blow to the Jaguar was the introduction in 1976 of the new 7 series BMW. Here the German company had further refined the lines originally seen in the 5 series and then successfully exploited the striking 633Csi of 1975. Three engine options were available; 2·8, 3·0 and 3·3 litre capacities and all were offered with fuel injection plus automatic transmission across the range.

When originally conceived the range was to have featured an all alloy V12 but the company wisely abandoned this direction in 1973 with the advent of the fuel crisis. Nevertheless both the 633Csi and the 3·3 litre 733 gave a creditable 200 bhp at 5000 rpm and returned respectable consumption even when driven hard. If there was any fault with the cars it lay in the rear suspension geometry of the coupé which allowed the car to break away fiercely on wet roads under certain camber conditions but this was later remedied with the 1982 models.

The company added a new small six cylinder single overhead cam engine to the range in 1978. Available first in 2 litre form, it appeared in both the 3 and 5 series shell. The following year the capacity was extended to 2·3 litres and was installed in the 3 series shell to give BMW the 2002 replacement that the faithful had been waiting for, the charismatic 323i.

As introduced the 323 was a hairy car with the same happily controllable oversteer of the 2002Ti. It sold to the man who wanted to outrun the sports car brigade and to the man who just wanted the best engineered small saloon he could lay hands upon. It hit just the right spot in the market offering a top speed of almost 130 mph and 1–60 mph in around the nine second mark.

It retained its bravado character even after the 3 Series had been repackaged into the E30 types of 1982 when the trailing arms of the rear suspension had been relocated to try to eliminate untoward cor-

BMW M635CSi
Country of origin: *Germany*
Engine: *2 × ohc S6*
Capacity: *3453cc*
Bore and stroke: *93·4 × 84·0 mm*
Power output: *286 bhp*
 @ 6500 rpm
Carburation: *DME-Motronic*
Number of gears: *5*

PERFORMANCE
Top speed: *255 km/h*
Acceleration (0–100 km/h): *6·4 sec*

DIMENSIONS
Length: *4·755 m*
Width: *1·725 m*
Height: *1·353 m*
Wheelbase: *2·625 m*
Doors: *2*
Seats: *4*
Fuel Capacity: *70 litres*

TWR
MOTUL
12
JAGUAR
MOTUL
TWR
MOTUL
DUNLOP

JAGUAR XJS3·6 AND XJS–SC3·6

Country of origin: *Great Britain*
Engine: *sohc S6*
Capacity: *3590cc*
Bore and stroke: *91·0 × 92·0 mm*
Power output: *228 bhp @ 5300 rpm*
Carburation: *Lucas digital injection*
Number of gears: *5*

PERFORMANCE

Top speed: *233 km/h (229 km/h SC)*
Acceleration (0–100 km/h): *7·6 sec*

DIMENSIONS

Length: *4·764 m*
Width: *1·793 m*
Height: *1·261 m*
Wheelbase: *2·591 m*
Doors: *2*
Seats: *2 + 2*
Fuel Capacity: *91 litres*

The XJS was a controversial successor to the E-Type 2+2, available initially only in coupé form

HOTEL SACHER
HOTEL SACHER

nering antics in the hands of the less sophisticated driver. While the 7 series was lined up to battle with the S Class Mercs and the Jaguars, the 323 lacked any real rival having to wait in the medium sector for the advent of the 190E downsized Merc. Even then it held its edge in the eyes that is of many confirmed BMW addicts.

The latter half of the seventies saw some hope for Jaguar against an otherwise gloomy background demonstrated by the fact that, for the first time, the Coventry marque was quietly being price discounted by its home dealers. To build confidence, Leyland decided to go racing. The car chosen was the glamorous XJC and the series was predictably the European Touring Car Championship. The result however was disastrous, not on the track but in the rule book.

To prepare the team cars Leyland approached Ralph Broad. Broad and his company Broadspeed had been synonymous with racing success since the early days of the Mini-Cooper. Drawing on the ideas of both Jaguar and the American sports car ace and Jaguar fanatic Bob Tullius, Broad built what was on paper the most sophisticated and competitive big cat ever to take to the tracks. In its original form it had dry sump lubrication, water cooled brakes, heavily modified suspension; the engine was overbored to slightly over 5·4 litres and the compression ratio increased to 11·5:1. Lucas fuel injection similar to that used successfully in contemporary Formula One cars was employed and the package sat on 13 inch front and 13½ inch rear tyres.

Surprisingly Broad managed to gain homologation for the coupé to use the five speed ZF gearbox although no such road going equipment was to be had from Jaguar. Unsurprisingly the water cooled brakes and dry sump engine were banned as rival manufacturers loudly protested at the magnificent beast's over-zealous preparation.

Without the water cooled brakes the situation was hopeless. The car's weight was close to two tons and, at the type of speeds the car was capable of, both brake fade and tyre failure due to heat build up were to cripple the team. Problems were

MERCEDES-BENZ 380SEC
Country of origin: *Germany*
Engine: *2 × ohc V8*
Capacity: *3839cc*
Bore and stroke: *88·0 × 78·9 mm*
Power output: *204 bhp*
 @ 5250 rpm
Carburation: *Bosch injection*
Number of gears: *Automatic*

PERFORMANCE
Top speed: *210 km/h*
Acceleration (0–100 km/h): *9·8 sec*

DIMENSIONS
Length: *4·910 m*
Width: *1·828 m*
Height: *1·406 m*
Wheelbase: *2·850 m*
Doors: *2*
Seats: *4*
Fuel Capacity: *90 litres*

MERCEDES-BENZ 500SEC
Country of origin: *Germany*
Engine: *2 × ohc V8*
Capacity: *4973cc*
Bore and stroke: *96·5 × 85·0 mm*
Power output: *231 bhp*
 @ 4750 rpm
Carburation: *Bosch injection*
Number of gears: *Automatic*

PERFORMANCE
Top speed: *225 km/h*
Acceleration (0–100 km/h): *8·1 sec*

DIMENSIONS
Length: *4·910 m*
Width: *1·828 m*
Height: *1·406 m*
Wheelbase: *2·845 m*
Doors: *2*
Seats: *4*
Fuel Capacity: *90 litres*

Far left: Mercedes 380 SEC coupé

Left: Mercedes 300 SEL

compounded by oil surge and after an abortive 1976 season in which a single entry expired in the TT, the programme was dropped towards the end of the 1977 season leaving the BMW 635Csi brigade to dominate the larger classes.

After the reforms brought in by Sir Michael Edwarde's tough style of management, the end of the decade saw the company even further towards reclaiming the prosperity and prestige enjoyed over its first three decades. The introduction of the Mark III version of the XJ saloons plus the adoption of the Mays heads, with their lean burn economy configuration adding a twenty per cent increase in combustion efficiency, had begun to refill the empty columns in the order books. Although the Mark III was more of a styling exercise than a full repackage, the fact that the Borg-Warner automatic box had made way for the smoother and more efficient General Motors unit went some way to answering the only criticism which could still generally be made in terms of ride and performance, that of snatchy changes.

Elsewhere the introduction of new pattern alloy wheels, new colours, a new higher roofline with increased glass area and a general refinement of the overall styling at last brought the car into line with rival products. It looked good and it was good. It was to need only one extra factor to confirm that it could stay good and this was added in April 1980 when the company acquired its own chairman again in the form of John Egan after a gap of five years and once again adopted the trading title Jaguar Cars Ltd.

That same year was one of enormous significance for Mercedes-Benz for it marked the launch of the third generation of S class cars. Already the refinement of the smaller cars had been undertaken with the W123 series of the mid seventies. The W126 series was to be the best family of saloon cars the company had ever marketed, at least in the opinion of the Mercedes-Benz.

Launched in August 1979, the new cars featured the latest development of the twin overhead cam 2·8 litre unit plus V8s of 3·8 and 5 litres. These larger engines featured all alloy construction, saving some ten per cent of the weight of the older iron block units, with a single overhead cam to each bank of the 90° V. In the case of the top of the range 4973cc unit some 240 bhp at 4750 rpm was available in standard fuel injected specification which was transmitted by the four speed torque converter box which Mercedes

also sell to Porsche for the 928.

Front suspension used the now familiar coil and wishbones at the front and semi-trailing wishbone and coil at the back. For those who preferred it, a self-levelling hydro-pneumatic option was available. Disc brakes all round finally brought the cars into the same class as their rivals in terms of stopping ability while attractive alloy wheels were a factory option with low profile tyres. Only the technology of the steering jarred with the retention of recirculating ball but, unlike the various Japanese models which still cling to this anachronism, the feel was fairly precise and, even with power assistance, allowed some road feel.

Stylistically it remains a matter of personal taste whether the newly smoothed aerodynamic shape is more attractive than the preceding cars, although a drag reduction of some twelve per cent is claimed. The grey plastic side panels which continue the line of the deep, impact-absorbing bumpers are certainly jarring to the eyes of most customers. In the early model life of the car almost all the specialist aerodynamic accessory manufacturers who built items such as spoilers and side skirts for the cars offered the option of repainting them into the body colour. It was a popular move.

Inside the cars display none of the sumptuousness of Rolls Royce or Jaguar favouring a stark look with few intrusions. All the instruments of importance are clustered in a binnacle. The seats are hard and bulky and back seat legroom is rather restricted but the L version takes care of this problem and these have so far proved the more desirable of the body options.

The 380 and 500SELs and the SEC versions which were introduced in early 1982 are set fair for production until the end of the eighties. Technically they are at the head of the field and are going to be a hard act to follow. Yet the market is changing and the last few years have seen the resurgence of a newly independent Jaguar while the management at BMW cannot be expected to run second to both companies at the top end of the prestige and performance markets for much longer. Meanwhile, with their delightful 9000 Turbo 16, Saab may well have declared a passing interest in taking sales away from all three. Nevertheless if one discounts the super-expensive cars such as the Bentley Mulsanne Turbo and the Lagonda, the names of Jaguar, Mercedes and BMW are still the three which best combine glamour with performance in the eyes of the world.

*7 In at
the small end*

Previous page: Citroen BX GT

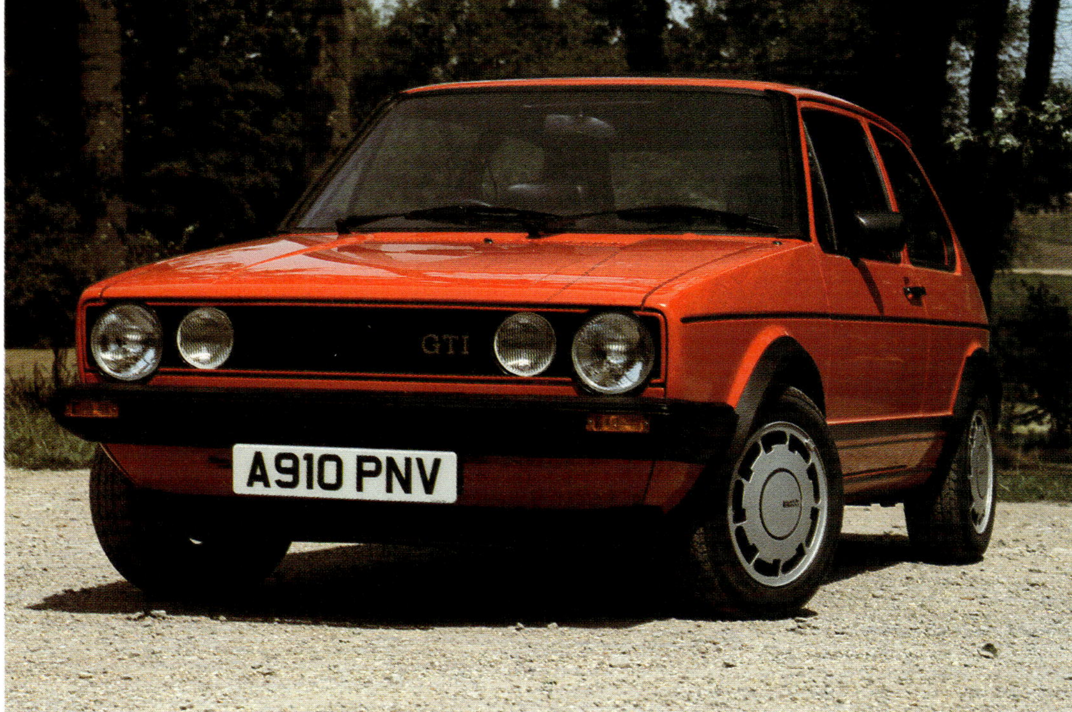

Right: VW's original Golf in GTi form was a market leader in the hot hatchback sales boom that began in the late 1970s

Below: Another product from the VAG combine was the sensational Audi Quattro which secured the prestigious world rally championship for the company

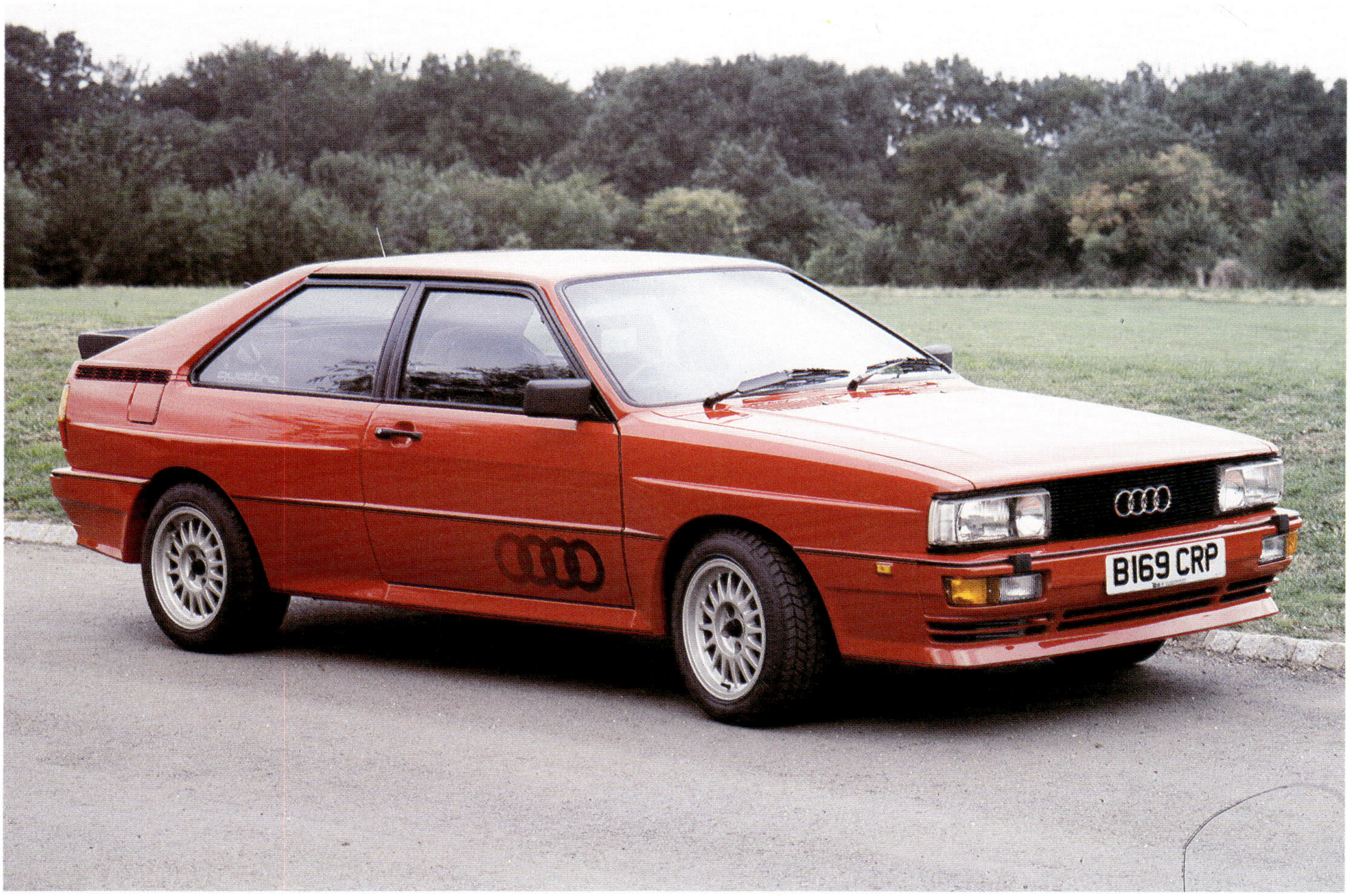

While from the early seventies onwards the Mercedes, BMW and Jaguar marques became established at the highest levels of desirability the period also marked an enormous leap forward for the world's mass manufacturers in the small and middle sized performance market with the emergence of the 'hot hatchback'. These were at last to shake the major companies out of their antiquated attitudes, and both Ford and General Motors eventually followed the front wheel drive, all independent suspension path pioneered for the mass market by Citroën and the British Motor Corporation.

The period also saw the car, more than ever before, become a political football. Post-oil-shock speed limits around the world were accompanied by anti-pollution and safety legislation which raised prices but generally brought about a much safer motoring environment. Public motoring awareness also grew greatly during the period, fuelled by the desire of the customer for more reliability, more value for money, more assurance against corrosion and depreciation and, in the face of ever rising costs, more performance for the money invested.

Without doubt, if the Mini was the small car of the sixties, the Volkswagen Golf (sold as the Rabbit in the USA) was to prove the car of the seventies. Since its introduction it has filled the slot left by the demise of the Beetle while becoming the standard by which the smaller cars of the world are judged. While the Mini was unique to its time the Golf represents a logical adoption of already well established trends combined with VW reliability and extremely shrewd international marketing.

Another trend of the period from 1970 to the present was the car's elevation to a symbol of nationalism. At two ends of the scale both the rise of the Japanese motor industry and the adoption by the Yugoslav government of the Fiat 128 both showed a feeling that to be a member of the affluent and influential nations which controll the world's resources, a car industry is one of the essentials. Once a nation develops a motor industry, the problem is one of sales. Today, as always, it is the manufacturer who can offer that extra glamour and performance at the most competitive price who attracts the most custom.

Ford had an excellent foundation in motor sport on which to build. With the introduction of the Escort in 1968 the Ford company had ensured that it had the ideal basis for saloon car competition at the lower end of the market and the performance derivatives were an integral factor in the subsequent success of the whole company.

Prior to the launch of the Escort a batch of twenty-five cars had been prepared to international competition regulations. These cars bore the badge 'Twin-Cam' and slightly flared arches with wider wheels, otherwise they seemed identical to the more mundane machinery available to the public. The basis of the car was the well proven Lotus-Cortina unit and the same close ratio gearbox was used. The type number J25 was given to these cars and with ever widening wheels and more aggressive body modifications, they were to dominate the following year's International Rally series.

The decision was taken to market the performance derivative of the car almost before public reaction to the basic version had been gauged. The first twenty-five units having been built entirely by hand, a separate production line for the customer replicas was created at Ford's giant Halewood plant. The first examples to find customers proved something of a mixed blessing for Ford as the average purchaser, finding himself with one of these superb handling and headily responsive cars, decided that they were potential competition machines and proceeded to take out unmodified straight-from-the-showroom cars which inevitably suffered under the rigours of competition use.

This phase passed and the company began to look for a weapon to defeat the BMW 2002 in competition. Thus in 1970 the RS1600 came into being. This was to mark the introduction of the Cosworth-developed BDA engine. At its announcement the engine displaced some 1599cc and offered 120 bhp at 6000 rpm, just 10 bhp less than the BMW 2002Ti had available in standard form in a lighter bodyshell. This engine, in both iron and alloy block form, was to claim for Ford the dominance in lesser formulas that the Ford-Cosworth DFV had achieved in Formula One.

In rally trim it ensured Ford success until the end of the decade while in Formula Two trim it broke the dominance of BMW when prepared by specialists such as Brian Hart, Cosworth themselves and Novamotor in Italy. It was, however, a highly specialised piece of equipment which was uneasy in its role as a fast, everyday road car and Ford needed something that the man in the street could use either wholeheartedly in competition or as a general, tractable sports saloon for business or pleasure.

The 1970 World Cup Rally provided them with just such a vehicle in the shape of the pushrod engined Escort Mexico. This car used the strengthened shell and uprated suspension from the RS with a tuned cross-flow version of the pushrod Kent engine found in the Cortina GT. Carburation was by twin 40 DCOE Webers and the close ratio box of the RS was available.

Ford was rationalising throughout Europe at this time and had committed large sums of money to the development of a new small saloon range in the US. This entailed the development of an all new 2 litre engine which took its name from the US range, the Pinto. In its emission-controlled US specification the engine was disappointing to say the least but when tweaked by the engineers at Ford development facilities it proved tractable, tuneable and extremely durable.

In 1973 the unit was incorporated into the Mark I Escort shell to give the first generation of the RS2000. It was not as hairy as the RS1600, neither was it as expensive, while the power output could easily be made to exceed that of the Mexico.

With the introduction of the updated Escort Mark II, bodyshell production of the RS was transferred to Saarlouis with the AVO (Advanced Vehicle Operations) facility which had taken over assembly from Halewood in 1970 closed down. The RS2000 was supplemented with an RS1800 version reverting once more to the superb BDA unit, and the company set out to regain lost ground in international rallying. This car featured standard looking bodywork in contrast to the less powerful RS2000 which incorporated a drooping nose line and built in spoilers, but it delivered the goods.

In road going form the RS1800 delivered a useful 115 bhp affording a genuine 111 mph maximum and a 0-60 mph time of seven seconds. Even so this was tame compared to the 170bhp plus that the factory obtained reliably from the unit for rallying, but the writing was already on the wall for the whole generation of performance Escorts for the decision had already been taken at Ford, even before the 1975 Mark II intro-

Above: The BMW 2002 a classic performance saloon of the early 1970s, and the car above all that Ford's hot Escorts were intended to beat on the racetrack

Right: The Escort Sport 'Harrier' of 1979, a pushrod engined derivative of the high performance Escorts at a budget price

The 1978 Escort RS 2000 had purposeful looking front end treatment and boot mounted spoiler but in fact was less powerful than the RS 1800

duction date, to fall into line with their world rivals and adopt front wheel drive configurations for its succeeding small and medium cars.

The development of the hot Escorts and the desire to beat BMW in the competition field was not a pattern confined to Ford. The rear wheel drive lower market offerings all across Europe and some from the Far East mirrored this last phase of conventional performance development.

Meanwhile some corporate efforts to endow smaller saloons with glamour seemed to verge on desperation. Such was the case with British Leyland's offering. This was a combination of a nine-year-old bodyshell with what was on paper one of the boldest engine developments the company was to produce to form the Triumph Dolomite Sprint.

The engine chosen for the Triumph assault on the performance saloon sector was the slant four overhead cam unit developed in conjunction with Saab. The talents of both Rover and Jaguar personnel were co-opted in the form of Spen King from the latter and Walter Hassan from the former. To aid them the abilities of Harry Mundy. who had been responsible for a good deal of the development work on the Ford ohc engines were also added, making up a team of proven talent possibly unmatched anywhere else in the industry at that time.

The basis 1850 unit was overbored to give 1998cc from a bore of 90·3 mm and a stroke of 78 mm and the head was completely re-developed into a sixteen valve configuration with a single overhead cam operating the valves by means of direct action on bucket tappets for the exhausts and crossover pushrods for the inlets. Induction was by two SUs and a figure of 127 bhp at 5700 rpm was quoted for the standard car.

The transmission from the larger Triumph 2·5 PI was used giving four forward speeds with optional overdrive on the top two. The bodyshell was the normal Dolomite article although, unlike the standard car, the independent rear suspension was replaced by a live axle located by four links while at the front coil and wishbone was used. A luxurious interior was standard with teak veneer and comfortable brushed nylon faced seats and Sprint badges, while special alloy wheels and a spoiler were added to the outside of the car.

From the first the car was well received by the press but the general lack of quality in the finish coupled with a tendency of the cylinder head to warp on the first production examples effectively killed its mass market chances. Nonetheless it was a first class racing saloon as developed by Ralph Broad, capable of outpacing the Group One 3 litre Capris which were matched against it. It lingered on in production until 1980 but in reality sales were disappointing and the bodyshell was never stressed well enough to take the power.

Matched against the Dolomite Sprint was the latest development from GM's Vauxhall division. This was based upon the floorpan

Top of the range Capri 3-litre. The Mark II redesign of 1973 gave the two door Capri a rear hatchback

of the 1972 HC Viva and utilised the 2·3 overhead cam Victor engine which was derived from a stillborn V8 development project. Fed by twin Stromberg carbs and incorporating a ZF box, the car was a coupé which had originally been designed to rival Ford's Capri and then, a limited number converted to performance specification, it was known as the Firenza.

That the car was fast was beyond doubt for even in standard tune, with its modified nose (which was to be adopted in the next generation of GM small saloons) which reduced drag by thirty per cent over the standard road car, it was capable of 118 mph with a 0-60 time of 8·5 seconds. Race prepared by Blydenstein the car was always a potential winner although only towards the end of its career could it really come within striking distance of the flying Dolomites. Even so it proved that the days of sitting on the sidelines of competition were well and truly over for General Motors' British division and opened the next chapter in GM's battle to gain European dominance in the mass market.

The early seventies were also to see both Nissan and Toyota making their first serious forays into the performance derivative field, the former with the 180SSS and the latter with the pretty little Celica. While the Datsun was more in keeping with the ideology behind the RS2000, the Celica was a small coupé looking for all the world like an amalgamation of all the styling gimmicks of the golden age of muscle cars reduced to miniature. It was fast though, especially in the sixteen valve twin overhead cam GT guise, but the company lost much European credibility by bringing in the pushrod engined 1600ST version earning it the reputation of a sheep in wolf's clothing.

The Datsun 180SSS looked and handled clumsily but it went. In triple carburettor configuration the car would comfortably exceed 100 mph and when the coupé received the attentions of Britain's Andy Dawson to the suspension it was a natural rally winner. The Japanese company were well aware of the potential of performance for in introducing the hairy 240Z they had captured the market which Britain had failed to exploit for powerful sports cars.

Even as the various companies turned out these performance derivatives time was running out for them. The trend was firmly toward front wheel drive for the masses yet there was still one last glamorous fling to come from Italy in the form of the rear wheel drive performance derivative. It arrived in 1974 in standard form and by 1975 the performance car was on the market. This was the Mirafiori 131 Abarth.

Carlo Abarth was born of Italian parents in Vienna in 1908. He studied as an engineer and by the late twenties was a keen motorcycle racer with a business manufacturing racing exhausts for a wide range of contemporary bikes. This knowledge of efficient exhaust management brought him to the attention of fellow Austrian Ferdinand Porsche who recruited him to the team Piero Dusio had brought together to build the Cisitalia Grand Prix team. In 1948, when this project folded, Abarth took some of his fellow workers and established premises in the Corso Marche, Turin, where he joined the ranks of the numerous Fiat improvers.

The 1960s saw Abarth operations expand to include complete cars. Understanding how to extract maximum power from minimum capacity, and using the Fiat 600 as a basis, he proceeded to transform the diminutive 'mouse', arriving at in the fearsome 1000TCR (Turismo Competizione Radiale) of the late sixties.

Abarth sold out to Fiat in 1971 but the company continued to use his name. In 1975 the go-ahead was given for the 'Abarth' treatment to be applied to the 131. After an eight month development period the Fiat Abarth 131 Rally came into being. Continuing tradition, Abarth's star sign of scorpio, the 'Scorpion', continued its occupation of the radiator grille and steering wheel centre boss.

Still in prototype form the car was entered for the Rallye Dei 100,000 Trabucchi (Rally of 100,000 corners) in Italy. In the closing stages of the 1975 season the car notched up another win in the Rallye Delle Valli Piacentine. Having seen these encouraging signs, Fiat hurriedly handed production of the Abarth to the Bertone workshops. Instructions were to produce a minimum batch of 400 cars, enabling the Abarth 131 Rally to be homologated for Group Four (Special GT) international motor sport.

Officially, Fiat discontinued participation with the Abarth in 1978, leaving rally and endurance racing to Lancia with Formula One in the capable hands of Ferrari. But even so, with German driver Walter Rohrl at the wheel of a re-liveried Abarth, the car won the 1980 Monte Carlo rally.

Naturally, a being a 'homologation special', the Abarth 131 Rally was never to sell in great numbers. In the late spring of 1979,

Fiat 130 Mirafiori Sport

however, cashing in on the Abarth's rally successes, Fiat introduced a mass production derivative of the Abarth 131 Rally. Called the 131 Racing in mainland Europe, due to antiquated ideas furnished by motor insurance underwriters, in Britain it was to be known as the 131 Sport.

It retained the 1995cc dohc engine but with Abarth's sixteen value cylinder head substituted by an eight valve head allied to a twin choke carburettor and greatly reduced compression ratio. Consequently, power dropped to 115 bhp.

The move towards hatchbacks and the trend towards front wheel drive had begun in earnest in the sixties. Although both were seen in various guises it was the combination of the two which wAS to prove the most enduring and practical small- and medium-sized car configuration as the decade wore on.

Perhaps unsurprisingly it was the French who were destined to set the pace in the hatchback market, first with the 1966 Renault 16 and then in the smaller sector with the 1968 Simca 1100. The Simca featured an alloy block 53 bhp overhead valve engine mounted transversely with the gearbox at the left driving the front wheels via driveshafts of unequal length. Suspension was independent all round by wishbones and torsion bars. The car was economical and cruised quite well but with the adoption of the 1294cc engine from their rear engined small performance model, the 1000 Rallye, it offered reasonable performance.

Two hot versions were available from 1971: the 1100 Special with single carburettor and the 1204 with twin Webers. Both featured a Porsche-designed gearbox and both could cruise indefinitely at speeds in the higher nineties. In 1972 the 1100 was France's best selling range and the rush was on among competitors to announce similar machinery.

Fiat were quick to announce a high performance hatchback derivative of their 128 with a 1300cc overhead cam engine while a 127 hatchback with the 'Sport' nametag arrived in 1972. As introduced some 75 bhp was available from the 1300 engine which gave both reasonable performance.

Peugeot, who already had a hatchback in the shape of the 204 coupé, entered the hot

Opel Manta GTE, GM Europe's reaction to the success of the Ford Capri

hatchback market in 1970 with the 1·3 litre 304 coupé which although seemingly rather solid and heavily built offered a top speed of almost 100 mph with independent suspension all round. The range was further enhanced by the super-mini sized 104 of 1973 with its 956cc ohc engine.

1973 was also to be the make or break year for Volkswagen. The famous Beetle had reached the end of its mass market dominance, even though it had had some reprieve with marketing concepts such as the denim-clad 'Jeans' Beetle and the 1303S performance derivatives. However, by the early seventies, the potential of any rear wheel driven car was severely limited.

Attempts to replace the aged model or supplement it with further rear wheel driven variants had failed dismally and, aware that time was running out, the company had laid plans for Porsche to design a replacement. On his arrival as chairman of VW, Rudolf Leiding was disconcerted to find that the Porsche replacement was as advanced in concept over the beetle as had been the Beetle over its crude beam-sprung, side valve contemporaries. It was a mono-

coque car with the same overall dimensions as the Beetle but with an in line overhead cam, all alloy engine mounted on its side beneath the rear seats driving the rear wheels through a transaxle set-up, Porsche's obvious rationale being to adapt the desirable qualities of the mid engine layout with the practicality of a saloon.

The project was speedily cancelled and during the remainder of 1973 the design staff at VW worked feverishly to produce a new front wheel drive car which had been originally conceived as the bottom end of the Audi-NSU part of the company using a straightforward water cooled, in line, four cylinder engine similar to that used in the Passat.

At the time the new model was under development, Giugiaro was styling a new high performance coupé for the company which was to emerge in 1974 as the Scirocco. The styling of the new Beetle replacement was also put into his capable hands and the result of all the co-operation made its debut in May 1974. Both the Golf and the Scirocco were instant best sellers. The millionth Golf was delivered in November 1976 and by 1979 the car was being assembled in the USA. Prior to this, however, the company had decided to complement the Scirocco with a more roomy performance version of the unashamedly sports package, designed specifically to attract the young executive who had been forced to come down in size by fuel cost increases.

The result of putting the Scirocco high performance package into the Golf shell made its debut in 1976 at the Frankfurt Autoshow. The 1588cc engine which had entered the range a year previously was retained but fitted with Bosch K-Jetronic fuel injection. A compression ratio of 9·5 : 1 and larger inlet valves gave a useful 110 bhp and the suspension was generally uprated all round. The initials GTi were adopted to denote both modification and the addition of fuel injection.

From the start the car reached a far wider customer base than the company had expected. In many ways it was the first truly 'classless' performance car since the demise of the Mini-Cooper in 1969.

Only the fact that the car could not stay in the race against the last of the rear wheel drive performance derivatives could be held against it.

This was in part remedied in 1979 when the four speed gearbox made way for the newer five speed which at least allowed high speed cruising to become a much more relaxed operation. Meanwhile the intermediate gears were closed up for better mid range reaction. This was further complemented with the introduction in 1982 of the new 1781cc 112 bhp engine which once again was also used in the updated Scirocco.

By 1983, however, having started the 'hot hatchback' craze, Volkswagen were due to replace the Golf and its GTi derivative. Two schools of thought had existed, one wanted to go for a new look, the other to maintain a strong family resemblance with the original Golf to avoid alienating existing customers.

Although the car was first shown in 1983, serious planning had been in progress since the spring of 1977. Ten designs were tendered, freelance and 'in-house', for Volkswagen's 'strategy commission' to preside over in late 1978 of which two were finally chosen and developed with the aid of a wind tunnel into almost finalised designs. Finally, in the spring of 1979, management chose the 'in-house' design that still strongly reflected the Mark 1's 'Giugiaro influence'.

In February 1983, with introduction a

VW Golf GTI II. The body shell was completely revised with increased interior room and luggage space. The 1781cc fuel injected engine from the Series-1 GTI was retained

matter of months away, a batch of three hundred pre-production Golfs was assembled, the majority going to their testing grounds at Ehra Lessien for a final shakedown. To criticisms of the original Golf, Volkswagen replied with a bodyshell enlarged overall increasing luggage capacity and interior passenger space. Increasing overall length and width, together with stretch in wheelbase and track (front and rear) transformed the Golf II. What had previously been a marginal four seat hatchback grew, literally, to become a full five seat 'family' hatchback.

The new range introduced two new 1093cc and 1272cc HCS (High Compression Squish) engines, borrowed from the Polo range and a carburettored version of the GTi's 1781cc engine as used in various Audis and Volkswagen's own Passat/Santana.

The GTi II retained its Kugelfischer injected 1781cc 112 bhp sohc engine without modification. Blessed with the ability to attain very high crankshaft speeds with exceptional smoothness, the engine kept the Golf GTi at the front of the hot hatchback

VOLKSWAGEN GOLF GTi II
Country of origin: *Germany*
Engine: *sohc S4*
Capacity: *1781cc*
Bore and stroke: *81·0 × 86·4 mm*
Power output: *112 bhp
@ 5500 rpm*
Carburation: *Injection*
Number of gears: *5*

PERFORMANCE
Top speed: *191 km/h*
Acceleration (0–100 km/h): *9·7 sec*

DIMENSIONS
Length: *3·985 m*
Width: *1·665 m*
Height: *1·415 m*
Wheelbase: *2·475 m*
Doors: *3*
Seats: *5*
Fuel Capacity: *55 litres*

TOYOTA COROLLA/SPRINTER 1600 GT

Country of origin: *Japan*
Engine: *sohc S4*
Capacity: *1587cc*
Bore and stroke: *81·0 × 77·0 mm*
Power output: *100 bhp @ 5600 rpm*
Carburation: *Injection*
Number of gears: *5*

PERFORMANCE

Top speed: *180 km/h*

DIMENSIONS

Length: *4·135 m*
Width: *1·635 m*
Height: *1·385 m*
Wheelbase: *2·430 m*
Doors: *4 or 5*
Seats: *5*
Fuel Capacity: *50 litres*

Toyota Corolla Coupé, a downsized sporting hatchback built on the floorpan of the already successful Corolla saloon

line-up against stiff competition.

Although bodyweight was up, as a result of superior aerodynamics the new GTi's performance increased. To counter the expected hard use, the disc/drum brake set-up of the original Golf was substituted by an all-disc system with ventilated front brakes.

The principal competition to the GTi arrived in 1980 with Ford's new Escort range. Having finally been convinced of the market viability of changing engineering direction away from its simplistic rear wheel drive policy, Ford's decision to alter the configuration of the smaller cars had first borne fruit with the Fiesta which entered the 'super-mini' battle in 1976.

Although the Fiesta had surprised even Ford by its popularity, it never quite achieved the mass market acceptance which had greeted first the Cortina and then the Escort. Even so, Ford had produced an extremely quick version of the car in the XR2 which used the 1600cc pushrodcross flow Kent engine first seen in the Mark II Cortina.

The Escort proved a sensation. It introduced two completely new engine configurations with the 1·3 and 1·6 single overhead cam CVH (Compound Value Angle Hemispherical Chamber) units.

The larger engined version was chosen to form the basis of the 'performance' version. The suspension was lowered and stiffened slightly and an anti-roll bar was incorporated at the rear coil and wishbone set-up. Weber carburation fed the fuel to the engine while front and rear spoilers, colour keyed grille and mirrors and special alloy wheels let the world know that the car was a 'special'.

Although the outgoing rear driven Escort had popularised the concept of the 'performance derivative' probably more effectively than any other single model, the new car, designed under the direction of Uwe Bahnsen, and named the XR3 in performance guise shattered the small sales volume expectation Ford had held for it outstripping in one year the whole of Rover's output in UK sales. Like the Golf it held a magic appeal across a broad spectrum of clients. Buyers ranged from boy racers to middle aged business executives who wanted something different.

A year later the package was improved by the addition of a fifth gear. For 1982 the car was improved still further by fitting Bosch K-Jetronic injection and the all important 'i' was added to the name. Power was increased

to 105 bhp from the original 96 bhp and a maximum speed of 116 mph was quoted.

In the meantime, General Motors had not been idle.

GM's hatchback contender, the Chevette, was embroiled in controversy within its second year of production. In November 1976, Bill Blydenstein's workshops at Shepreth near Cambridge prepared a Chevette 2300 HS rally car equipped with a Lotus sixteen valve cylinder head and Magnum 2·3 litre block for Dealer Team Vauxhall (DTV). As a condition of its continuing Group Four class rally participation homologation was required, and here the problems began. The necessary road going 2300HS appeared in January 1978 with an important deviation from the homologation sheets. Vauxhall had substituted the original Lotus sixteen valve cylinder head for one based on Vauxhall's own design and although fundamentally similar, the Vauxhall head broke the spirit of the homologation rules. The Lotus head, it

FORD ESCORT XR3i
Country of origin: *Great Britain/Germany*
Engine: *sohc S4*
Capacity: *1567cc*
Bore and stroke: *80·0 × 80·0 mm*
Power output: *105 bhp
@ 6000 rpm*
Carburation: *Bosch K-Jetronic injection*
Number of gears: *5*

PERFORMANCE
Top speed: *186 km/h*
Acceleration (0–100 km/h): *9·6 sec*

DIMENSIONS
Length: *3·970 m*
Width: *1·640 m*
Height: *1·369 m*
Wheelbase: *2·402 m*
Doors: *3*
Seats: *5*
Fuel Capacity: *48 litres*

had to be argued, allowed very limited access to the exhaust valves and camshaft. Vauxhall quickly returned to ranks by fitting the road car-developed Blydenstein head to the competition car. So the higher performance Chevette had been in the unique position of being developed as a competition rally car first, and second as a road car.

Under the bonnet, both cars shared the Blydenstein-headed twin cam 2279cc engine driving through a Getrag gearbox in the rally car and ZF unit in the road car, both with five close-set ratios. As well as a dry sump lubrication system and raised compression ratio, the rally car differed in carburation, replacing the two Dellorto twin choke carburettors by a pair of Stromberg carburettors. Power output for the road car was 135 bhp compared with the rally version's 240 bhp.

Both versions of the 2300HS have, over the years, enjoyed a great deal of success in motor rallying, from humble club events to full international championship rallies.

Having seen a semblance of standardisation applied to the rear driven Kadett and Chevette, General Motors continued their rationalisation programme to envelop the new 'T car' range.

Though based in Russelheim in West Germany, GM's European design studio was headed by British born Wayne Cherry. His styling influence formed the basis of an updated corporate identity, Vauxhall especially needing a timely shot in the arm. Seeing the VW Golf's growing success, GM introduced the brand new front wheel drive Opel Kadett in late 1979 as a direct rival to the Golf.

All production was based at Russelheim, originally limited to Opel-badged Kadetts, but through pure badge engineering, Vauxhall acquired a new model range for Britain in the form of the Astra. Other than badges, both cars were identical. For a number

With the XR3i Ford branded a performance Escort as a street machine aimed straight at the executive market. The exercise proved an outstanding success

of years the British buyer was confronted with the supposed choice of buying the British Vauxhall or the German Opel, more likely than not ignorant of the car's single origins.

Two main groups of power units were offered. At the lower end, the choice was between a 1·0 and 1·2 litre ohv engine, both from the outgoing rear driven Kadett. Concurrently, the larger-engined versions relied on totally new 'Family II' 1·3 and 1·6 litre carburated sohc engines with hydraulic tappets.

In early 1983, GM unveiled the Kadett SRi/Astra GTE. Sharing a 1·8 litre derivative of the 'Family II' engine with its lesser brethren, though now fuel injected, 9M had finally delivered something to take on the Golf GTi in the marketplace.

The slab sided Astra GTE got off to a controversial start. With the hot hatchback standard now being five closely stacked gears, the Astra went it alone in offering an overdriven gearbox. Met by a general outcry, GM back-pedalled and revised the gearing to provide a true close-ratio box. Sporting a healthy 115 bhp with the aid of Bosch fuel injection, the Astra claimed 115 mph top speed.

Then, seeing the Golf II appear in late 1983 GM, who were already gently progressing with their Mark II T car in the form of T85 (the codename given to the rebodied Kadett/Astra), brought forward their launch date. The T85's lines had become rounded in the quest for aerodynamic efficiency, although unkind critics flouted them with the nickname 'jelly mould'. Nevertheless with prominent body appendages front and rear, the new wind-cheating rebodied

Opel Kadett GTE. The slab sided bodyshell was only in production for some eighteen months before the launch of the 'jelly-mould' T-series with aerodynamically more efficient body shape

The new bodyshell may have offended some but certainly not the increase in top speed afforded by the new wind-cheating shape

OPEL KADETT 1·8GSi/ASTRA GTE
Country of origin: *Great Britain/Germany*
Engine: *sohc S4*
Capacity: *1796cc*
Bore and stroke: *84·8 × 79·5 mm*
Power output: *115 bhp*
  @ 5800 rpm
Carburation: *Bosch LE-Jetronic*
Number of gears: *5*

PERFORMANCE
Top speed: *203 km/h*
Acceleration (0–100 km/h): *9·0 sec*

DIMENSIONS
Length: *3·998 m*
Width: *1·663 m*
Height: *1·400 m*
Wheelbase: *2·520 m*
Doors: *3 or 5*
Seats: *5*
Fuel Capacity: *42 litres*

Astra GTE had body drag reduced to a Cd figure of 0·30, with an increase in top speed to a spectacular, for the class, 126 mph.

Mechanically nothing had changed, just the application of Wayne Cherry's design skills in attempting to defy air whilst revised suspension mounting points and detail improvements have refined what was originally an extremely attractive package.

While Ford and General Motors marked each other's product ranges and shuffled production around various European plants in an attempt to beat VW quality and price, Europe's indigenous manufacturers began to develop their own hot hatchbacks.

Renault had the perfect base in their R5. This had been on sale for three years by the time the Alpine tuned version was offered in 1975. Apart from uprating the suspension, which was by torsion bars and wishbones at the front and longitudinal swinging arms with transverse torsion bars at the rear, and the addition of an anti-roll bar, the little car needed very little modification to accept the overbored 93 bhp unit.

The 1984 Renault 5 TSE introduced a performance model into the R5 line-up with the tidied up bodyshell

The result was a veritable road burner with its appearance enhanced by the addition of special alloy wheels, side stripes and deep front spoiler with a matching rear air dam soon available as an option.

More was to come, however, for Renault decided to go rallying in 1979 and marketed a mid engined version using the 1397cc overhead valve Alpine engine with a Garrett T3 turbocharger and Bosch K-Jetronic injection. This was the car which allowed the factory to take on the might of the Lancia and Audi teams with a fair degree of success.

To cope with the 160 bhp at 6000 rpm and the torque of 163 lb/ft at 3250 rpm, a twin plate clutch took the power to the five speed box while revised rear suspension by coil and wishbone transmitted the power to the road. To cope with the 5 inch front and 7½ inch rear wheel rim widths specially flared arches were incorporated, the rear ones incorporating the air intakes for the engine and intercooler. Although originally planned merely as a limited run homologation special, the car remains in the Renault catalogue.

The next variation was the 110 bhp Alpine turbo. This again utilised the Garrett T3 but this time acting through a Weber 32 DIR 75 downdraft carburettor and the engine remained in its original front mounted position. A maximum speed of 116 mph was attainable. This model became available in 1980 and was marketed in Britain as the Gordini (as had been the original Alpine, due to PSA owning the Alpine designation). It became an immediate success rivalling the Golf GTi and the XR3i with the 'go fast' set.

Citroën for their effort in the small car sector chose their 1977 Visa to which to add performance to and did it with panache, producing first the Chrono, a limited special

After a series of performance derivative R5s including a Gordini model and a mid engined turbo, the Laureate Turbo was a special edition marking the end of production of the old body style

Above: Citroen Visa Mille Pistes, a four wheel drive rally car, 200 of which were offered for open sale to conform with homologation rules

Right: Peugeot's 205 GTi featured a fuel injected engine delivering 105 bhp in a shortened body shell. The resulting car had dazzling performance and handling

PEUGEOT 205GTi

Country of origin: *France*
Engine: *sohc S4*
Capacity: *1580cc*
Bore and stroke: *83·0 × 73·0 mm*
Power output: *105 bhp*
    @ 6250 rpm
Carburation: *Bosch L-Jetronic injection*
Number of Gears: *5*

PERFORMANCE

Top speed: *190 km/h*
Acceleration (0–100 km/h): *9·5 sec*

DIMENSIONS

Length: *3·705 m*
Width: *1·589 m*
Height: *1·355 m*
Wheelbase: *2·420 m*
Doors: *3*
Seats: *4*
Fuel Capacity: *50 litres*

performance edition for the French market, followed by the GT and then the four wheel drive Mille Pistes in 1983 complete with Garrett turbocharging.

While the GT produced a healthy 80 bhp at 5800 rpm from its overhead cam, all alloy 1360cc engine it was not exactly a shatteringly quick car. The Mille Pistes however was in a different class being nothing more or less than a full blooded homologation special which needed virtually nothing except full harness, safety cage and fire extinguisher to allow it out onto the rally ground. Unfortunately only 200 of these interesting little cars were built but at just over 90,000 Francs, they epitomised the type of machine which the basic clubman could well turn to good and inexpensive competition use.

Peugeot took their 1982 offering, the 205, and adopting VW type designation built the GTi. To improve road holding, save weight and increase the appeal of the car the same route of chopping the car short that was employed in the creation of the 80 bhp 104Z was taken. Into this attractive shell was placed the largest engine in the range, the overhead cam 1580cc unit giving 105 bhp at 6250 rpm.

The suspension of the less powerful mem-bers of the family, MacPherson strut front and trailing arm transverse torsion bar rear, was uprated with a rear anti-roll bar fitted. Maximum speed was quoted as 118 mph but it was the faultless handling which caught the imagination of the motoring trade press.

Like Renault, Peugeot decided to make a mid engined rallying version. Unlike Renault they decided to follow the Audi-inspired path of fitting four wheel drive. The resulting homologation special with its sixteen valve head and turbocharger was without doubt the sensation of the 1984 Geneva show as far as saloons were concerned.

K-Jetronic fuel injection was utilised plus a KKK turbocharger with twin belt driven overhead camshafts in the all alloy unit. A Ferguson viscous coupling type transmission was driven through a five speed box with a single plate clutch. A ZF limited slip differential was used at the rear and surprisingly also at the front.

The suspension was double wishbone front and rear with coil over shocks and front and rear anti-roll bars while nine inch ventilated discs all round took care of the stopping department. In luxury road going

521 END 75

trim, with a choice of one colour, metallic graphite grey, the car was priced at £25,000 for one of the limited edition of 200 available. A bargain, no doubt, for serious collectors. As a rally device the car was to prove its effectiveness with two major international wins in its first ever season.

Meanwhile further south in Italy the transition from the early seventies to the present was to prove something of a trial for all concerned.

For the smaller Alfa Romeos, the seventies wars a period of missed opportunities tempered by startling innovation. The decade started on a keenly optimistic note with the introduction of the pretty and advanced Alfasud built in the new Arese plant near Naples. Originally introduced in 1176cc form the car was destined to grow into a whole range offering 1·2, 1·3 and 1·5 litre variants on the double overhead cam, flat four boxer engine theme along with two and four door saloons and latterly three and five door hatchbacks, plus from 1979 onwards an extremely attractive Sprint Ti variant which was a scaled down version of the larger GTV.

Unfortunately labour troubles at the Arese plant prevented full production ever being reached while the super mini sector of the market at which the cars were aimed was totally oversubscribed by such rivals as the Peugeot 104, the Fiat 127 and the Polo. This, added to the model's early reputation for an unstable mechanical temperament and unlimited potential for corrosion, boded ill for the little car.

Pleasant to drive and appealing to the eye it might have been but the 'Sud for one reason or another cost Alfa dear and the losses had to be made good. This brought about the almost unthinkable when the brilliant boxer engine in its smallest 1186cc guise wars dropped into the tackily styled Nissan Cherry bodywork to create the 1983 Arna. As yet another facet of overall model rationalisation 1984 saw the by now excellent and class leading 1·3 and 1·5 variants disappear in saloon and hatchback form leaving only the 1·5 Sprint Ti of the original well conceived yet badly presented range.

Britain, which had created the first small hatchback in the form of the Austin A40 countryman, saw the seventies in with the idiotic decision by British Leyland to drop the Mini-Cooper. Its replacement was a detuned version of the 1275cc engine (at a time when the customer wanted more power) dropped into in the hastily updated Mini Clubman shell sold at the 1275GT.

Alfa Romeo 33. A worthy successor to the charismatic Alfasud, the Alfa 33 was found somewhat stodgy by devotees of the 'Sud but seems set for a successful and long production life

While BL's rationalisation programme killed off MG as a separate marque, the august name was readily applied to performance derivatives of the company's new generation of standard saloons, in effect repeating the process by which MG started in the first place. The MG Metro Turbo proved a true hot hatchback worthy of the name while the 1994cc engined MG Maestro EFi with electronic fuel injection was marginally faster

Only the introduction of the Ford Fiesta in its XR2 version offered any hope of a genuine revival in British small performance car fortunes, and even then only the engine was actually built in Britain. Nevertheless the little road rocket found itself extremely welcome when it arrived somewhat belatedly in 1980. The well proven 1598cc Kent engine with electronic ignition gave a useful 84 bhp in standard Weber carburated form, enough to give the little car a 9·3 second 0-60 time with a top speed of over 105 mph.

Leyland's answer to the hot Ford super mini came two years later in May 1982. The

MG MAESTRO AND MAESTRO EFi

Country of origin: *Great Britain*
Engine: *sohc S4*
Capacity: *1576cc*
Bore and stroke: *76·2 × 87·6 mm*
Power output: *99 bhp*
  @ 6000 rpm
Carburation: *1 × Weber 40 DCNF*
(Electronic fuel injection Efi)
Number of gears: *5*

PERFORMANCE

Top speed: *175 km/h*
Acceleration (0–100 km/h): *10·2 sec*

DIMENSIONS

Length: *4·049 m*
Width: *1·687 m*
Height: *1·429 m*
Wheelbase: *2·507 m*
Doors: *5*
Seats: *5*
Fuel Capacity: *54 litres*

MG METRO TURBO

Country of Origin: *Great Britain*
Engine: *ohv S4*
Capacity: *1275cc*
Bore and Stroke: *70·6 x 81·3 mm*
Power Output: *90 bhp   6130 rpm*
Carburation: *SU with Garrett turbo*
Number of Gears: *4*

PERFORMANCE

Top speed: *180 km/h*
Acceleration (0-100 km/h): *10·2 sec*

DIMENSIONS

Length: *3·403 m*
Width: *1·563 m*
Height: *1·359 m*
Wheelbase: *2·250 m*
Doors: *3*
Seats: *4*
Fuel Capacity: *30 litres*

corporation had revived the MG marque and returned it to its original role of providing tuned versions of current production cars — in this instance the Mini Metro, introduced in standard form in 1981. The tired A series 1275cc ohv engine was retained as was SU carburation. With only 72 bhp on offer the car was certainly not in the same league as the Renault 5 Alpine or the 1·3 Alfasud. Nevertheless it was the best Leyland could manage and as such received fair treatment from the press who singled out the gearchange and the road holding as being areas of exceptional merit.

More was needed and the only way to achieve it was to turbocharge the by now obsolete engine. This duly arrived a year later with the introduction of the MG Metro Turbo. This used the attractive outer body treatment of the MG Metro and offered a heady 93 bhp at an easily attainable 6350 rpm. The four speed VW Golf box was retained and in standard form, 0-60 mph came up in 9·9 seconds and the car topped out at 112 mph.

Leyland's other hatchback offering, the Maestro, was also available in MG trim and tune. More was on offer here due to the use

of the 1600cc overhead valve engine with its alloy head. A top speed of 109 mph was claimed and power from the twin Weber carburated unit was quoted as 102 bhp at 6000 rpm. Like the Metro the car still suffered from some anachronistic thinking in the engine department.

This was to some extent remedied with the introduction of the 1994cc option and the addition of Lucas L type fuel injection with a fuel engine management system including anti-knock and electronic ignition. Even if with its cast iron block the O Series engine was not the much needed British answer to foreign technological superiority, the 155 bhp output made the car quite lively while the five speed Honda gearbox was light and effective. The claimed company figures for the Maestro were 0-60 mph in 8·5 seconds and a maximum of 115 mph. Hardly the stuff of which nightmares were made for the marketing men behind the 1800 GTi at VW but an attempt to catch up just the same.

Britain's own branch of the giant PSA group was also involved in the hot small car market with the Talbot Sunbeam-Lotus, a real performance hybrid in the traditional sense of the word.

Introduced in the autumn of 1977, the Chrysler, later to become Talbot, Sunbeam set out to become a modern hatchback derivative of the Chrysler Avenger. The Sunbeam retained the Avenger's running gear (MacPherson struts up front and a live axle at the rear) together with its 1295cc and 1598cc all iron ohv engine, with a third engine option, the all alloy, chain driven sohc 928cc Climax engine used in the Imp.

In a blaze of publicity consisting of celebrity challenge car races in the spring of 1979, Chrysler introduced the higher performance 1·6 Ti derivative. Equipped with what have now become virtually mandatory 'go faster' fittings, front and rear spoilers. the Ti certainly looked the part. To match the looks, Chrysler uprated the 1·6 litre engine to give it some 'go' — the well tried solution of bolting a pair of Weber twin choke carburettors certainly worked, the 'hot' Sunbeam producing a healthy 100 bhp.

Talbot were not standing still. Though aired as nothing more than an intriguing concept at the March 1979 Geneva motor show, by the autumn the Lotus-engined Sunbeam had become more than a concept — it was for real. Talbot proceeded to homologate the Sunbeam-Lotus for Group Four motor rallying, after all, as well as the image boost given by the tie-up with Lotus to

The Sunbeam Lotus launched the Talbot company into international rallying with a world championship win. Production of this pioneering 'hot hatchback' ended in 1982

the Sunbeam range, a powerful reason for the car's existence centred around its sporting aspirations. A condition of Group Four participation was the need to manufacture a minimum batch of 400 cars, although not necessarily to sell them. This joint venture between Talbot and Lotus therefore stipulated that Lotus should provide a total of 4500 complete engines over a period of three years.

Derived from the 2·0 litre four cylinder type 907 sixteen valve engine, the type 911 boasted an increased capacity of 2172cc due to a lengthened stroke. Breathing through a pair of Dellorto twin choke carburettors, and with the emphasis on torque with increased flexibility at the expense of outright power, the horse power dropped by 10 bhp to 150 bhp. Driving flat

out utilising a 3·89 final drive implied a slight overgearing — the maximum speed of 125 mph occurred just below peak power revs.

Elsewhere in the range the Talbot company also offered the indecently quick and delightfully chuckable French built Samba Rallye. The latter device gave a useful 90 bhp from its single overhead cam 1219cc Weber fed engine. In this guise the super mini turned in a creditable 109 mph top speed with excellent economy. At the larger end the Horizon range offered five doors and formed the basis for the Dodge Omni series in the USA.

A fanatical insistence on building technically innovative cars found Lancia in the unenviable position of having to be bought out to survive. Pressured by the Italian gov-

ernment, Fiat were persuaded to intervene and buy the famous company (with its enormous debts) in 1969.

Coming in under the wing of Fiat had its advantages for Lancia financially and technically. Having in the past resorted to numerous 'unique' engine configurations — the narrow V4 Fulvia engine being a perfect example, Lancia were now able to take advantage of the availability of Fiat's wide range of dohc engines. The Beta of 1972, borrowing a name first used in 1909, was Lancia's first car to benefit from the takeover.

An overlap of 'old' and 'new' Lancia schools of thought occurred between the Beta's introduction in 1972 and the eventual demise of the Fulvia in 1976. The Fessia-inspired Fulvia, and its successor, in the form of the Giugiaro-designed Delta, occupied that market niche so well known to Lancia, that of the medium sized luxury/sporting saloon.

The Beta although extremely attractive in its coupé and HPE variants was an unhappy experience for Lancia and an embarrassing one to the whole Italian motor industry because of its inclination to rust in the engine mountings. The subsequent damage was not just structural for the sub-frame was capable of moving when corroded and breaking the steering mechanism. To the company's credit they recalled all the suspect cars and owners were offered the chance of selling affected cars back at the market rate, but the damage to the marque was vast.

Another spin off from the Fiat takeover

LANCIA DELTA 1600GT

Country of origin: *Italy*
Engine: *2 × ohc S4*
Capacity: *1584cc*
Bore and stroke: *84·0 × 71·5 mm*
Power output: *105 bhp @ 5800 rpm*
Carburation: *1 × Weber 34 DAT*
Number of gears: *5*

PERFORMANCE

Top speed: *180 km/h*
Acceleration (0–100 km/h): *10·2 sec*

DIMENSIONS

Length: *3·895 m*
Width: *1·620 m*
Height: *1·380 m*
Wheelbase: *2·475 m*
Doors: *5*
Seats: *5*
Fuel Capacity: *45 litres*

was the Gamma, the Fiat group's replacement for the beautiful 130 range with its Ferrari-designed overhead cam V6 engine. The Gamma was pure Lancia in the best traditions of the founder. Under the functional bodywork lay the world's largest boxer engine. It displaced 2½ litres and, with transistorised ignition, proved a smooth and willing unit. A coupé was also offered and must rate as one of the most beautiful modern production designs. Yet the Gamma was doomed by poor finishing and a general lack of development.

The Delta was first shown at the 1979 Frankfurt motor show and won the 1980 'Car of the Year' award. It was originally available with a choice of transversely mounted 1301cc and 1498cc belt-driven sohc engines — the sporting driver had to wait until the spring of 1983 for a true performance derivative. Utilising the standard bodyshell, but with modified running gear in the form of an all disc brake set-up, updated suspension and dohc engine, Lancia introduced the Delta GT1600. In this form, the Fiat-derived 1585cc twin cam engine with a single Weber twin choke carburettor boasted a power output of 105 bhp. Equipped with a 3:58 ratio final drive and a true close-ratio set of gears, its 112 mph maximum speed coincided with peak power.

Though in GT1600 form the Delta could be considered a paragon of understatement, the same could not be said for the HF Turbo which followed close behind. With both flanks festooned in blue and red Lancia-Martini stripes, and prominent 'Turbo' logos on each C-pillar, white bodied HF Turbos could not have been more extravagant.

Retaining the GT's basic mechanics, with a much lowered compression ratio, the HF relied on American turbocharging technology with a Garret T3 turbo unit and an air-to-air intercooler boosting power to a healthy 130 bhp. In view of this power, and a potential 124 mph maximum speed, overall gearing rose with the inclusion of a 3:4 final drive and an uprated ZF gearbox.

Fiat's own venture into the hot hatchback market was the Ritmo/Strada. In a world of lookalike hatchbacks the Ritmo, at its launch in 1978, stood out in terms of styling at least.

The car was initially available with 1116cc, 1301cc and 1498cc transversely mounted belt driven sohc engines. Within the first twelve months of production the range grew by one with the addition of the Brazil-built 1049cc version. Given the go-ahead in July 1978 to produce a performance derivative, Mario Colucci, Head of Preparation at Abarth, had to have a car ready for the end of September to commence testing. The 1498cc engine proved well able to take the increase in power from the original 75 bhp to the quoted 157 bhp at 8200 rpm with Kugelfischer fuel injection and a compression ratio of 11·0:1 to produce a top

FIAT RITMO/STRADA 105TC

Country of origin: *Italy*
Engine: *2 × ohc S4*
Capacity: *1585cc*
Bore and stroke: *84·0 × 71·5 mm*
Power output: *105 bhp*
 @ 6100 rpm
Carburation: *1 × Weber 34 DMTR*
Number of gears: *5*

PERFORMANCE

Top speed: *178 km/h*
Acceleration (0–100 km/h): *9·5 sec*

DIMENSIONS

Length: *4·014 m*
Width: *1·663 m*
Height: *1·390 m*
Wheelbase: *2·444 m*
Doors: *3*
Seats: *4*
Fuel Capacity: *55 litres*

FIAT RITMO/STRADA ABARTH 130TC

Country of origin: *Italy*
Engine: *2 × ohc S4*
Capacity: *1995cc*
Bore and stroke: *84·0 × 90·0 mm*
Power output: *130 bhp*
 @ 5900 rpm
Carburation: *2 × Weber 40 DCOE*
Number of gears: *5*

PERFORMANCE

Top speed: *195 km/h*
Acceleration (0–100 km/h): *8·0 sec*

DIMENSIONS

Length: *4·014 m*
Width: *1·663 m*
Height: *1·374 m*
Wheelbase: *2·432 m*
Doors: *3*
Seats: *4*
Fuel Capacity: *55 litres*

speed of over 120 mph.

Using the group's 1585cc belt-driven dohc engine producing 105 bhp, and a three door Ritmo bodyshell, in the spring of 1981 Fiat sought to enlarge the sporting pedigree of their new big seller, and have their initial foray into the hotly contested hot hatchback market. The Ritmo 105TC had arrived.

In its new guise the 105TC was distinguished from lesser brethren by the addition of a deeper front spoiler, wheel arch extensions and tail spoiler. To maximise the engine's already 'gutsy' character, overall gearing remained low with a 3·77:1 final drive, enabling the engine, even in fifth gear, to run well into the red to obtain a 109 mph maximum speed.

Fiat Strada Abarth 130 TC

For a short period, Fiat sought to boost the Ritmo to greater heights with the introduction of the Abarth 125TC. Introducing the car early in 1982, perhaps optimistically, Fiat aimed it at the Porsche 924/Alfetta GTV buyer.

Using the evergreen Fiat 1995cc twin cam engine breathing through a single Weber twin choke carburettor, power was increased to 125 bhp. Although fundamentally identical, the front suspension and running gear differed from other Ritmos in having variable-ratio springing and ventilated disc brakes. At the rear, a single varying-thickness transverse leaf spring substituted the normal twin ply spring, although retained drum brakes.

Late 1982 saw the introduction of the Ritmo II. Although at first sight it sported merely a redesigned nose and rear end, actual redesign work extended to the whole structure, and at the 1983 Geneva motor show, Fiat introduced the performance derivative of the redesigned model, the Ritmo II 105TC. The car retained the 1585cc dohc, 105 bhp engine, but improved aerodynamics saw the 105TC top 112 mph.

For the real performance buff however, good news was also imminent. Again reverting to the Corso Marche premises Abarth were put to work, the fruition of which appeared late in 1983. Though endowed with no less looks than the other Ritmos, the resulting Ritmo Abarth 130TC conspired to radiate a brutish beauty.

It had been an open secret that Fiat, when developing the 130TC, had had the Volkswagen Golf GTi firmly in their sights. Retaining the 1995cc engine previously found in the 125TC, Abarth increased the power to 130 bhp using a pair of Weber 40 DCOE or Solex C40 twin choke side draught carburettors. With fuel injection so popular in other sporting cars, the arrangement bore out Abarth's genius at understanding and perfecting a conventional induction system. Reverting to a five speed transmission with ZF-manufactured internals, driving through a 3·4:1 final drive, quoted maximum speed for the 130TC was in the order of 122 mph.

The late seventies brought two worthy challengers from the Far East in the shape of the Daihatsu Charade and the Mazda 323 GT while Honda enjoyed a love affair with the media following the introduction of its Scirocco copy in the form of the 1980 Prelude to be carried on by the 1982 CRX coupé.

The Daihatsu, apart from being a charming little car in its own right, formed the basis of Alessandro De Tomaso's rediscovery of the old Innocenti hatchback mini concept when he adopted the five speed gearbox and the neat little three cylinder 993cc overhead cam engine of the Charade as the basis for a performance derivative. In turbocharged form this engine gave a sparkling 80 bhp and 99 mph in a cheerful and comfortable economy package squeezed into a tiny envelope.

The Mazda 323 became available in 1977 and to promote it the company launched a series of single model championships on the world's racetracks. Unlike similar Japanese products this well finished hatchback both looked and felt good, frighteningly good to the majority of the world's small car manufacturers. In 1980 the 323GT was launched to capitalise on this success receiving little short of rapturous reviews. Subsequently the series was updated and, with the addition of 1500XG Turbo with its 1490cc, 115 bhp engine and 112 mph top speed, the range must seriously rate consideration against the best European products.

The range of small hot cars from Honda is too numerous to encapsulate here but the Prelude EX of 1983 and the Honda CRX seem to indicate that the Japanese company, which once issued an official statement to the effect that in the age of mass electronics they would be offering everyone the chance to afford Mercedes-Benz type quality, lacks little in expertise when it comes to pleasing the world's motoring press. It remains to be seen, however, whether any truly discerning European motorist would sacrifice proven reputations and cachet to drive the rather ill proportioned Japanese offerings for any other reason than bargain price.

8 The eighties: Design for performance

Previous page: The crisply functional dash layout of the Lancia Thema

While the motoring world was awakening to the joys of the downsized performance saloon and its hot hatchback stablemate, the middle market was going through a series of convulsions as it frantically sought direction. At the end of the sixties most of the performance cars between 1600cc and 2800cc already had the features which the smaller car buyers were now demanding. All round discs may have been something of a rarity but all round independent suspension was not. Overhead cam alloy block engines were not necessarily the order of the day but with the first major fuel crisis of 1973 they ceased to be an exotic rarity.

Fuel injection was beginning to creep in throughout the middle weight sector while the search for better aerodynamics, better cabin ergonomics and lowered noise and fatigue levels had been pioneered by Rover, Mercedes and Volvo since the onset of unitary construction, or at least the advent of the pioneering Citroën DS19.

For the first three years of the seventies the British motor industry reaped the benefit of the innovations of the early and middle sixties. British Leyland had the middle weight sector well covered with such machinery as the Triumph 2·5 PI and the Rover 2000 and 3500 even if BL's overall corporate policy, such as it was, meant the elevation of Jaguar into a new higher price bracket.

Ford for their part offered fair performance with their E (for executive) badged cars and, for those who wanted a slightly enhanced performance version without the luxury trimming, all their cars except the very largest came in GT form with uprated suspension and the almost mandatory

Weber carburettor.

In Sweden Volvo offered a 3 litre version of their pleasant 144 range which had entered the market in 1967 and been brought into the newly fashionable 2 litre class in 1969 by enlarging the original 1800 overhead valve engine. The cars were tough, by any standards, and reflecting the company's policy of long model life they were designed from the outset with a view to constant modification and long product life.

Like their close neighbours Saab, Volvo incorporated stainless steel where most rivals used chromium plate while Swedish companies were well to the forefront in corrosion prevention techniques due to the stringent Swedish government inspection techniques which could take even a two-year-old car from the road if any rust damage was found.

Although the performance of the range was certainly not far behind their obvious European rivals, the company had earned a reputation for building staid and unimaginative cars. 'Who wants to drive around in an armoured personnel carrier?' was the type of comment generally levelled at with Volvo and even the 115 mph plus of the 3 litre was not enough to silence such remarks.

Saab too had a contender for the 2 litre market when the slant four overhead cam engine which they had developed in conjunction with Triumph was bored out from its original 1850cc displacement. Even in this form, however, few could see that the eccentrically styled 99 was destined to become one of the most influential cars of the decade.

This smooth running, aerodynamic, front wheel drive car owed little to conventional thinking except perhaps that in its front wheel drive configuration and monocoque construction it was a natural means of capitalising on their original rally winning 92/94 model range. These delightful cars with their three cylinder engines, known as cucumbers in their native country, showed a good turn of pace when in rally tune. Their advanced aerodynamics, evolved in conjunction with the aircraft production arm of the company, allowed extremely good high speed cruising.

This original model, as well as giving Saab a reputation in the rally field, also built up goodwill in the export markets, gaining a wholly justified reputation for reliability and toughness. The build quality, as with Bristol, was all that one could

Nissan Leopard Turbo ZGX, typical of the quality performance cars from Japan that would come to hotly contest European predominance in this sector in the 1980s

expect from a company which had devolved into cars from the manufacture of aircraft. When the company dropped the original three cylinder two stroke engine and adopted the German Ford V4 in 1966, the car went on to make many new friends for the company.

The Saab 99 featured suspension by coil and wishbone at the front but, interestingly, the rear was by a solid rear axle trailing radius arms and coil springs. Stromberg carburation was used and with the exception of some weak spots in the gearbox and transmission of the earlier models, the 99 carried on the reputation built by the earlier cars.

Like the contemporary Volvo, Saab followed Jaguar practice by incorporating all round disc brakes from the beginning while new regulations in Sweden dictated dual circuitry. Other safety features were built into the exceptionally rigid monocoque such as the ingenious bonnet design which lifted and swung forward before it could be raised from the front. This feature was a straightforward adoption from aircraft practice and as well as offering an extremely rigid and safe structure (from the point of view that accidental opening while the car was in motion was almost impossible), it helped to spread any frontal accident impact load the length of the car. The air-

craft mentality could also be seen in an overall shape designed in the wind tunnel and owing little or nothing to contemporary styling trends.

By 1975 the car had gained a hatchback stablemate available in three and five door configurations and, in the top of the range EMS, it had acquired fuel injection giving 118 bhp, outperforming many more 'sporting' rivals from the larger makers with its secure handling characteristics.

In that year Volvo dropped the straight

Top: Rover took to the racetrack again in 1982 with the outstanding success both in the British Saloon Car Championship and in Europe

Above: Saab 99, pioneer 'hot hatchback'

Ford of America's performance team for the 1980s includes the Thunderbird (**below**), the Escort Turbo (**below left**) and the Mercury Cougar XR-7 (**left**). The American Escort shares engine and drivetrain with its European counterpart

Chrysler following its corporate reconstruction still lays claim to a substantial part of the US performance market with some products for the 1980s which directly evoke the great days of the 'muscle cars' including the Plymouth Duster (**below right**), the Chrysler Laser (**far right**) and Chrysler Sunbird Turbo (**right**)

Peugeot 505 Turbo Injection. The French company has introduced performance technology right across its model range

six 3 litre unit and introduced the 244 series. Externally it seemed little had changed but under the bonnet was a new single overhead cam engine while the structure surrounding it had been even more reinforced. The new engine displaced some 2·1 litres as introduced and was destined to grow through 2·2 litres to 2·4 yet it still left the heavy car feeling sluggish, even in fuel injected form. Like Peugeot, who had developed their striking 2 litre 504 to its maximum realistic level of performance, the company needed a new engine and in conjunction with Peugeot and Renault, who lacked anything more powerful than the 16TX unit which had been used to power the top of the range 17 coupé, they embarked on a development programme designed to give them a performance engine with development potential to take them into the last decade of the century.

Renault had seen the seventies in with two new performance orientated coupés which were the company's subtly gallicised response to the success of the Capri. Introduced in 1972 the 15 and the 17 both offered the 1565cc cross flow pushrod unit originally seen in the 16TS of 1968. In the top of the range 17 it utilised the fuel injection set-up from the 16 to give 120 bhp, giving the French car enough power to compete with all but the 3 litre Capri. Yet Renault had plans for far more ambitious moves into the executive and performance markets, and pleasing as the cars were, they were to disappear before the end of the decade.

Peugeot on the other hand had developed one of the best all round propositions in the 2 litre class with the 504. Although the engine displaced only 1·8 litres, being directly derived from the cross flow pushrod unit in the 404, in standard tune the power output of 82 bhp gave it a healthy and economical high nineties cruising speed and in fuel injected form the car could exceed, just, the magic ton. It was not, however, equipped to take on the 2·5 PI or the Rovers from a performance standpoint even in the extremely beautiful coupé and cabriolet versions. More important, neither Renault nor Peugeot had an answer to the new generation of medium saloons from

Audi, with their 115 bhp coupé and top of the range 100 model, and the NSU Ro80.

Sadly, the Wankel-engined Ro80, with its clean styling and free revving rotary engine, was destined to die off as both the public and the management at VAG realised the limited life span of the Wankel and with it the accelerated rate at which it used fuel as the rotor tips wore. The Audi 100, however, was to remain a potent force in the cheaper performance medium saloon market taking custom, at one end of the spectrum, from the man who wanted to enhance his image from Ford or GM products, and from the other from the established 'quality' builders such as Peugeot, Rover and Volvo.

The arrival, therefore, in 1975 of the advanced V6 engine from the Douvrin plant of PRV (Peugeot-Renault-Volvo) was of crucial importance to the three manufacturers. Even the continuing fuel shortages of the time which made people seriously consider moving down the power and size scale, worked in the triumvirate's favour for the unit was remarkably frugal for its 150 plus bhp output.

Alliances between Europe's major car manufacturers were not unusual. Citroën and Maserati had joined forces in the early seventies to produce the glamorous and over-engineered SM and even before the shotgun marriage of Triumph and Rover, they had co-operated briefly on a project which brought forth each company's 2000 offering. The interesting facet of the Douvrin project was its demonstration that such co-operation could work and be beneficial to all involved.

Equally interesting was the manner in which each of the three participants in the V6 project utilised the upper range flexibility it offered. For Peugeot it was a good opportunity to put some much needed muscle into their 504 coupé and cabriolet while a year later the company launched the sumptuously equipped and reasonably quick 604 built around the carburettor version of the engine. This was a head-on attempt to capture the upper executive and diplomatic market in Europe while at the same time offering its fanatically loyal customer base in French-speaking Africa a viable alternative both to Mercedes-Benz and the larger Japanese saloons which were making deep inroads into the developing nations.

For Renault the engine meant a new top of the line hatchback in the shape of the 30TS while the company's Le Mans-winning sporting image could be further fortified by incorporating the engine into the beautiful Alpine A310. This gave the French company a challenger to the Porsche range while the 30TS and its smaller engined stablemate the 20TS (which used an all alloy single overhead cam Douvrin-built 1995cc unit which was later to power the Peugeot 505) kept faith with the type of customer who had made the 16 such a rousing success. Volvo, for its part, used the engine to replace the old straight six at the top of its range but also offered the engine in a long wheelbase saloon aimed at the diplomatic market and known as the 264TE.

Yet 1975 was not just the year of the PRV engine. The Triumph and Rover models which had virtually created the middle executive luxury performance class were on their last legs. In the case of the Triumph its reputation had never recovered from the battering it had received by being the first mass produced saloon to incorporate the Lucas fuel injection system, while defects such as the lack of luggage space and high overall replacement and maintenance costs were damaging the Rover 2200, as it had become, and its larger 3500 variant.

Three superb products of the Japanese motor industry, outpacing European manufacturers in areas they long regarded as their own, the Honda Prelude XX (**right**), Nissan Liberta 1500 SSS and Toyota Corolla GT (**below left and right**). Perhaps most significant is the Toyota Corolla which outperforms and undercuts in price most European competition

The car with which Leyland was to replace all its ageing executive and middle luxury saloons in the over 2·2 litre market was announced in 1976. For once the company seemed to have got it right. Using the trusty ex-Buick 3500 V8 served by twin SU carbs and giving a moderate 155 bhp, the new Rover SD1 amply justified the tag 'Solihull Citroën'. The nose was reminiscent of the Ferrari Daytona but the rest of the ill proportioned shell could well have originated from the drawing board of any junior stylist at Javel.

Gone was the sophisticated De Dion rear axle arrangement with its inboard disc brakes used on the previous cars for, in an effort to simplify the car and keep servicing costs reasonable, the company had adopted a rigid rear axle with coils located by Watts linkage. The front suspension featured MacPherson struts with lower trailing links and coils. Nevertheless it was a well equipped and good handling package and rave press reviews soon had long waiting lists building for the car.

Once again the inability of Leyland to market adequately developed motor cars was to end this happy state of affairs as a host of teething troubles manifested themselves in the early models. As well as these the continuous strikes and stoppages both at Leyland and its component suppliers soon disenchanted overseas buyers while the introduction in 1978 of the single overhead cam straight six engined 2600 and 2400 versions served to knock sales at the top of the range for, apart from the badging, they were virtually identical.

Not until the early eighties could it be said that the cars were fully 'sorted'. By then a

fortunate rule adjustment in international saloon car classes and Leyland's newly enlightened competition policy began to move the big hatchback to the forefront of the market. This achieved, the introduction of the top of the range Vitesse model in 1982 produced the car which the Rover should have been right from the start.

With the alloy 3528cc engine giving 190 bhp with the adoption of Lucas L electronic ignition, the car was capable of a 0–60 mph time of a mere 7·1 seconds, faster than the Mercedes 500SEL. Maximum speed was some 135 mph while lowered suspension did much to enhance the looks of the car when coupled with the deep chin spoiler and rear hatch mounted polyurethane 'tea tray'. As befits a car which was intended from the start to catch up with the products of BMW, it comes lavishly equipped including pretty alloy wheels and low profile tyres. Yet even as the cars dominate the racetracks the question still has to be asked: 'Why did it take so long?'

The Rover SDI illustrates the virtues of long term development and the desirability of a large, torquey and relatively simple multi-cylinder engine. Other companies meanwhile had their sights firmly set upon the middle luxury performance slot but without the finances of the PRV consortium or the shrewd long term development which had gone into the Mercedes and Rover powerplants, some drastically revised engineering thinking was called for.

Audi solved the problem neatly and pragmatically for their 100 which was introduced in a newly evolved bodystyle in 1977. In effect they added an extra cylinder to their already highly developed and

ROVER VITESSE

Country of origin: *Great Britain*
Engine: *ohv V8*
Capacity: *3528cc*
Bore and stroke: *88·9 × 71·1 mm*
Power output: *193 bhp
@ 5280 rpm*
Carburation: *Lucas–Bosch digital
injection*
Number of gears: *5*

PERFORMANCE

Top speed: *211 km/h*
Acceleration (0–100 km/h): *7·3 sec*

DIMENSIONS

Length: *4·730 m*
Width: *1·770 m*
Height: *1·410 m*
Wheelbase: *2·820 m*
Doors: *5*
Seats: *5*
Fuel Capacity: *66 litres*

extremely tractable overhead cam four to give them a five cylinder set-up. This was introduced as maintaining the economy of a four while offering the smoother running characteristics of a six. Its front wheel drive and neutral handling characteristics soon marked this range as one to watch, while the policy of producing an up market coupé version (in common with all the other German manufacturers) augured well for further production developments.

This was not long in coming although one vital ingredient had first to gain market acceptance. The introduction of the Saab 99 Turbo in 1978 heralded an explosion in the performance market unlike any seen before.

Like many fine ideas, turbocharging — the principle of using the waste energy of the exhaust gases to drive a compressor — had been around for many years waiting for the right combination of circumstances to make it viable. In the early twenties Major Frank Halford had built such devices into the engines he used in his Aston Martin based Grand Prix racers but had been defeated by the metallurgical unsophistication of the day.

The Second World War saw turbocharging applied on a wide scale in US aircraft engines but in most cases, to gain the right amount of boost, the equipment had to be made on a scale which made it altogether too unwieldy for automotive use. The breakthrough had come in the diesel truck markets, largely at the instigation of Ford, in the sixties after Cummins had gained a fair amount of publicity by entering a turbocharged diesel at the 1952 Indianapolis 500 which took the fastest qualifying time.

In 1960 General Motors took the decision to adopt turbocharging on the ill fated Chevrolet Corvair flat six which after two years of development was made publicly available in the form of the Corvair Monza Spyder of 1962. Oldsmobile followed with a turbocharged GTO which, although more sophisticated than its Chevrolet stablemate in that it featured a wastegate and fail-safe by-pass valves, was too complicated for the mechanics of the day.

By 1978 diagnostic tuning equipment was

Alfa GTV 6, 2.5, a consistent racetrack star performer. With its 2+2 configuration and slippery good looks, the GTV 6 is reminiscent of some of the great Alfas of the past

advanced to the 'plug in, read out and adjust' stage and even a mediocre mechanic could in theory work the latest electronic systems so that consideration of complexity ceased to apply in the majority of cases. Taking their lead from the extremely hairy BMW 2002 Turbo of 1973/74, Saab boldly went into the mass performance market and carved out a niche which was to see them on the way to challenging the prestigious BMW, Mercedes and Jaguar market in the affections of many US and European performance enthusiasts.

While BMW had produced only 1672 examples of their 2002 Turbo and had seen fit to equip it with bolt-on plastic spoilers and air dams, Saab made it clear from the introduction that the Turbo was no boy racers special. While the BMW had been boosted to some 170 bhp from its combination of KKK Turbo and Shafer injection, the Saab was content to rest with a more manageable 145 bhp from its Garrett installation.

To make the most of the power a five speed box now resided in the 99, a feature

which was to spread through all models of the range by 1982, and the suspension was slightly uprated from that of the 99EMS. More importantly for Saab the Turbo allowed them to market a larger car without having to develop a completely new engine. This arrived a few months after the Turbo was launched with the model nomenclature 900.

Even before the advent of the Saab Turbo the press had been cheerfully making the point that, compared with the equivalent models of the preceding decade any mid seventies car, outside the USA where emission controls had reversed the process, could be classed as a performance saloon. Better engines, alloy blocks and heads, fuel injection, more efficient carburation, better aerodynamics and better tyres had all educated a mass market in the importance of engineering which was relentlessly put to the fore in advertising campaigns. The resultant turbo boom was to build on this new awareness while at the same time new areas of technological development were beginning to open up.

While such companies as Alfa Romeo had always sought to minimise weight and equalise distribution by using a high percentage of alloy in their cars, the weight saving trend which had begun in the smaller cars of the early sixties continued to accelerate aided by increasing the use of the various high quality plastics becoming available. In the middle luxury sector of the market this kind of innovation was needed not just to offer increased performance but to improve economy.

The upsurge in these offerings by technologically advanced makers left many traditional performance makes slightly lost as the desperate struggle to gain lost ground began. While the Japanese, with their usual thoroughness, turbocharged anything which could move with some fairly drastic results, makers such as Alfa and Citroën explored other ways of attaining the market's blessing.

In 1972 Alfa Romeo, realising that their twin overhead cam engine was still competitive and likely to remain so for many years, brought out the first of theirs modern generation Alfettas. This used the 1750cc engine from the Giulietta but coupled it with a transaxle five speed gearbox mounted in the De Dion rear axle.

Although offering a robust 122 bhp and handling well up to the accepted standards of the day, the car proved slightly disappointing to the company and the subse-

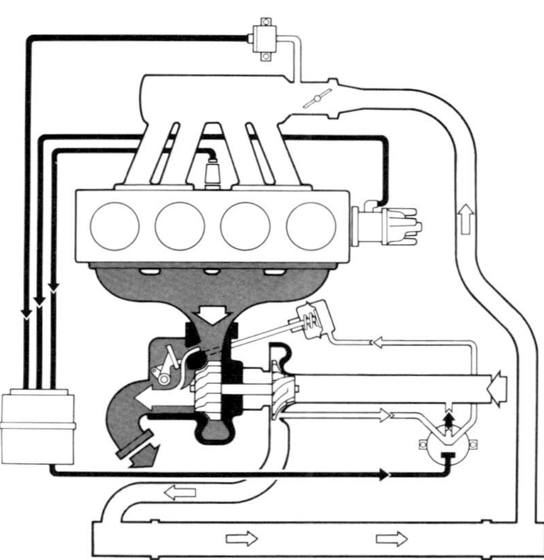

The mysteries of turbocharging revealed in this schematic of the Saab 9000 turbo set up. Hot exhaust gasses drive a turbine at up to ten times engine speed. This in turn drives a compressor which forces air under pressure into the fuel injection system boosting both torque and bhp with very small penalty in fuel consumption. Efficient waste-gate engineering and the use of smaller turbos has cut the 'turbo-lag' inherent in first generation designs

Alfa Romeo Giulietta Turbo. Last of the classic Alfas perhaps, the notchback Giuliettas were a graceful variation on a long running theme

quent uprating of the engine to 2 litres hardly altered the fact that other manufacturers were usurping the glamour of the marque. The result was the delightful little Giulietta of 1976 with the 1600cc engine and the same basic transmission package.

This was more in keeping with the flamboyant reputation of the marque and the means to capitalise on it soon became available with all the optional sizes of the twin cam engine on offer. At its best, and in real terms that meant the vehicles assembled in the South African plant, this car vied with the smaller products of BMW and could well have been the major Italian contender

of its class. It handled superbly, the engine was willing and free revving giving 130 bhp at 5400 rpm but an unenviable reputation for unreliability due to poor build quality doomed the beauty.

Nor was Alfa's contender for the upper end of the saloon market as well subscribed as it should have been. The Alfa Six which the world saw in 1979 represented an ill conceived challenge to Munich, Stuttgart and Coventry. With an overhead cam 2·5 litre V6 aspirated by six Dellorto carburetors and carrying its gearbox in the conventional location, the car was too far removed from the traditional concept of the fiery

Even diesels can be performance cars as evidenced by the Alfa Romeo Alfetta turbo-diesel

manoeuvrable products for which the Milanese company was respected. Once more build quality was suspect and a high initial purchase price was not enough to save the company embarrassment over this and its 2 litre variant.

This apart the incorporation of the V6 into the coupé derivative of the Giulietta produced a real firebreather. The GTV6 2·5 again featured a rear mounted gearbox and comfortable accommodation for four. It answered critics of the original 1750cc and 2 litre versions who wanted more power and at the same time delivered it in a wonderfully relaxed and controllable format. Perhaps its greatest moments have been in the hands of Andy Rouse in saloon car races in which it took the 1983 British championship for group A in its two plus two configuration. With its good power to weight ratio, it is reminiscent of some of the great Alfas of the past.

The engine also represents another logical step forward in Alfa design philosophy in its use of a single overhead cam per bank operating directly upon the inlet valves and by pushrods on the exhausts. With Bosch L-Jetronic injection in the GTV6, a reliable 160 bhp is achieved, delivered with an overall economy of something akin to 26 mpg.

The Alfa 33 range, designed to replace the top end of the Alfasud range and the bottom end of the Giulietta, is however a different story. Unlike either of the two ranges it supplants it is not immediately visually stimulating while even in 1·5 litre Quadifoglio Oro guise it remains somewhat lacking in all departments when compared to the Alfasud 1·5 Ti. This lack of immediate sparkle may well be merely a temporary phase. Private tuning specialists such as Bell and Colville and Westune in Britain have obtained fine results from turbocharging the engine in the 'Sud, so perhaps the factory can learn.

The future for Alfa in the highly competitive world of the performance saloon is firmly bound up with the 60 and the 90. Both have the unmistakable Alfa touch which was so lacking in the Alfetta and the 33 and both represent a continuation of tradition. They retain many of the features which were successful from the older ranges, adding the lessons of the last few years plus a wealth of new production technology.

Although important in their own right, the new Alfas are also part of a new and vital corporate framework, hopefully one which will ensure the survival of the type of car Alfa has built so wonderfully in the past. Along with Fiat, Lancia and Saab (who later withdrew) Alfa formed the consortium to build the Tipo 4. Regardless of their withdrawal some sixteen castings in the Saab 9000 were related to the product while Lancia's Thema also sprang from it.

Alfa 90, the car on which so many of Alfa's hope to get firmly back into the performance markets depends

Beneath the bonnet of the 90 is a twin overhead cam 2-litre engine with electronic fuel injection

ALFA ROMEO ALFA 90 2·0

Country of origin: *Italy*
Engine: *2 × ohc S4*
Capacity: *1962cc*
Bore and stroke: *84·0 × 88·5 mm*
Power output: *130 bhp*
  @ 5400 rpm
Carburation: *Motronic injection*
Number of gears: *5*

PERFORMANCE
Top speed: *190 km/h*
Acceleration (0–100 km/h): *9·7 sec*

DIMENSIONS
Length: *4·391 m*
Width: *1·638 m*
Height: *1·420 m*
Wheelbase: *2·510 m*
Doors: *4*
Seats: *5*
Fuel Capacity: *49 litres*

Lancia Thema

Lancia Thema on home ground

As if to carry the co-operation theme still further, the Thema as well as offering the Fiat/Lancia range of engines also carries a slightly modified Douvrin PRV V6. The rationale of the Lancia product team was that although the V6 gives perhaps 15 bhp less than the turbocharged 2 litre, it does it in a more relaxed way and at the same time has more than a passing appeal to those who prefer the simplicity of normal aspiration.

The Thema itself represents the luxury arm of Fiat at its best. MacPherson strut suspension with self-levelling rear struts ABS, transverse mounted engine and every other fashionable gimmick have been thrown together in a bodyshell carefully calculated not to offend anyone and very thoroughly guaranteed against corrosion from the inside resulting in a fine package with which to stem the tide of Japanese imports and challenge the medium sized cars from Munich.

Lancia are not alone in wanting to find some reasonable hardware to aim at this market. Even Mercedes-Benz have noted the progressive increases in quality from BMW and, no doubt taking into account the marque loyalty inherent in the customer for the 3 Series, produced their own attempt at flattery in the shape of the 190.

LANCIA THEMA 2·8 V6

Country of origin: *Italy*
Engine: *ohv V6*
Capacity: *2849cc*
Bore and stroke: *91·0 × 73·0 mm*
Power output: *150 bhp*
Carburation: *Bosch K‑Jetronic*
Number of gears: *4*

PERFORMANCE

Top speed: *190 km/h*
Acceleration (0–100 km/h): *9·5 sec*

DIMENSIONS

Length: *4·590 m*
Width: *1·755 m*
Height: *1·433 m*
Wheelbase: *2·660 m*
Doors: *4*
Seats: *5*
Fuel Capacity: *70 litres*

The Thema's 2-litre turbocharged engine cut away from the turbocharger side showing the valve gear and exhaust driven turbo set up. Blowing boosts the power output from 120 bhp to 165 bhp at maximum output

Unlike the past cars to bear the designation, the present 190 is a proper scaled down quality car. Available in standard trim with a single Stromberg 175 CDT carburettor aspirating the 1997cc single overhead cam engine the car is reputed to give 90 bhp at 5000 rpm. In E designation with the ubiquitous Bosch providing the induction it gives 122 bhp at 5100 rpm. Only on the top model where the magic of Cosworth has been called into play does the car really sparkle.

Here the company which provided Chapman with his Lotus-Cortina engine and built the two most successful major league racing engines of all time in the DFV and the DFX units has given Mercedes the benefit of its experience in this specialist field by providing a twin cam head which transforms an otherwise ordinary engine into a true rival to the 323i. Using Bosch KE fuel injection the Cosworth engine gives 185 bhp endowing the small Merc with a handy 143 mph top speed.

Obviously this is done at a price, yet the

The top of the Mercedes 190 range, the 190E 2.3-16 in its natural Autobahn habitat where the Cosworth prepared engine capable of delivering 185 bhp comes into its own

Stuttgart company has always been able to charge high prices for its wares without eroding its stolidly middle class following.

Another company which has always retained a solid middle class presence and has benefited from co-operation (although in this case enforced by economic disaster) is Citroën. While the company has always been at the forefront of technical innovation and judged by the standards of their time the cars have been fairly speedy, only in 1984 did the French company fully capital-ise on the potential of its superb CX.

Produced as a replacement for the DS in 1975 the CX is still one of the sleekest cars on the market. Even in GTi form it offered fair performance from its 2·5 litre L-Jetronic injected engine but, with the uprating of its hydropneumatic suspension, the addition of stiffer anti-roll bars and a well executed Garrett T3 installation, the car became one of the great performance saloons.

With a higher ratio five speed gearbox than the standard GTi plus twenty-two per

MERCEDES-BENZ 190E 2·3–16
Country of origin: *Germany*
Engine: *2 × ohc S4*
Capacity: *2299cc*
Bore and stroke: *95·0 × 80·3 mm*
Power output: *185 bhp*
  @ 6200 rpm
Carburation: *Bosch injection*
Number of gears: *5*

PERFORMANCE
Top speed: *230 km/h*
Acceleration (0–100 km/h): *7·5 sec*

DIMENSIONS
Length: *4·430 m*
Width: *1·706 m*
Height: *1·361 m*
Wheelbase: *2·665 m*
Doors: *4*
Seats: *5*
Fuel Capacity: *70 litres*

cent more power (168 bhp against 138 bhp) and maximum torque coming in at 3250 rpm where it makes overtaking a positive pleasure, the car is naturally in competition with some of the finest cars on the market. With performance similar to that of the Audi 200 Turbo and an interior which is arguably the finest available in terms of ergonomics the GTi Turbo brings the 1975 shape into contention with the very latest products of the world's industry and so good was the original concept that the car is immediately competitive.

As if this were not enough the French company also took the latest of their progeny, the BX, and by incorporating the Peugeot light alloy 2 litre unit created the chic and exhilarating BX19GT. If there is one car in the market which feels inherently right for the future the BX19GT must be that car. A combination of hydropnuematic and MacPherson strut suspension provides a ride which almost matches that of the Saab 900, while the road holding bears comparison with any car in the performance market once the odd feeling of roll on high G force corners becomes familiar.

A top speed of some 115 mph and 105 bhp at 5600 rpm from the normally aspirated engine may sound tame yet the car is capable of carrying five adults plus luggage in comfort. Some of the exhilaration comes from the relative lightness of the car for its size for as well as the use of alloy in the engine and transmission casings good use has been made of plastics and composites in

CITROËN CX25 GTi TURBO
Country of origin: *France*
Engine: *ohv S4*
Capacity: *2482cc*
Bore and stroke: *93·0 × 92·0 mm*
Power output: *166 bhp*
@ 5000 rpm
Carburation: *Bosch LE-Jetronic*
Number of gears: *5*

PERFORMANCE
Top speed: *217 km/h*
Acceleration (0–100 km/h): *9·5 sec*

DIMENSIONS
Length: *4·659 m*
Width: *1·770 m*
Height: *1·360 m*
Wheelbase: *2·845 m*
Doors: *5*
Seats: *5*
Fuel Capacity: *68 litres*

Citroen CX 25 GTI. With turbocharging this decade old design is still one of the most potent performance saloons of the mid 1980s

the body structure. This gives a ratio of some 107 bhp per ton, a superior power to weight figure than some of the turbo-charged exotics on offer.

The fact that like all smaller Citroëns the car represents astounding value for money and that the oddities usually found mas-querading as instruments in front of the Citroën driver have been replaced by dials, help to give the car the purposeful air that many Citroëns with sporting pretensions lacked in previous years. With the company ready to admit that the possibility of both fuel injection and turbocharging in the future is a very real one the car needs only the addition of self-cancelling indicators to make it untouchable in the small 2 litre class.

Citroen BX 19 GT, one of the best performers in the under 2-litre class

Audi 200 Quattro. The technology which allowed Audi to produce the awe-inspiring Quattro coupé has been incorporated throughout the range to produce this four wheel drive, sure footed executive express capable of 140 mph

Across the border from France in the little town of Ingolstadt, Audi have also been busy creating cars which may well point the way to the future. The combination of the bodyshell from the 80 Coupé, the engine from the top of the range 200 Turbo and the four wheel drive system from the VAG group's military Iltis to form the Quattro has done as much for all wheel traction as the introduction of the 99 Turbo did for forced induction.

Yet the continuing preoccupations of Audi do not merely rest with producing the ideal, civilised, all wheel drive family of cars. The introduction in 1982 of the third generation 100 with its flush fitting glass and low Cd factor marked the movement of the company even further into the domain of the big three prestige makers. The 200 Turbo variant with its 182 bhp and 143 mph top speed coupled with an overall average fuel consumption of some 30 mpg is a sure

fire way of giving headaches to the opposition.

The fact that this type of technical excellence is coupled with extremely high build and finish quality, extending across the whole product range, bodes well for the up-market arm of VAG. The stated aim of the company is to be able to offer a high performance full sized saloon with the economy of the Series I VW Golf. Without doubt they will achieve this.

In Sweden the Volvo 760 Turbo has been developed into a useful saloon car championship contender while Saab have introduced the 9000. Both cars offer full accommodation for five passengers and are designed to survive into long term production, returning figures for economy which would have been wishful thinking on the part of the marketing department just five years ago.

Almost every manufacturer is taking

Saab 9000, the Swedish manufacturer's car for the 21st century. The package may look conventional but advanced engineering throughout includes use of new composite material technology and aircraft-derived body stress studies to produce a light but very strong bodyshell

Far right: The 700 series Volvos may have broken some styling rules of the time but the distinguished if ponderous lines of the car belie a true performance potential, especially in the top of the range 760 Turbo, capable of over 200 km/h

advantage of electronics to build the type of engine management system into their cars which allows automatic advance and retard at critical points in the power curve. In some instances this can achieve a compression ratio as high as 17 : 1 in motorway cruising conditions. The combination of advances in electronic ignition efficiency and light alloy metallurgy has led to a veritable deluge of delectable power plants.

Again Saab are front runners with their latest sixteen valve development for the Turbo 16 engine employed in both the 1984 900 range and the 9000. Yet others have adopted the traditional four valve per cylinder layout. As well as the Mercedes-Cosworth, Toyota have proved just how close they can come to the ideal small performance coupé with the delightful twin cam sixteen valve Corolla Coupé while marking the top of the range Capri with their V6 Celica GT with its 2·8 litre fuel injected 175 bhp engine.

Nissan too with their performance range

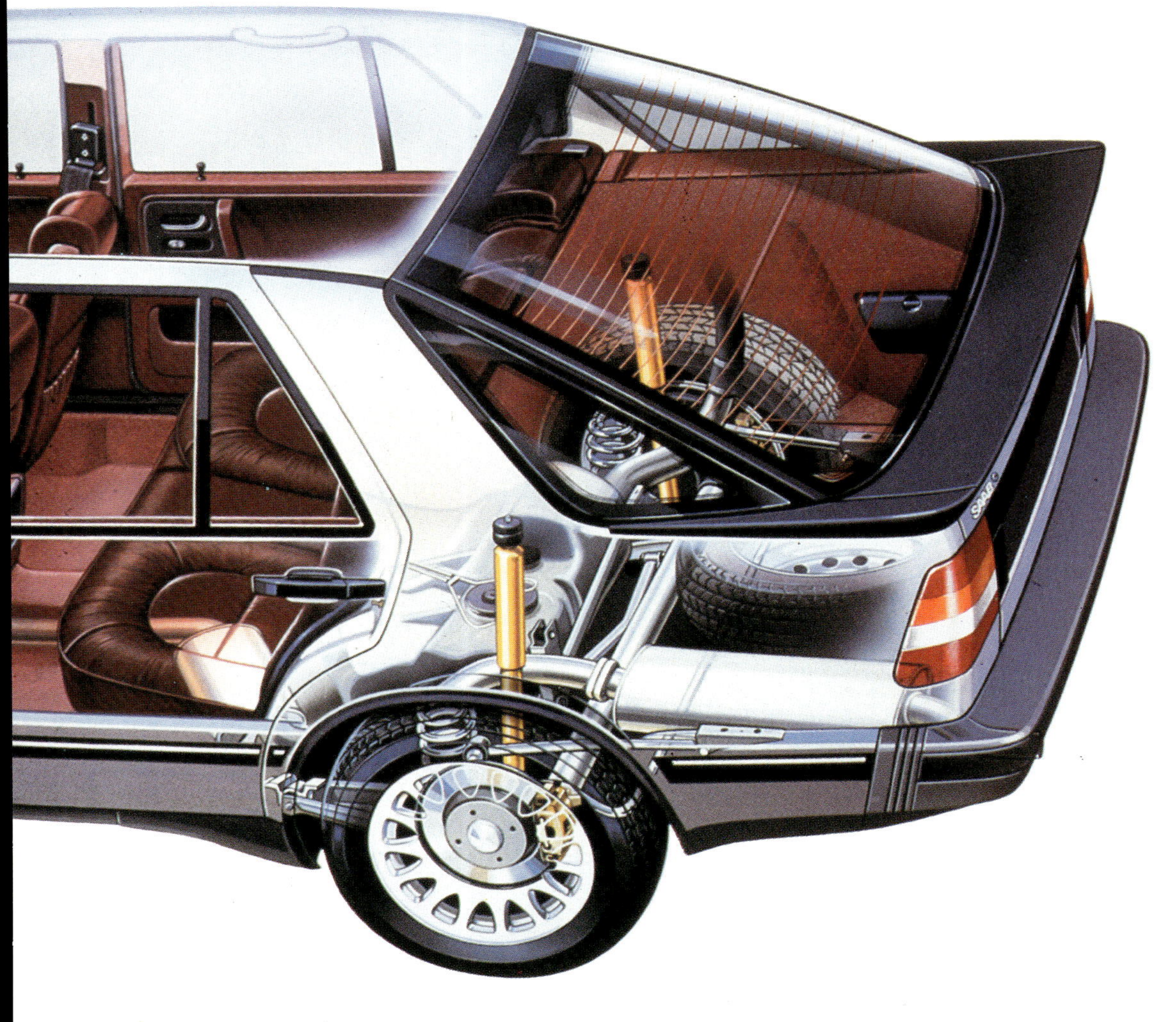

SAAB 9000 TURBO 16
Country of origin: *Sweden*
Engine: *2 × ohc S4*
Capacity: *1985cc*
Bore and stroke: *90·0 × 78·0 mm*
Power output: *175 bhp
 @ 5300 rpm*
Carburation: *Bosch LH-injection with
 turbo*
Number of gears: *5*

PERFORMANCE
Top speed: *220 km/h*
Acceleration (0–100 km/h): *8·3 sec*

DIMENSIONS
Length: *4·620 m*
Width: *1·764 m*
Height: *1·430 m*
Wheelbase: *2·672 m*
Doors: *5*
Seats: *5*
Fuel Capacity: *68 litres*

are proving adept at learning from criticism with the result that, although the 300ZX is still more of a pastiche than a Porsche, in the well styled and well equipped Silvia Turbo they have a car no European manufacturer would be too ashamed of having brought to the market.

The Mitsubishi range is another which has learned from adverse market reaction and is moving well into contention in the performance market with the Lancer Turbo and the Starion coupé. The latter has even shown well in saloon racing and the Japanese have an enviable marketing history of being able to tailor individual products to the national markets they are aimed at.

Of the rest of Europe's larger manufacturers Renault joined the middle range Turbo club with their 1980 18 Turbo, their Cortina/Ascona competitor which utilises the rather outdated uprated version of the 16 pushrod engine. This was joined by the Fuego Turbo in 1983 and the 11 Turbo in early 1984. With the latter car the resulting package looks set to capitalise on the success of the AMC-built Alliance in the USA.

While Fiat have yet to announce their middle class contender there is virtually no doubt that it will retain the economic and pleasing twin cam engine. The group responded to the outbreak of Turbos by releasing the Volumex supercharging system into the market in the form of supercharged versions of the Beta HPE and the Beta Coupé. Their attempts to uprate the unlovely and unloved 132 Argenta with the system came too late in the day to save its reputation for lack of power and bad handling, yet must have gained the Italian Company valuable expertise in the supercharged market.

In the international market the continuing battle between the European arms of Ford and General Motors has escalated almost to the status of war, each seeking to find a market niche or exploit one that its rival has found with all the enthusiasm of a hungry vampire.

Range and production rationalisation in the late seventies coupled with a vast improvement in the Vauxhall Cavalier/Opel Ascona range, which was amply demonstrated both in the showroom and later upon the international rally circuit of the early eighties, have seen the performance derivatives locked closely into battle for sales.

Moreover as the Opel Ascona/Vauxhall Cavalier range began to gain ground in the battle with Ford for the affections of the lower company exec market, both companies began to field fuel injected or high performance derivatives of their ranges. Ford preferred to stay with large engines in the Cortina days but with the introduction of the Sierra with its unconventional bodystyle they opted for the BMW-baiting sophistication of the XR4i with its high specification and commensurate high price while GM offered the tamer but more practical Cavalier/Ascona SRi with a lower spec and output but more affordable insurance premiums and original purchase price. While the 2·8 litre XR4i conquered a whole new market for Ford, the SRi certainly stirred product loyalty in their traditionally strong market areas while reinforcing GM sales in others.

At the top of the market Opel currently holds sway with its superb Monza yet the new large Fords herald a counter-attack as the company takes great pains to stress that their new post-Granada large car for the upper executive market will outdo Audi claims by offering the economy of the Series 1 Fiesta.

So good is the drive train of the Monza that just as British specialist high performance makers have adopted the Ford V6, the exclusive German specialist manufacturer Bitter have taken the engine and some chassis components from GM's top car for the basis of the exclusive SC coupé in both its coupé and Cabrio versions. The success and continued survival of Bitter is in itself a symptom of a trend which has come too late for many of the great names of motoring, the desire for something very exclusive indeed in motor cars. No better examples can be found in the world of the exotic than the Maserati Quattroporte or the dashingly elegant Aston-Martin Lagonda.

Indeed both cars represent the same design philosophy with sleek and enduringly beautiful four door coachwork, and incredibly sumptuous interiors being propelled at rates which exceed every world speed limit in an unruffled way by highly tuned V8 engines. Both cars represent the type of performance and roadholding which would have been available only from a very top of the range Ferrari in the early seventies, while neither is anything but the epitome of indulgence for the super rich.

Further down the scale the resurgence of the Maserati marque has been abetted by the Biturbo in its 2 litre and 2·5 litre guise. These cars use the small block Maserati V6 originally developed in conjunction with Citroën and later seen in the Merak, aspirated by a Weber carburettor and two IHI turbos controlled by a Maserati-developed electronic engine management system. In 2 litre form the engine offers some 180 bhp at 6000 rpm while in 2·5 litre form 200 bhp at 5500 rpm is quoted. Unlike its larger brother the Quattroporte which uses MacPherson struts only at the front the Biturbo boasts them at all four corners coupled with light and precise rack and pinion steering.

While Maserati suffered from the traditional problem of limited demand for its

The dramatic coupe styling and double rear spoilers of the XR4i proclaimed its distance from the more prosaic Sierra

FORD SIERRA XR4i
Country of origin: *Great Britain/Germany*
Engine: *ohv V6*
Capacity: *2772cc*
Bore and stroke: *93·0 × 68·5 mm*
Power output: *150 bhp*
 @ 5700 rpm
Carburation: *Bosch K-Jetronic*
Number of gears: *5*

PERFORMANCE
Top speed: *210 km/h*
Acceleration (0–100 km/h): *8·4 sec*

DIMENSIONS
Length: *4·459 m*
Width: *1·728 m*
Height: *1·392 m*
Wheelbase: *2·608 m*
Doors: *3*
Seats: *5*
Fuel Capacity: *60 litres*

more exotic products the demand for the Biturbo overwhelmed the company and in its first year of production quality suffered as a result. Yet while the Quattroporte and the Lagonda have to appeal to the Arabian princes and the rock and roll superstars to justify their existence, the Biturbo has cut firmly into territory previously held by larger less exotic rivals.

Obviously the success of the Biturbo has eased the problems of Alessandro De Tomaso in saving the respected name of Maserati, yet even before he added the cars of the Trident to his stable he was offering up market performance under his own name. The De Tomaso Deauville carries on this tradition using the 5763cc American Ford V8 in an attractive bodyshell which, like the more complex Quattroporte, uses MacPherson struts at the front and double coil over shocks at each rear corner. The use of the American engine without the ZF five speed manual gearbox and limited slip differential option of the Quattroporte allows thus a cheaper expression of the same philosophy while the same basic pack-age in two plus two form pads out the range in the form of the Longchamp.

While these pure bred exotics hold sway in the less conservative sector of the super rich categories the rekindling of Bentley's individuality has added a whole new dimension to the upper price bracket. When the Rolls Royce company narrowly escaped becoming part of either Ford or Mercedes-Benz during the financial crash of the aero engine division in 1971, it was to rise quickly from its corporate mire, split off as a separate company and launch the elegant Corniche. Then as now the company had few rivals for this sector of the market and the two door car with its slightly uprated suspension and engine began to recapture sporting ground lost to rivals such as Bristol and Jensen.

Throughout the decade the coupé theme was to remain a highly innovative area for the company and 1975 saw this further exploited with the introduction of the Pininfarina-styled Camargue.

The eighties, however, saw the company needing a replacement for the Silver

Discreet 'turbo' badging and a deep front spoiler hint at the performance potential of the stately Bentley Mulsanne Turbo. A 6.7 litre turbocharged engine affords the big, superbly engineered car breathtaking acceleration and top speed

Shadow and in 1981 the Silver Spirit and the longer wheelbased Silver Spur were added. Under the new bodyshell very little had changed. The alloy engine had by now been enlarged marginally to 6750cc and four wheel discs were standardised with some revision to the suspension to cope with the heavier and wider bodywork yet, although the cars immediately became the object of adulation, the well tried RR policy of gradual improvement and development meant that very few major innovations were incorporated.

As usual the Bentley variant of the Spirit was a badge engineered version but with a new name, Mulsanne. However, the Rolls Royce Motors company had become the property of another traditional British corporation, Vickers, who felt that the interests of the marque could best be served by reviving some of the Bentley name's former raffish glamour.

In 1983 the first steps were taken with the introduction of the Mulsanne Turbo. Although the all alloy engine remained ostensibly the same, the addition of a Garrett T3 Turbo with a single down-draught Solex A1 carburettor fed by a

Bosch fuel delivery system transformed the performance of the two ton car. Uprating the traditional self-levelling suspension gave the car more purchase on the road while discreet 'Turbo' badging gave away the fact that the car was somewhat enhanced over the cooking models.

The overall result was simply sensational. Capable of over 135 mph and with acceleration at times reminiscent of the Porsche 928, the Turbo at a stroke solved the problem of marque identity. So successful was the move that the marque was further enhanced in 1984 with the announcement of the normally aspirated Bentley Eight. For the first time since 1934 the original wire mesh grille of the W.O. Bentleys was adopted on a current Rolls Royce product. Once more the uprated suspension from the Mulsanne was in evidence yet although the price was almost ten per cent down on the Mulsanne, the new car lost none of the craftsmanship which marked the Roll Royce as a car apart.

To revive the superb reputation of the fifties cars the company also took the trouble to rename the Corniche variant, with its Bentley badge, as the latter day Continental.

The Bentley Eight reintroduced the characteristic mesh grille of the great pre-war Bentleys

BENTLEY MULSANNE TURBO

Country of origin: *Great Britain*
Engine: *ohv V8*
Capacity: *6750cc*
Bore and stroke: *104·1 × 99·1 mm*
Power output: *More than adequate*
Carburation: *Solex A41 with turbo*
Number of Gears: *Automatic*

PERFORMANCE

Top speed: *216 km/h*
Acceleration (0–100 km/h): *7·4 sec*

DIMENSIONS

Length: *5·310 m*
Width: *1·890 m*
Height: *1·490 m*
Wheelbase: *3·060 m*
Doors: *4*
Seats: *5*
Fuel Capacity: *107 litres*

Carrying on in a great tradition, the products of the Bristol Car Company for the 1980s include the Bristol Brigand and flamboyant open Beaufighter.

Adhering to the tradition of big Chrysler engines and hand built craftmanship, the cars' styling remains eccentric but appealing

MPH 100

While this means nothing in terms of engineering, the policy of the company was to appeal to the younger man about town — the latter day equivalent of the 'Chelsea set' who had made the R Type Continental such an astounding success. Meanwhile, although the company are adamant that such a project is many years from fruition, rumours began to grow of a real sports saloon in the manner of the great cars of the late twenties and early thirties. Somehow such a car seems fitting, both to mark the company as the leader in a new age of technical progress and as an example of the traditional merits of the best of the British motor industry.

While Bristol have kept alive a tradition of using the best in American engines combined with the finest available British craftsmanship and Lagonda have taken the luxury performance carriage firmly into the electronics age, nothing could please either the British enthusiasts or the world's motoring connoisseurs more than a rebirth of the magnificent Bentley 'Le Mans' tradition.

Meanwhile as the names Maserati, Ferrari, Bristol, Lagonda and Bentley carry a special kind of performance motoring forward, perhaps the revival of Chrysler fortunes under the dynamic guidance of Lee Iacocca will herald the rebirth of the great American roadsters. Perhaps not in the shape of a reborn Duesenberg or Packard (realistically, who could afford to build that way?) but a revival of the fast and elegant machines which the Americans loved so well in the years before Detroit decreed that the mass market ruled would enhance the Naderised conformity which pervades the world's makers.

Saab have proved that a safe car need not be dull. The continued success of Jaguar means that a certain kind of customer still aspires to grace and pace. The car is a means of asserting individuality and if the major manufacturers lose sight of this, there may well be specialist customisers who will rise as Jaguar and BMW did to provide the kind of performance the motorist will always demand.

Below: The Bitter SC four door saloon. Powered by Opel, these limited production, hand built cars have found a top market niche to themselves commended by reliability and superb finish

Bottom: Ferrari 400i — the nearest thing to a saloon ever to emerge from Il Commendatore's factory

9 Data section

ABBREVIATIONS

ohc – overhead cam
sohc – single overhead cam
ohv – overhead valve
S4 – straight four cylinders in-line
rpm – revolutions per minute
2 × ohc – twin overhead cam

CONVERSIONS

Capacity – cubic centimetres to
cubic inches = × 0.061
Bore and stroke – mm to inches
 = × 0.0394
Top speed – km/h to mph
 = × 0.621
Dimensions – metres to feet
 = × 3.28
Fuel capacity – litres to gallons
 = × 0.22

CZECHOSLOVAKIA

Tatra 613 Special

Skoda Rapid 130

TATRA 613-SPECIAL

Country of origin: *Czechoslovakia*
Engine: *2 × ohc V8*
Capacity: *3495cc*
Bore and stroke: *85·0 × 77·0 mm*
Power output: *168 bhp*
 @ 5200 rpm
Carburation: *2 × Jikov*
Number of gears: *4*

PERFORMANCE
Top speed: *190 km/h*
Acceleration (0–100 km/h): *12·7 sec*

DIMENSIONS
Length: *5·185 m*
Width: *1·800 m*
Height: *1·440 m*
Wheelbase: *3·130 m*
Doors: *4*
Seats: *4*
Fuel Capacity: *72 litres*

SKODA 130L

Country of origin: *Czechoslovakia*
Engine: *sohv S4*
Capacity: *1289cc*
Bore and stroke: *75·5 × 72·0 mm*
Power output: *62 bhp*
 @ 5000 rpm
Carburation: *1 × 2 Vikov*
Number of gears: *5*

PERFORMANCE
Top speed: *150 km/h*
Acceleration (0–100 km/h): *14·0 sec*

DIMENSIONS
Length: *4·200 m*
Width: *1·610 m*
Height: *1·400 m*
Wheelbase: *2·400 m*
Doors: *4*
Seats: *5*
Fuel Capacity: *37 litres*

SKODA RAPID 130

Country of origin: *Czechoslovakia*
Engine: *sohv S4*
Capacity: *1289cc*
Bore and stroke: *75·5 × 72·0 mm*
Power output: *62 bhp*
 @ 5000 rpm
Carburation: *1 × 2 Vikov*
Number of Gears: *5*

PERFORMANCE
Top speed: *153 km/h*
Acceleration (0–100 km/h): *14·0 sec*

DIMENSIONS
Length: *4·200 m*
Width: *1·610 m*
Height: *1·380 m*
Wheelbase: *2·400 m*
Doors: *2*
Seats: *2 + 2*
Fuel Capacity: *37 litres*

FRANCE

CITROEN BX19GT
Country of origin: *France*
Engine: *sohc S4*
Capacity: *1891cc*
Bore and stroke: *83·0 × 98·0 mm*
Power output: *102 bhp*
  @ 5600 rpm
Carburation: *1 × Solex*
Number of gears: *5*

PERFORMANCE
Top speed: *185 km/h*
Acceleration (0–100 km/h): *10·0 sec*

DIMENSIONS
Length: *4·230 m*
Width: *1·660 m*
Height: *1·361 m*
Wheelbase: *2·655 m*
Doors: *5*
Seats: *5*
Fuel Capacity: *52 litres*

CITROEN VISA GT
Country of origin: *France*
Engine: *sohc S4*
Capacity: *1360cc*
Bore and stroke: *75·0 × 70·0 mm*
Power output: *79 bhp*
  @ 5800 rpm
Carburation: *2 × Solex 35*
Number of gears: *5*

PERFORMANCE
Top speed: *168 km/h*
Acceleration (0–100 km/h): *10·9 sec*

DIMENSIONS
Length: *3·730 m*
Width: *1·530 m*
Height: *1·410 m*
Wheelbase: *2·426 m*
Doors: *5*
Seats: *5*
Fuel Capacity: *40 litres*

CITROEN CX GTi: *See page 148*

PEUGEOT 205GT
Country of origin: *France*
Engine: *sohc S4*
Capacity: *1360cc*
Bore and stroke: *75·0 × 77·0 mm*
Power output: *80 bhp*
  @ 5800 rpm
Carburation: *2 × Solex*
Number of gears: *5*

PERFORMANCE
Top speed: *170 km/h*
Acceleration (0–100 km/h): *11·6 sec*

DIMENSIONS
Length: *3·705 m*
Width: *1·572 m*
Height: *1·365 m*
Wheelbase: *2·240 m*
Doors: *5*
Seats: *5*
Fuel Capacity: *50 litres*

PEUGEOT 205 GTi: *See page 113*

PEUGEOT 505 TURBO INJECTION
Country of origin: *France*
Engine: *sohc S4*
Capacity: *2155cc*
Bore and stroke: *91·7 × 81·6 mm*
Power output: *155 bhp*
  @ 5200 rpm
Carburation: *Bosch L-Jetronic and turbo*
Number of gears: *5*

PERFORMANCE
Top speed: *205 km/h*
Acceleration (0–100 km/h): *8·6 sec*

DIMENSIONS
Length: *4·580 m*
Width: *1·730 m*
Height: *1·424 m*
Wheelbase: *2·740 m*
Doors: *4*
Seats: *5*
Fuel Capacity: *70 litres*

PEUGEOT 505GTi
Country of origin: *France*
Engine: *sohc S4*
Capacity: *2165cc*
Bore and stroke: *88·0 × 89·0 mm*
Power output: *123 bhp*
  @ 5500 rpm
Carburation: *Bosch L-Jetronic injection*
Number of gears: *5*

PERFORMANCE
Top speed: *185 km/h*
Acceleration (0–100 km/h): *10·0 sec*

DIMENSIONS
Length: *4·580 m*
Width: *1·720 m*
Height: *1·432 m*
Wheelbase: *2·740 m*
Doors: *4*
Seats: *5*
Fuel Capacity: *70 litres*

RENAULT R25 V6 INJECTION
Country of origin: *France*
Engine: *sohc V6*
Capacity: *2664cc*
Bore and stroke: *88·0 × 73·0 mm*
Power output: *141 bhp*
  @ 5500 rpm
Carburation: *Bosch injection*
Number of gears: *5*

PERFORMANCE
Top speed: *201 km/h*
Acceleration (0–100 km/h): *10·0 sec*

DIMENSIONS
Length: *4·649 m*
Width: *1·772 m*
Height: *1·405 m*
Wheelbase: *2·723 m*
Doors: *4*
Seats: *5*
Fuel Capacity: *72 litres*

Renault 25 V6 Turbo

RENAULT R25TS, R25GTS
Country of origin: *France*
Engine: *sohc S4*
Capacity: *1995cc*
Bore and stroke: *88·0 × 82·0 mm*
Power output: *101 bhp*
 @ 5500 rpm
Carburation: *1 × Weber 28/36 DARA*
Number of gears: *5*

PERFORMANCE
Top speed: *182 km/h*
Acceleration (0–100 km/h): *11·5 sec*

DIMENSIONS
Length: *4·623 m*
Width: *1·772 m*
Height: *1·405 m*
Wheelbase: *2·718 m (TS) 2·723 m (GTS)*
Doors: *4*
Seats: *5*
Fuel Capacity: *67 litres*

RENAULT R11 TURBO
Country of origin: *France*
Engine: *ohv S4*
Capacity: *1397cc*
Bore and stroke: *76·0 × 77·0 mm*
Power output: *105 bhp*
 @ 5500 rpm
Carburation: *1 × Solex 32 DIS and turbo*
Number of gears: *5*

PERFORMANCE
Top speed: *186 km/h*
Acceleration (0–100 km/h): *9·0 sec*

DIMENSIONS
Length: *3·958 m*
Width: *1·634 m*
Height: *1·380 m*
Wheelbase: *2·483 m*
Doors: *3*
Seats: *4*
Fuel Capacity: *47 litres*

RENAULT R18 TURBO
Country of origin: *France*
Engine: *ohv S4*
Capacity: *1565cc*
Bore and stroke: *77·0 × 84·0 mm*
Power output: *125 bhp*
 @ 5500 rpm
Carburation: *1 × Solex 32*
Number of gears: *5*

PERFORMANCE
Top speed: *195 km/h*
Acceleration (0–100 km/h): *10·0 sec*

DIMENSIONS
Length: *4·394 m*
Width: *1·696 m*
Height: *1·410 m*
Wheelbase: *2·438 m*
Doors: *4*
Seats: *5*
Fuel Capacity: *53 litres*

RENAULT FUEGO TURBO
Country of origin: *France*
Engine: *ohv S4*
Capacity: *1565cc*
Bore and stroke: *77·0 × 84·0 mm*
Power output: *132 bhp*
 @ 5500 rpm
Carburation: *1 × Solex 32 and turbo*
Number of gears: *5*

PERFORMANCE
Top speed: *198 km/h*
Acceleration (0–100 km/h): *9·5 sec*

DIMENSIONS
Length: *4·385 m*
Width: *1·692 m*
Height: *1·328 m*
Wheelbase: *2·440 m*
Doors: *3*
Seats: *4*
Fuel Capacity: *57 litres*

RENAULT R25GTX
Country of origin: *France*
Engine: *sohc S4*
Capacity: *2165cc*
Bore and stroke: *88·0 × 89·0 mm*
Power output: *121 bhp*
 @ 5250 rpm
Carburation: *Renix electronic injection*
Number of gears: *5*

PERFORMANCE
Top speed: *195 km/h*
Acceleration (0–100 km/h): *10·3 sec*

DIMENSIONS
Length: *4·623 m*
Width: *1·772 m*
Height: *1·405 m*
Wheelbase: *2·723 m*
Doors: *4*
Seats: *5*
Fuel Capacity: *72 litres*

RENAULT 5 TSE: *See page 111*

Renault 11 Turbo

Renault Fuego Turbo

FEDERAL REPUBLIC OF GERMANY

AUDI 80GTE

Country of origin: *Germany*
Engine: *sohc S4*
Capacity: *1781cc*
Bore and stroke: *81·0 × 86·4 mm*
Power output: *112 bhp*
 @ 5800 rpm
Carburation: *Injection*
Number of gears: *5*

PERFORMANCE
Top speed: *187 km/h*
Acceleration (0–100 km/h): *9·2 sec*

DIMENSIONS
Length: *4·406 m*
Width: *1·682 m*
Height: *1·340 m*
Wheelbase: *2·538 m*
Doors: *2*
Seats: *5*
Fuel Capacity: *68 litres*

AUDI 90

Country of origin: *Germany*
Engine: *sohc S5*
Capacity: *2226cc*
Bore and stroke: *81·0 × 86·4 mm*
Power output: *136 bhp*
 @ 5700 rpm
Carburation: *Injection*
Number of gears: *5*

PERFORMANCE
Top speed: *200 km/h*
Acceleration (0–100 km/h): *9·0 sec*

DIMENSIONS
Length: *4·465 m*
Width: *1·682 m*
Height: *1·365 m*
Wheelbase: *2·525 m*
Doors: *4*
Seats: *5*
Fuel Capacity: *68 litres*

AUDI 80 QUATTRO

Country of origin: *Germany*
Engine: *sohc S4*
Capacity: *1781cc*
Bore and stroke: *81·0 × 86·4 mm*
Power output: *90 bhp*
 @ 5200 rpm
Carburation: *Injection*
Number of gears: *5*

PERFORMANCE
Top speed: *170 km/h*
Acceleration (0–100 km/h): *12·0 sec*

DIMENSIONS
Length: *4·406 m*
Width: *1·682 m*
Height: *1·376 m*
Wheelbase: *2·525 m*
Doors: *2 or 4*
Seats: *5*
Fuel Capacity: *70 litres*

AUDI 90 QUATTRO

Country of origin: *Germany*
Engine: *sohc S5*
Capacity: *2226cc*
Bore and stroke: *81·0 × 86·4 mm*
Power output: *136 bhp*
 @ 5700 rpm
Carburation: *Injection*
Number of gears: *5*

PERFORMANCE
Top speed: *200 km/h*
Acceleration (0–100 km/h): *9·0 sec*

DIMENSIONS
Length: *4·465 m*
Width: *1·682 m*
Height: *1·376 m*
Wheelbase: *2·687 m*
Doors: *4*
Seats: *5*
Fuel Capacity: *70 litres*

AUDI 200 TURBO: *See page 151*

Above: Audi 90

Left: Audi 90 Quattro

AUDI 200 QUATTRO

Country of origin: *Germany*
Engine: *sohc S5*
Capacity: *2144cc*
Bore and stroke: *79·5 × 86·4 mm*
Power output: *182 bhp*
    @ 5700 rpm
Carburation: *Injection*
Number of gears: *5*

PERFORMANCE

Top speed: *230 km/h*
Acceleration (0–100 km/h): *8·1 sec*

DIMENSIONS

Length: *4·807 m*
Width: *1·814 m*
Height: *1·422 m*
Wheelbase: *2·687 m*
Doors: *4*
Seats: *5*
Fuel Capacity: *80 litres*

AUDI COUPE GT

Country of origin: *Germany*
Engine: *sohc S5*
Capacity: *2226cc*
Bore and stroke: *79·5 × 86·4 mm*
Power output: *136 bhp*
    @ 5700 rpm
Carburation: *Injection*
Number of gears: *5*

PERFORMANCE

Top speed: *202 km/h*
Acceleration (0–100 km/h): *8·6 sec*

DIMENSIONS

Length: *4·421 m*
Width: *1·682 m*
Height: *1·350 m*
Wheelbase: *2·538 m*
Doors: *2*
Seats: *5*
Fuel Capacity: *68 litres*

AUDI QUATTRO

Country of origin: *Germany*
Engine: *sohc S5*
Capacity: *2144cc*
Bore and stroke: *79·5 × 86·4 mm*
Power output: *200 bhp*
    @ 5500 rpm
Carburation: *Injection*
Number of gears: *5*

PERFORMANCE

Top speed: *222 km/h*
Acceleration (0–100 km/h): *7·1 sec*

DIMENSIONS

Length: *4·404 m*
Width: *1·723 m*
Height: *1·344 m*
Wheelbase: *2·524 m*
Doors: *2*
Seats: *5*
Fuel Capacity: *70 litres*

Audi Quattro

Audi 200 Quattro

AUDI QUATTRO SPORT
Country of origin: *Germany*
Engine: *sohc S5*
Capacity: *2133cc*
Bore and stroke: *79·3 × 86·4 mm*
Power output: *300 bhp*
 @ 6500 rpm
Carburation: *Injection*
Number of gears: *5*

PERFORMANCE
Top speed: *222 km/h*
Acceleration (0–100 km/h): *7·1 sec*

DIMENSIONS
Length: *4·164 m*
Width: *1·803 m*
Height: *1·345 m*
Wheelbase: *2·204 m*
Doors: *2*
Seats: *2 + 2*
Fuel Capacity: *90 litres*

BILTER SC COUPE
Country of origin: *Germany*
Engine: *sohc S6*
Capacity: *3848cc*
Bore and stroke: *95·0 × 90·5 mm*
Power output: *210 bhp*
 @ 5100 rpm
Carburation: *Bosch L-Jetronic*
Number of gears: *4*

PERFORMANCE
Top speed: *215 km/h*
Acceleration (0–100 km/h): *8·5 sec*

DIMENSIONS
Length: *4·910 m*
Width: *1·820 m*
Height: *1·350 m*
Wheelbase: *2·683 m*
Doors: *2*
Seats: *4*
Fuel Capacity: *75 litres*

BMW 528i
Country of origin: *Germany*
Engine: *sohc S6*
Capacity: *2788cc*
Bore and stroke: *86·0 × 80·0 mm*
Power output: *184 bhp*
 @ 5800 rpm
Carburation: *Bosch LE-Jetronic*
Number of gears: *5*

PERFORMANCE
Top speed: *215 km/h*
Acceleration (0–100 km/h): *8·4 sec*

DIMENSIONS
Length: *4·620 m*
Width: *1·700 m*
Height: *1·415 m*
Wheelbase: *2·625 m*
Doors: *4*
Seats: *5*
Fuel Capacity: *70 litres*

BMW 635CSi
Country of origin: *Germany*
Engine: *sohc S6*
Capacity: *3430cc*
Bore and stroke: *92·0 × 86·0 mm*
Power output: *218 bhp*
 @ 5500 rpm
Carburation: *DME-Motronic*
Number of gears: *5*

PERFORMANCE
Top speed: *229 km/h*
Acceleration (0–100 km/h): *7·4 sec*

DIMENSIONS
Length: *4·755 m*
Width: *1·725 m*
Height: *1·365 m*
Wheelbase: *2·630 m*
Doors: *2*
Seats: *4*
Fuel Capacity: *70 litres*

BMW 635 CSi

Mercedes 380 SEC

BMW 745i
Country of origin: *Germany*
Engine: *sohc S6*
Capacity: *3430cc*
Bore and stroke: *92·0 × 86·0 mm*
Power output: *252 bhp*
  @ 4900 rpm
Carburation: *DME-Motronic*
Number of gears: *Automatic*

PERFORMANCE
Top speed: *227 km/h*
Acceleration (0–100 km/h): *7·9 sec*

DIMENSIONS
Length: *4·860 m*
Width: *1·800 m*
Height: *1·430 m*
Wheelbase: *2·795 m*
Doors: *4*
Seats: *5*
Fuel Capacity: *70 litres*

BMW M535i: *See page 83*
BMW M635i: *See page 87*
BMW M323i: *See page 85*

MERCEDES-BENZ 190E
Country of origin: *Germany*
Engine: *sohc S4*
Capacity: *1997cc*
Bore and stroke: *89·0 × 80·3 mm*
Power output: *122 bhp*
  @ 5100 rpm
Carburation: *Bosch injection*
Number of gears: *4 or 5*

PERFORMANCE
Top speed: *195 km/h*
Acceleration (0–100 km/h): *10·5 sec*

DIMENSIONS
Length: *4·420 m*
Width: *1·678 m*
Height: *1·383 m*
Wheelbase: *2·665 m*
Doors: *4*
Seats: *5*
Fuel Capacity: *55 litres*

MERCEDES-BENZ 280 E
Country of origin: *Germany*
Engine: *2 × ohc S6*
Capacity: *2746cc*
Bore and stroke: *86·0 × 76·8 mm*
Power output: *185 bhp*
  @ 5800 rpm
Carburation: *Bosch injection*
Number of gears: *4 or 5*

PERFORMANCE
Top speed: *200 km/h*
Acceleration (0–100 km/h): *9·9 sec*

DIMENSIONS
Length: *4·725 m*
Width: *1·786 m*
Height: *1·438 m*
Wheelbase: *2·795 m*
Doors: *4*
Seats: *5*
Fuel Capacity: *80 litres*

MERCEDES-BENZ 280CE
Country of origin: *Germany*
Engine: *sohc S6*
Capacity: *2746cc*
Bore and stroke: *86·0 × 78·8 mm*
Power output: *185 bhp*
  @ 5800 rpm
Carburation: *Bosch K-Jetronic*
Number of gears: *4 or 5*

PERFORMANCE
Top speed: *200 km/h*
Acceleration (0–100 km/h): *9·9 sec*

DIMENSIONS
Length: *4·640 m*
Width: *1·786 m*
Height: *1·395 m*
Wheelbase: *2·710 m*
Doors: *2*
Seats: *5*
Fuel Capacity: *80 litres*

Mercedes 500 SEL

Opel Ascona 1.8i

MERCEDES-BENZ 280SE
Country of origin: *Germany*
Engine: *2 × ohc S6*
Capacity: *2746cc*
Bore and stroke: *86·0 × 78·8 mm*
Power output: *185 bhp*
 @ 5800 rpm
Carburation: *Bosch injection*
Number of gears: *4 or 5*

PERFORMANCE
Top speed: *210 km/h*
Acceleration (0–100 km/h): *10·0 sec*

DIMENSIONS
Length: *4·995 m*
Width: *1·820 m*
Height: *1·430 m*
Wheelbase: *2·935 m*
Doors: *4*
Seats: *5*
Fuel Capacity: *90 litres*

MERCEDES-BENZ 380SEL
Country of origin: *Germany*
Engine: *2 × ohc V8*
Capacity: *3839cc*
Bore and stroke: *88·0 × 78·9 mm*
Power output: *204 bhp*
 @ 5250 rpm
Carburation: *Bosch injection*
Number of gears: *Automatic*

PERFORMANCE
Top speed: *210 km/h*
Acceleration (0–100 km/h): *9·8 sec*

DIMENSIONS
Length: *5·135 m*
Width: *1·820 m*
Height: *1·440 m*
Wheelbase: *3·075 m*
Doors: *4*
Seats: *5*
Fuel Capacity: *90 litres*

MERCEDES-BENZ 500SEL
Country of origin: *Germany*
Engine: *2 × ohc V8*
Capacity: *4973cc*
Bore and stroke: *96·5 × 85·0 mm*
Power output: *231 bhp*
 @ 4750 rpm
Carburation: *Bosch injection*
Number of gears: *Automatic*

PERFORMANCE
Top speed: *225 km/h*
Acceleration (0–100 km/h): *8·1 sec*

DIMENSIONS
Length: *5·135 m*
Width: *1·820 m*
Height: *1·440 m*
Wheelbase: *3·070 m*
Doors: *4*
Seats: *5*
Fuel Capacity: *90 litres*

OPEL ASCONA 1·8i
Country of origin: *Germany*
Engine: *sohc S4*
Capacity: *1796cc*
Bore and stroke: *84·8 × 79·5 mm*
Power output: *115 bhp*
 @ 5800 rpm
Carburation: *Bosch LE-Jetronic*
Number of gears: *5*

PERFORMANCE
Top speed: *187 km/h*
Acceleration (0–100 km/h): *10·5 sec*

DIMENSIONS
Length: *4·360 m*
Width: *1·668 m*
Height: *1·395 m*
Wheelbase: *2·574 m*
Doors: *2, 4 or 5*
Seats: *5*
Fuel Capacity: *61 litres*

OPEL MANTA 400
Country of origin: *Germany*
Engine: *2 × ohc S4*
Capacity: *2410cc*
Bore and stroke: *95·0 × 85·0 mm*
Power output: *144 bhp at 5200 rpm*
Carburatin: *Bosch L-Jetronic*
Number of gears: *5*

PERFORMANCE
Top speed: *210 km/h*
Acceleration (0–100 km/h): *7·5 sec*

DIMENSIONS
Length: *4·475 m*
Width: *1·670 m*
Height: *1·320 m*
Wheelbase: *2·518 m*
Doors: *2*
Seats: *5*
Fuel Capacity: *50 litres*

OPEL MONZA 3.0i GSE
Country of origin: *Germany*
Engine: *sohc S6*
Capacity: *2969cc*
Bore and stroke: *95·0 × 69·8 mm*
Power output: *180 bhp @ 5800 rpm*
Carburation: *Bosch LE-Jetronic*
Number of gears: *5*

PERFORMANCE
Top speed: *215 km/h*
Acceleration (0–100 km/h): *8·5 sec*

DIMENSIONS
Length: *4·72 m*
Width: *1·722 m*
Height: *1·380 m*
Wheelbase: *2·668 m*
Doors: *3*
Seats: *5*
Fuel Capacity: *70 litres*

VW SCIROCCO 16V
Country of origin: *Germany*
Engine: *2 × ohc S4*
Capacity: *1781cc*
Bore and stroke: *81·0 × 86·4 mm*
Power output: *138 bhp @ 6300 rpm*
Carburation: *Injection*
Number of gears: *5*

PERFORMANCE
Top speed: *210 km/h*
Acceleration (0–100 km/h): *8·0 sec*

DIMENSIONS
Length: *4·050 m*
Width: *1·625 m*
Height: *1·280 m*
Wheelbase: *2·400 m*
Doors: *3*
Seats: *5*
Fuel Capacity: *55 litres*

Opel Monza

Opel Manta GTE

GREAT BRITAIN

ASTON MARTIN–LAGONDA
Country of origin: *Great Britain*
Engine: *4 × ohc V8*
Capacity: *5340cc*
Bore and stroke: *100·0 × 85·0 mm*
Power output: *305 bhp
@ 5000 rpm*
Carburation: *4 × Weber 42 DCNF*
Number of gears: *Automatic*

PERFORMANCE
Top speed: *225 km/h*
Acceleration (0–100 km/h): *8·8 sec*

DIMENSIONS
Length: *5·283 m*
Width: *1·816 m*
Height: *1·302 m*
Wheelbase: *2·908 m*
Doors: *4*
Seats: *5*
Fuel Capacity: *128 litres*

BENTLEY CORNICHE/ROLLS ROYCE CORNICHE
Country of origin: *Great Britain*
Engine: *ohv V8*
Capacity: *6750cc*
Bore and stroke: *104·1 × 99·1 mm*
Power output: *Adequate*
Carburation: *Solex A41*
Number of gears: *Automatic*

PERFORMANCE
Top speed: *198 km/h*
Acceleration (0–100 km/h): *Not available*

DIMENSIONS
Length: *5·200 m*
Width: *1·820 m*
Height: *1·520 m*
Wheelbase: *3·050 m*
Doors: *2*
Seats: *4*
Fuel Capacity: *107 litres*

BENTLEY MULSANNE AND BENTLEY 8
Country of origin: *Great Britain*
Engine: *ohv V8*
Capacity: *6750cc*
Bore and stroke: *104·1 × 99·1 mm*
Power output: *Adequate*
Carburation: *2 × SU HIF 7*
Number of gears: *Automatic*

PERFORMANCE
Top speed: *193 km/h*
Acceleration (0–100 km/h): *Not available*

DIMENSIONS
Length: *5·310 m*
Width: *1·890 m*
Height: *1·490 m*
Wheelbase: *3·060 m*
Doors: *4*
Seats: *5*
Fuel Capacity: *107 litres*

BENTLEY MULSANNE TURBO: *See page 157*

Aston Martin Lagonda

Bentley Mulsanne Turbo

BRISTOL BRITANNIA/BRIGAND
Country of origin: *Great Britain*
Engine: *ohv V8*
Capacity: *5898cc*
Bore and stroke: *101·6 × 90·93 mm*
Power output: *not specified*
Carburation: *1 × 4 Carter (Brigand with Turbo)*
Number of gears: *Automatic*

PERFORMANCE
Top speed: *225 km/h (240 km/h)*
Acceleration (0–100 km/h): *7·2 sec (5·9 sec)*

DIMENSIONS
Length: *4·91 m*
Width: *1·77 m*
Height: *1·43 m*
Wheelbase: *2·90 m*
Doors: *2*
Seats: *4*
Fuel Capacity: *82 litres*

FORD FIESTA XR2
Country of origin: *Great Britain/Germany*
Engine: *sohc S4*
Capacity: *1567cc*
Bore and stroke: *80·0 × 80·0 mm*
Power output: *96 bhp
@ 6000 rpm*
Carburation: *1 × Weber*
Number of gears: *5*

PERFORMANCE
Top speed: *180 km/h*
Acceleration (0–100 km/h):

DIMENSIONS
Length: *3·648 m*
Width: *1·620 m*
Height: *1·334 m*
Wheelbase: *2·288 m*
Doors: *3*
Seats: *5*
Fuel Capacity: *40 litres*

FORD ESCORT XR 3i: *See page*
FORD SIERRA XR4i: *See page 155*
FORD CAPRI 2.8i: *See page*

FORD CAPRI 2·8i
Country of origin: *Great Britain/Germany*
Engine: *ohv V6*
Capacity: *2772cc*
Bore and stroke: *93·0 × 68·5 mm*
Power output: *160 bhp
@ 5700 rpm*
Carburation: *Bosch K-Jetronic*
Number of gears: *5*

PERFORMANCE
Top speed: *210 km/h*
Acceleration (0–100 km/h): *8·3 sec*

DIMENSIONS
Length: *4·376 m*
Width: *1·698 m*
Height: *1·323 m*
Wheelbase: *2·608 m*
Doors: *2*
Seats: *4*
Fuel Capacity: *58 litres*

Jaguar XJS HE

MG Metro Turbo

JAGUAR HE SOVEREIGN
Country of origin: *Great Britain*
Engine: *2 × ohc V12*
Capacity: *5343cc*
Bore and stroke: *90·0 × 70·0 mm*
Power output: *299 bhp*
  @ 5500 rpm
Carburation: *Lucas–Bosch L-Jetronic*
Number of gears: *Automatic*

PERFORMANCE
Top speed: *225 km/h*
Acceleration (0–100km/h): *8·4 sec*

DIMENSIONS
Length: *4·959 m*
Width: *1·770 m*
Height: *1·377 m*
Wheelbase: *2·865 m*
Doors: *4*
Seats: *5*
Fuel Capacity: *91 litres*

JAGUAR XJS HE
Country of origin: *Great Britain*
Engine: *2 × ohc V12*
Capacity: *5343cc*
Bore and stroke: *90·0 × 70·0 mm*
Power output: *299 bhp*
  @ 5500 rpm
Carburation: *Lucas–Bosch L-Jetronic*
Number of gears: *Automatic*

PERFORMANCE
Top speed: *240 km/h*
Acceleration (0–100 km/h): *7·6 sec*

DIMENSIONS
Length: *4·743 m*
Width: *1·790 m*
Height: *1·260 m*
Wheelbase: *2·590 m*
Doors: *2*
Seats: *2 + 2*
Fuel Capacity: *91 litres*

JAGUAR XJ6 4·2
Country of origin: *Great Britain*
Engine: *2 × ohc S6*
Capacity: *4235cc*
Bore and stroke: *92·0 × 106·0 mm*
Power output: *205 bhp*
  @ 5000 rpm
Carburation: *Lucas–Bosch L-Jetronic*
Number of gears: *5*

PERFORMANCE
Top speed: *198 km/h*
Acceleration (0–100 km/h): *10·5 sec*

DIMENSIONS
Length: *4·959 m*
Width: *1·770 m*
Height: *1·377 m*
Wheelbase: *2·865 m*
Doors: *4*
Seats: *5*
Fuel Capacity: *91 litres*

ITALY

ALFA ROMEO 33 QUADRIFOGLIO VERDE
Country of origin: *Italy*
Engine: *2 × ohc S4*
Capacity: *1474cc*
Bore and stroke: *84·0 × 67·2 mm*
Power output: *105 bhp @ 6000 rpm*
Carburation: *2 × Weber*
Number of gears: *5*

PERFORMANCE
Top speed: *185 km/h*
Acceleration (0–100 km/h): *11·2 sec*

DIMENSIONS
Length: *4·022 m*
Width: *1·612 m*
Height: *1·340 m*
Wheelbase: *2·455 m*
Doors: *5*
Seats: *5*
Fuel Capacity: *50 litres*

ALFA ROMEO GIULIETTA 1·6
Country of origin: *Italy*
Engine: *2 × ohc S4*
Capacity: *1567cc*
Bore and stroke: *78·0 × 82·0 mm*
Power output: *108 bhp @ 5600 rpm*
Carburation: *2 × Dellorto*
Number of gears: *5*

PERFORMANCE
Top speed: *175 km/h*
Acceleration (0–100 km/h): *13·0 sec*

DIMENSIONS
Length: *4·210 m*
Width: *1·650 m*
Height: *1·400 m*
Wheelbase: *2·510 m*
Doors: *4*
Seats: *5*
Fuel Capacity: *50 litres*

ALFA ROMEO GIULIETTA 2·0
Country of origin: *Italy*
Engine: *2 × ohc S4*
Capacity: *1962cc*
Bore and stroke: *84·0 × 88·5 mm*
Power output: *130 bhp @ 5400 rpm*
Carburation: *2 × Solex C40*
Number of gears: *5*

PERFORMANCE
Top speed: *185 km/h*
Acceleration (0–100 km/h): *9·7 sec*

DIMENSIONS
Length: *4·210 m*
Width: *1·650 m*
Height: *1·400 m*
Wheelbase: *2·510 m*
Doors: *4*
Seats: *5*
Fuel Capacity: *50 litres*

ALFA ROMEO ALFETTA QUADRIFOGLIO
Country of origin: *Italy*
Engine: *2 × ohc S4*
Capacity: *1962cc*
Bore and stroke: *84·0 × 88·5 mm*
Power output: *130 bhp @ 5400 rpm*
Carburation: *2 × Solex C40*
Number of gears: *5*

PERFORMANCE
Top speed: *185 km/h*
Acceleration (0–100 km/h): *10·0 sec*

DIMENSIONS
Length: *4·385 m*
Width: *1·640 m*
Height: *1·430 m*
Wheelbase: *2·510 m*
Doors: *4*
Seats: *5*
Fuel Capacity: *49 litres*

ALFA ROMEO GTV6 2·5
Country of origin: *Italy*
Engine: *2 × ohc V6*
Capacity: *2492cc*
Bore and stroke: *88·0 × 68·3 mm*
Power output: *158 bhp @ 5600 rpm*
Carburation: *Bosch L-Jetronic*
Number of gears: *5*

PERFORMANCE
Top speed: *205 km/h*
Acceleration (0–100 km/h): *8·3 sec*

DIMENSIONS
Length: *4·260 m*
Width: *1·664 m*
Height: *1·330 m*
Wheelbase: *2·400 m*
Doors: *3*
Seats: *2 + 2*
Fuel Capacity: *75 litres*

ALFA ROMEO 33: *See page 143*

Alfa Romeo Giulietta Turbo

Alfa Romeo GTV6, 2.5

ALFA ROMEO ALFA 90 2·5 QUADRIFOGLIO ORO
Country of origin: *Italy*
Engine: *2 × ohc V6*
Capacity: *2492cc*
Bore and stroke: *88·0 × 68·3 mm*
Power output: *158 bhp*
  @ 5600 rpm
Carburation: *Bosch L-Jetronic*
Number of gears: *5*

PERFORMANCE
Top speed: *200 km/h*
Acceleration (0–100 km/h): *Not available*

DIMENSIONS
Length: *4·391 m*
Width: *1·638 m*
Height: *1·420 m*
Wheelbase: *2·510 m*
Doors: *4*
Seats: *5*
Fuel Capacity: *49 litres*

DE TOMASO DEAUVILLE
Country of origin: *Italy*
Engine: *ohv V8*
Capacity: *5763cc*
Bore and stroke: *101·6 × 88·9 mm*
Power output: *270 bhp*
  @ 6000 rpm
Carburation: *4 barrel Motocraft*
Number of gears: *Automatic*

PERFORMANCE
Top speed: *230 km/h*
Acceleration (0–100 km/h): *9·7 sec*

DIMENSIONS
Length: *4·925 m*
Width: *1·878 m*
Height: *1·368 m*
Wheelbase: *2·770 m*
Doors: *4*
Seats: *5*
Fuel Capacity: *100 litres*

Ferrari 400i

Lancia Delta

FERRARI 400i
Country of origin: *Italy*
Engine: *4 × ohc V12*
Capacity: *4823cc*
Bore and stroke: *81·0 × 78·0 mm*
Power output: *315 bhp*
  @ 6400 rpm
Carburation: *Bosch K-Jetronic*
Number of gears: *5*

PERFORMANCE
Top speed: *235 km/h*
Acceleration (0–100 km/h): *6·9 sec*

DIMENSIONS
Length: *4·810 m*
Width: *1·798 m*
Height: *1·314 m*
Wheelbase: *2·700 m*
Doors: *2*
Seats: *4*
Fuel Capacity: *120 litres*

FIAT RITMO 105TC: *See page 122*
FIAT RITMO 130TC: *See page 122*

INNOCENTI TURBO
Country of origin: *Italy*
Engine: *sohc S3*
Capacity: *993cc*
Bore and stroke: *76·0 × 73·0 mm*
Power output: *72 bhp*
  @ 6200 rpm
Carburation: *Nippondenso Turbo*
Number of gears: *5*

PERFORMANCE
Top speed: *160 km/h*
Acceleration (0–100 km/h): *10·8 sec*

DIMENSIONS
Length: *3·138 m*
Width: *1·530 m*
Height: *1·340 m*
Wheelbase: *2·048 m*
Doors: *3*
Seats: *4*
Fuel Capacity: *40 litres*

LANCIA DELTA TURBO HF
Country of origin: *Italy*
Engine: *2 × ohc S4*
Capacity: *1585cc*
Bore and stroke: *84·0 × 71·5 mm*
Power output: *130 bhp*
  @ 5600 rpm
Carburation: *1 × Weber and turbo*
Number of gears: *5*

PERFORMANCE
Top speed: *195 km/h*
Acceleration (0–100 km/h): *8·9 sec*

DIMENSIONS
Length: *3·895 m*
Width: *1·620 m*
Height: *1·380 m*
Wheelbase: *2·475 m*
Doors: *5*
Seats: *4*
Fuel Capacity: *45 litres*

LANCIA DELTA 1600GT: *See page 121*

LANCIA A112 ABARTH
Country of origin: *Italy*
Engine: *ohv S4*
Capacity: *1049cc*
Bore and stroke: *67·2 × 74·0 mm*
Power output: *70 bhp*
  @ 6600 rpm
Carburation: *1 × Weber 32 DMTR*
Number of gears: *5*

PERFORMANCE
Top speed: *154 km/h*
Acceleration (0–100 km/h): *13·6 sec*

DIMENSIONS
Length: *3·268 m*
Width: *1·480 m*
Height: *1·360 m*
Wheelbase: *2·038 m*
Doors: *3*
Seats: *4*
Fuel Capacity: *30 litres*

MASERATI BITURBO 2500 (EXECUTIVE)/BITURBO 425
Country of origin: *Italy*
Engine: *2 × ohc V6*
Capacity: *2491cc*
Bore and stroke: *91·6 × 63·0 mm*
Power output: *190 bhp @ 5500 rpm (2500) 200 bhp @ 5500 rpm (425)*
Carburation: *IHI and turbo*
Number of gears: *5*

PERFORMANCE
Top speed: *212 km/h (2500) 215 km/h (425)*
Acceleration (0–100 km/h): *6·6 sec (2500) 6.9 sec (425)*

DIMENSIONS
Length: *4·153 m (2500) 4·400 m (425)*
Width: *1·714 m (2500) 1·730 m (425)*
Height: *1·305 m (2500) 1·360 m (425)*
Wheelbase: *2·514 m (2500) 2·600 m (425)*
Doors: *2 (2500) 4 (425)*
Seats: *5*
Fuel Capacity: *82 litres*

MASERATI BITURBO 2000/2000S
Country of origin: *Italy*
Engine: *2 × ohc V6*
Capacity: *1895cc*
Bore and stroke: *82·0 × 63·0 mm*
Power output: *205 bhp @ 6500 rpm (S) 185 bhp @ 6000 rpm (2000)*
Carburation: *IHI and turbo*
Number of gears: *5*

PERFORMANCE
Top speed: *221 km/h (S) 215 km/h (2000)*

DIMENSIONS
Length: *4·153 m*
Width: *1·714 m*
Height: *1·305 m*
Wheelbase: *2·514 m*
Doors: *2*
Seats: *5*
Fuel Capacity: *80 litres*

MASERATI QUATTROPORTE
Country of origin: *Italy*
Engine: *4 × ohc V8*
Capacity: *4930cc*
Bore and stroke: *93·9 × 89·0 mm*
Power output: *280 bhp*
  @ 5600 rpm
Carburation: *4 × Weber 42 DCNF 6*
Number of gears: *5*

PERFORMANCE
Top speed: *230 km/h*

DIMENSIONS
Length: *4·980 m*
Width: *1·790 m*
Height: *1·350 m*
Wheelbase: *2·800 m*
Doors: *4*
Seats: *5*
Fuel Capacity: *100 litres*

JAPAN

DAIHATSU CHARADE TURBO
Country of origin: *Japan*
Engine: *sohc S3*
Capacity: *993cc*
Bore and stroke: *76·0 × 73·0 mm*
Power output: *80 bhp
@ 5500 rpm*
Carburation: *Twincarb and turbo*
Number of gears: *5*

PERFORMANCE
Top speed: *165 km/h*

DIMENSIONS
Length: *3·600 m*
Width: *1·395 m*
Height: *1·390 m*
Wheelbase: *2·320 m*
Doors: *3*
Seats: *5*
Fuel Capacity: *50 litres*

HONDA CITY TURBO
Country of origin: *Japan*
Engine: *sohc S4*
Capacity: *1231cc*
Bore and stroke: *66 × 99 mm*
Power output: *100 bhp @ 5500 rpm*
Carburation: *Injection*
Number of gears: *5*

PERFORMANCE
Top speed: *175 km/h*
Acceleration (0–100 km/h) 8·6 sec

DIMENSIONS
Length: *34·2 m*
Width: *1·625 m*
Height: *1·46 m*
Wheelbase: *2·22 m*
Doors: *3*
Seats: *5*
Fuel Capacity: *41 litres*

HONDA CIVIC COUPE CRX
Country of origin: *Japan*
Engine: *sohc S4*
Capacity: *1477cc*
Bore and stroke: *74·0 × 86·5 mm*
Power output: *100 bhp
@ 5750 rpm*
Carburation: *PGM injection*
Number of gears: *5*

PERFORMANCE
Top speed: *190 km/h*
Acceleration (0–100 km/h): *8·9 sec*

DIMENSIONS
Length: *3·675 m*
Width: *1·625 m*
Height: *1·290 m*
Wheelbase: *2·200 m*
Doors: *2*
Seats: *4*
Fuel Capacity: *41 litres*

Honda Ballade/Civic Sports CRX 1.5i

HONDA PRELUDE EX
Country of origin: *Japan*
Engine: *sohc S4*
Capacity: *1829cc*
Bore and stroke: *80·0 × 91·0 mm*
Power output: *105 bhp*
  @ 5500 rpm
Number of gears: *5*

PERFORMANCE
Top speed: *183 km/h*
Acceleration (0–100 km/h): *9·8 sec*

DIMENSIONS
Length: *4·295 m*
Width: *1·690 m*
Height: *1·295 m*
Wheelbase: *2·450 m*
Doors: *2*
Seats: *4*
Fuel Capacity: *60 litres*

HONDA ACCORD/VIGOR 1800Fi
Country of origin: *Japan*
Engine: *sohc S4*
Capacity: *1829cc*
Bore and stroke: *80·9 × 91·0 mm*
Power output: *130 bhp*
  @ 5800 rpm
Carburation: *injection*
Number of gears: *5*

PERFORMANCE
Top speed: *180 km/h*

DIMENSIONS
Length: *4·255 m*
Width: *1·665 m*
Height: *1·355 m*
Wheelbase: *2·450 m*
Doors: *3 or 4*
Seats: *5*
Fuel Capacity: *60 litres*

ISUZU PIAZZA TURBO
Country of origin: *Japan*
Engine: *sohc S4*
Capacity: *1994cc*
Bore and stroke: *88·0 × 82·0 mm*
Power output: *180 bhp*
  @ 5400 rpm
Number of gears: *5*

PERFORMANCE
Top speed: *180 km/h*

DIMENSIONS
Length: *4·385 m*
Width: *1·660 m*
Height: *1·300 m*
Wheelbase: *2·440 m*
Doors: *3*
Seats: *5*
Fuel Capacity: *58 litres*

ISUZU FLORIAN ASKA 2000 TURBO
Country of origin: *Japan*
Engine: *sohc S4*
Capacity: *1994cc*
Bore and stroke: *88·0 × 82·0 mm*
Power output: *150 bhp*
  @ 5400 rpm
Number of gears: *5*

PERFORMANCE
Top speed: *180 km/h*

DIMENSIONS
Length: *4·440 m*
Width: *1·670 m*
Height: *1·375 m*
Wheelbase: *2·580 m*
Doors: *4*
Seats: *5*
Fuel Capacity: *56 litres*

MAZDA 323GT
Country of origin: *Japan*
Engine: *sohc S4*
Capacity: *1479cc*
Bore and stroke: *77·0 × 80·0 mm*
Power output: *88 bhp*
  @ 6000 rpm
Carburation: *1 × Hitachi*
Number of gears: *5*

PERFORMANCE
Top speed: *168 km/h*

DIMENSIONS
Length: *3·965 m*
Width: *1·630 m*
Height: *1·375 m*
Wheelbase: *2·365 m*
Doors: *3*
Seats: *5*
Fuel Capacity: *42 litres*

MAZDA COSIMO 12A TURBO (ROTARY)
Country of origin: *Japan*
Engine: *Twin rotor Wankel*
Capacity: *2292cc*
Power output: *165 bhp*
  @ 6500 rpm
Number of gears: *5*

PERFORMANCE
Top speed: *180 km/h*

DIMENSIONS
Length: *4·640 m*
Width: *1·690 m*
Height: *1·340 m*
Wheelbase: *2·615 m*
Doors: *4 or 2*
Seats: *5*
Fuel Capacity: *60 litres*

Isuzu Florian Aska 2000 Turbo

MISTUBISHI CORDIA 1600 Turbo

Country of origin: *Japan*
Engine: *sohc S4*
Capacity: *1570cc*
Bore and stroke: *76·9 × 86·0 mm*
Power output: *114 bhp*
  @ 5500 rpm
Carburation: *Stromberg and turbo*
Number of gears: *4*

PERFORMANCE
Top speed: *183 km/h*
Acceleration (0–100 km/h): *not specified*

DIMENSIONS
Length: *4·275 m*
Width: *1·660 m*
Height: *1·320 m*
Wheelbase: *2·445 m*
Doors: *4*
Seats: *2*
Fuel Capacity: *50 litres*

MITSUBISHI COLT 1600 TURBO EC1

Country of origin: *Japan*
Engine: *sohc S4*
Capacity: *1597cc*
Bore and stroke: *76·9 × 86·0 mm*
Power output: *125 bhp*
  @ 5500 rpm
Carburation: *Nippon Denso*
Number of gears: *5*

PERFORMANCE
Top speed: *193 km/h*
Acceleration (0–100 km/h): *8·6 sec*

DIMENSIONS
Length: *3·995 m*
Width: *1·635 m*
Height: *1·360 m*
Wheelbase: *2·380 m*
Doors: *3*
Seats: *5*
Fuel Capacity: *45 litres*

MITSUBISHI GALANT 2000 TURBO EC1

Country of origin: *Japan*
Engine: *sohc S4*
Capacity: *1983cc*
Bore and stroke: *85·0 × 88·0 mm*
Power output: *150 bhp*
  @ 5500 rpm
Carburation: *Mikuni fuel injection and turbo*
Number of gears: *5*

PERFORMANCE
Top speed: *200 km/h*

DIMENSIONS
Length: *4·560 m*
Width: *1·695 m*
Height: *1·385 m*
Wheelbase: *2·600 m*
Doors: *4*
Seats: *5*
Fuel Capacity: *60 litres*

MITSUBISHI STARION TURBO

Country of origin: *Japan*
Engine: *sohc S4*
Capacity: *1983cc*
Bore and stroke: *85·0 × 88·0 mm*
Power output: *170 bhp*
  @ 5500 rpm
Carburation: *Turbo*
Number of Gears: *5*

PERFORMANCE
Top speed: *220 km/h*
Acceleration (0–100 km/h): *9·0 sec*

DIMENSIONS
Length: *4·425 m*
Width: *1·705 m*
Height: *1·315 m*
Wheelbase: *2·435 m*
Doors: *2*
Seats: *2 + 2*
Fuel Capacity: *75 litres*

NISSAN SILVIA

Country of origin: *Japan*
Engine: *2 × ohc S4*
Capacity: *1977cc*
Bore and stroke: *89·0 × 80·0 mm*
Power output: *145 bhp*
  @ 6400 rpm
Carburation: *L-Jetronic*
Number of gears: *5*

PERFORMANCE
Top speed: *205 km/h*
Acceleration (0–100 km/h): *9·6 sec*

DIMENSIONS
Length: *4·350 m*
Width: *1·660 m*
Height: *1·330 m*
Wheelbase: *2·425 m*
Doors: *3*
Seats: *2 + 2*
Fuel Capacity: *53 litres*

Mitsubishi Cordia 4WD Turbo

Mitsubishi Galant 2000 Turbo

NISSAN 300ZX

Country of origin: *Japan*
Engine: *2 × ohc V6*
Capacity: *2940cc*
Bore and stroke: *87·0 × 83·0 mm*
Power output: *170 bhp*
  @ 5600 rpm
Carburation: *L-Jetronic*
Number of gears: *5*

PERFORMANCE

Top speed: *220 km/h*
Acceleration (0–100 km/h): *9·1 sec*

DIMENSIONS

Length: *4·540 m*
Width: *1·725 m*
Height: *1·310 m*
Wheelbase: *2·220 m*
Doors: *3*
Seats: *2 + 2*
Fuel Capacity: *77 litres*

NISSAN SILVIA 2000RS TURBO

Country of origin: *Japan*
Engine: *2 × ohc S4*
Capacity: *1990cc*
Bore and stroke: *89·0 × 80·0 mm*
Power output: *190 bhp*
  @ 6400 rpm
Carburation: *Injection*
Number of gears: *5*

PERFORMANCE

Top speed: *180 km/h*

DIMENSIONS

Length: *4·350 m*
Width: *1·660 m*
Height: *1·330 m*
Wheelbase: *2·425 m*
Doors: *2 or 3*
Seats: *5*
Fuel Capacity: *60 litres*

NISSAN BLUEBIRD 1800 TURBO SSS

Country of origin: *Japan*
Engine: *sohc S4*
Capacity: *1809cc*
Bore and stroke: *83·0 × 83·6 mm*
Power output: *135 bhp*
  @ 6000 rpm
Carburation: *Injection*
Number of gears: *5*

PERFORMANCE

Top speed: *180 km/h*

DIMENSIONS

Length: *4·500 m*
Width: *1·690 m*
Height: *1·395 m*
Wheelbase: *2·550 m*
Doors: *4*
Seats: *5*
Fuel Capacity: *60 litres*

Nissan Bluebird 1800 Turbo SSS

Nissan Skyline 2000 RS Turbo

NISSAN SKYLINE 2000RS TURBO

Country of origin: *Japan*
Engine: *2 × ohc S4*
Capacity: *1990cc*
Bore and stroke: *89·0 × 80·0 mm*
Power output: *205 bhp*
  @ 6400 rpm
Carburation: *Injection*
Number of gears: *5*

PERFORMANCE

Top speed: *180 km/h*

DIMENSIONS

Length: *4·620 m*
Width: *1·675 m*
Height: *1·360 m*
Wheelbase: *2·615 m*
Doors: *4 or 2*
Seats: *5*
Fuel Capacity: *60 litres*

NISSAN FAIRLADY Z2300

Country of origin: *Japan*
Engine: *sohc V6*
Capacity: *2960cc*
Bore and stroke: *87·0 × 83·0 mm*
Power output: *230 bhp*
  @ 5200 rpm
Carburation: *Injection*
Number of gears: *5*

PERFORMANCE

Top speed: *180 km/h*

DIMENSIONS

Length: *4·530 m*
Width: *1·690 m*
Height: *1·310 m*
Wheelbase: *2·520 m*
Doors: *2*
Seats: *2 + 2*
Fuel Capacity: *72 litres*

Toyota Celica Coupe GT

TOYOTA COROLLA/SPRINTER 1600 GT

Country of origin: *Japan*
Engine: *sohc S4*
Capacity: *1587cc*
Bore and stroke: *81·0 × 77·0 mm*
Power output: *100 bhp @ 5600 rpm*
Carburation: *Injection*
Number of gears: *5*

PERFORMANCE

Top speed: *180 km/h*

DIMENSIONS

Length: *4·135 m*
Width: *1·635 m*
Height: *1·385 m*
Wheelbase: *2·430 m*
Doors: *4 or 5*
Seats: *5*
Fuel Capacity: *50 litres*

TOYOTA CELICA XX2000GT TWIN CAM

Country of origin: *Japan*
Engine: *2 × ohc S6*
Capacity: *1988cc*
Bore and stroke: *75·0 × 75·0 mm*
Power output: *160 bhp @ 6400 rpm*
Carburation: *Injection*
Number of gears: *5*

PERFORMANCE

Top speed: *180 km/h*

DIMENSIONS

Length: *4·460 m*
Width: *1·685 m*
Height: *1·315 m*
Wheelbase: *2·615 m*
Doors: *2 or 3*
Seats: *5*
Fuel Capacity: *61 litres*

NISSAN LEOPARD 2000 TURBO

Country of origin: *Japan*
Engine: *sohc S6*
Capacity: *1998cc*
Bore and stroke: *78·0 × 69·7 mm*
Power output: *145 bhp @ 5600 rpm*
Carburation: *Injection*
Number of gears: *5*

PERFORMANCE

Top speed: *180 km/h*
Acceleration (0–100 km/h): *not specified*

DIMENSIONS

Length: *4·64 m*
Width: *1·69 m*
Height: *1·345 m*
Wheelbase: *2·625 m*
Doors: *2 or 4*
Seats: *5*
Fuel Capacity: *65 litres*

TOYOTA CELICA COUPE GT

Country of origin: *Japan*
Engine: *2 × ohc S4*
Capacity: *1587cc*
Bore and stroke: *81·0 × 77·0 mm*
Power output: *124 bhp @ 6600 rpm*
Number of gears: *5*

PERFORMANCE

Top speed: *190 km/h*
Acceleration (0–100 km/h): *10·5 sec*

DIMENSIONS

Length: *4·435 m*
Width: *1·665 m*
Height: *1·320 m*
Wheelbase: *2·500 m*
Doors: *2*
Seats: *5*
Fuel Capacity: *61 litres*

TOYOTA CELICA XX2800GT

Country of origin: *Japan*
Engine: *2 × ohc S6*
Capacity: *2759cc*
Bore and stroke: *83·0 × 85·0 mm*
Power output: *175 bhp @ 5600 rpm*
Carburation: *Injection*
Number of gears: *5*

PERFORMANCE

Top speed: *180 km/h*

DIMENSIONS

Length: *4·460 m*
Width: *1·685 m*
Height: *1·315 m*
Wheelbase: *2·615 m*
Doors: *3*
Seats: *5*
Fuel Capacity: *61 litres*

SOVIET UNION

GAZ TCHAIKA GAZ-14
Country of origin: *Soviet Union*
Engine: *sohc V8*
Capacity: *5529cc*
Bore and stroke: *100·0 × 88·0 mm*
Power output: *220 bhp
@ 4200 rpm*
Number of gears: *Automatic*

PERFORMANCE
Top speed: *175 km/h*
Acceleration (0–100 km/h): *15·0 sec*

DIMENSIONS
Length: *6·115 m*
Width: *2·020 m*
Height: *1·580 m*
Wheelbase: *3·450 m*
Doors: *4*
Seats: *5 or 7*
Fuel Capacity: *120 litres*

SWEDEN

SAAB 900 TURBO
Country of origin: *Sweden*
Engine: *sohc S4*
Capacity: *1985cc*
Bore and stroke: *90·0 × 78·0 mm*
Power output: *145 bhp
@ 5000 rpm*
Carburation: *Bosch CL-Injection with
turbo*
Number of gears: *5*

PERFORMANCE
Top speed: *195 km/h*
Acceleration (0–100 km/h): *9·0 sec*

DIMENSIONS
Length: *4·740 m*
Width: *1·690 m*
Height: *1·425 m*
Wheelbase: *2·517 m*
Doors: *3, 4 or 5*
Seats: *5*
Fuel Capacity: *63 litres*

SAAB 900 TURBO 16/16S
Country of origin: *Sweden*
Engine: *2 × ohc S4*
Capacity: *1985cc*
Bore and stroke: *90·0 × 78·0 mm*
Power output: *175 bhp @
5300 rpm*
Carburation: *Bosch LH-Injection with
turbo*
Number of gears: *5*

PERFORMANCE
Top speed: *205 km/h*
Acceleration (0–100 km/h): *8·7 sec*

DIMENSIONS
Length: *4·740 m*
Width: *1·690 m*
Height: *1·425 m*
Wheelbase: *2·517 m*
Doors: *3, 4 or 5*
Seats: *5*
Fuel Capacity: *63 litres*

VOLVO 360GLE
Country of origin: *Sweden*
Engine: *sohc S4*
Capacity: *1986cc*
Bore and stroke: *88·9 × 80·0 mm*
Power output: *115 bhp
@ 5700 rpm*
Carburation: *Bosch LE-Jetronic*
Number of gears: *5*

PERFORMANCE
Top speed: *185 km/h*
Acceleration (0–100 km/h): *11·0 sec*

DIMENSIONS
Length: *4·415 m*
Width: *1·660 m*
Height: *1·435 m*
Wheelbase: *2·400 m*
Doors: *4*
Seats: *5*
Fuel Capacity: *57 litres*

VOLVO 240 TURBO
Country of origin: *Sweden*
Engine: *sohc S4*
Capacity: *2127cc*
Bore and stroke: *92·0 × 80·0 mm*
Power output: *155 bhp
@ 5500 rpm*
Carburation: *Bosch K-Jetronic*
Number of gears: *5*

PERFORMANCE
Top speed: *190 km/h*
Acceleration (0–100 km/h): *8·9 sec*

DIMENSIONS
Length: *4·785 m*
Width: *1·707 m*
Height: *1·435 m*
Wheelbase: *2·640 m*
Doors: *5*
Seats: *5*
Fuel Capacity: *60 litres*

VOLVO 760 TURBO: *See page 152*

Volvo 360 GLE Injection

BUICK SKYHAWK 1·8 TURBO

Country of origin: *USA*
Engine: *sohc S4*
Capacity: *1796cc*
Bore and stroke: *84·8 × 79·5 mm*
Power output: *152 bhp*
  @ 5600 rpm
Carburation: *Bosch-Jetronic*
Number of gears: *4*

PERFORMANCE

Top speed: *150 km/h*
Acceleration (0–100 km/h): *10·2 sec*

DIMENSIONS

Length: *4·453 m*
Width: *1·575 m*
Height: *1·372 m*
Wheelbase: *2·570 m*
Doors: *2*
Seats: *5*
Fuel Capacity: *52 litres*

BUICK REGAL 3·8 TURBO

Country of origin: *USA*
Engine: *sohc V6*
Capacity: *3791cc*
Bore and stroke: *96·5 × 86·4 mm*
Power output: *203 bhp*
Carburation: *Injection*
Number of gears: *Automatic*

PERFORMANCE

Top speed: *205 km/h*
Acceleration (0–100 km/h): *8·5 sec*

DIMENSIONS

Length: *5·094 m*
Width: *1·816 m*
Height: *1·386 m*
Wheelbase: *2·745 m*
Doors: *2*
Seats: *6*
Fuel Capacity: *79 litres*

CHEVROLET CAMARO 228 5·0 HO

Country of origin: *USA*
Engine: *ohv V8*
Capacity: *5002cc*
Bore and stroke: *94·9 × 88·4 mm*
Power output: *193 bhp*
  @ 4800 rpm
Carburation: *1 × 4 Rochester*
Number of gears: *5*

PERFORMANCE

Top speed: *205 km/h*
Acceleration (0–100 km/h): *8·0 sec*

DIMENSIONS

Length: *4·771 m*
Width: *1·829 m*
Height: *1·264 m*
Wheelbase: *2·566 m*
Doors: *2*
Seats: *4*
Fuel Capacity: *61 litres*

1985 Chevrolet Camaro Z28

Dodge Omni GLH

CHRYSLER LeBARON 2·2 TURBO

Country of origin: *USA*
Engine: *sohc S4*
Capacity: *2213cc*
Bore and stroke: *87·5 × 92·0 mm*
Power output: *144 bhp*
  @ 5600 rpm
Carburation: *Chrysler–Bosch injection*
Number of gears: *Automatic*

PERFORMANCE
Top speed: *177 km/h*
Acceleration (0–100 km/h): *9·5 sec*

DIMENSIONS
Length: *4·564 m*
Width: *1·740 m*
Height: *1·344 m*
Wheelbase: *2·538 m*
Doors: *2*
Seats: *4-6*
Fuel Capacity: *53 litres*

CHRYSLER LASER 2·2 TURBO

Country of origin: *USA*
Engine: *sohc S4*
Capacity: *2213cc*
Bore and stroke: *87·5 × 92·0 mm*
Power output: *144 bhp*
  @ 5600 rpm
Carburation: *Chrysler–Bosch-injection*
Number of gears: *5*

PERFORMANCE
Top speed: *182 km/h*
Acceleration (0–100 km/h): *9·0 sec*

DIMENSIONS
Length: *4·445 m*
Width: *1·745 m*
Height: *1·298 m*
Wheelbase: *2·461 m*
Doors: *2*
Seats: *4*
Fuel Capacity: *49 litres*

DODGE OMNI 2·2 GLH

Country of origin: *USA*
Engine: *sohc S4*
Capacity: *2213cc*
Bore and stroke: *87·5 × 92·0 mm*
Power output: *111 bhp*
  @ 5600 rpm
Carburation: *1 × 2 Holley*
Number of gears: *5*

PERFORMANCE
Top speed: *180 km/h*
Acceleration (0–100 km/h): *9·0 sec*

DIMENSIONS
Length: *4·187 m*
Width: *1·670 m*
Height: *1·349 m*
Wheelbase: *2·520 m*
Doors: *5*
Seats: *5*
Fuel Capacity: *49 litres*

DODGE SHELBY CHARGER

Country of origin: *USA*
Engine: *sohc S4*
Capacity: *2213cc*
Bore and stroke: *87·5 × 92·0 mm*
Power output: *111 bhp*
  @ 5600 rpm
Carburation: *1 × 2 Holley*
Number of gears: *5*

PERFORMANCE
Top speed: *190 km/h*
Acceleration (0–100 km/h): *8·8 sec*

DIMENSIONS
Length: *4·412 m*
Width: *1·694 m*
Height: *1·290 m*
Wheelbase: *2·456 m*
Doors: *3*
Seats: *5*
Fuel Capacity: *49 litres*

1985 Ford Mustang GT

FORD ESCORT 1·6 TURBO
Country of origin: *USA*
Engine: *sohc S4*
Capacity: *1598cc*
Bore and stroke: *80·0 × 79·5 mm*
Power output: *90 bhp*
  @ 5200 rpm
Carburation: *Injection*
Number of gears: *5*

PERFORMANCE
Top speed: *185 km/h*
Acceleration (0–100 km/h): *9·0 sec*

DIMENSIONS
Length: *4·162 m*
Width: *1·673 m*
Height: *1·353 m*
Wheelbase: *2·393 m*
Doors: *3 or 5*
Seats: *4*
Fuel Capacity: *49 litres*

FORD MUSTANG 2·3 TURBO
Country of origin: *USA*
Engine: *sohc S4*
Capacity: *2301cc*
Bore and stroke: *96·0 × 79·4 mm*
Power output: *147 bhp*
  @ 4600 rpm
Carburation: *Injection*
Number of gears: *5*

PERFORMANCE
Top speed: *185 km/h*
Acceleration (0–100 km/h): *9·0 sec*

DIMENSIONS
Length: *4·540 m*
Width: *1·750 m*
Height: *1·320 m*
Wheelbase: *2·550 m*
Doors: *2 or 3*
Seats: *4*
Fuel Capacity: *58 litres*

FORD MUSTANG 4·9
Country of origin: *USA*
Engine: *sohc V8*
Capacity: *4942cc*
Bore and stroke: *101·0 × 76·0 mm*
Power output: *208 bhp*
  @   rpm
Carburation: *1 × 4 holley*
Number of gears: *5*

PERFORMANCE
Top speed: *230 km/h*
Acceleration (0–100 km/h): *6·5 sec*

DIMENSIONS
Length: *4·549 m*
Width: *1·754 m*
Height: *1·319 m*
Wheelbase: *2·550 m*
Doors: *2 or 3*
Seats: *4*
Fuel Capacity: *58 litres*

10 Index

PICTURE CREDITS

½-title: *Bitter*, Title: *Opel*, 6: *Lancia*, 7: *AC Cars*, 8: *NMM*, 9: *NMM*, 10: *Vauxhall*, 10 below: *NMM*, 14 top: *NMM*, 14 middle: *Coys Ltd*, 14 below: *Coys Ltd*: 16 top: *NMM*, 16 below: *Coys Ltd*, 18: *NMM*, 21 top: *NMM*, 21 below: *BMW*, 23: *Pininfarina*, 24: *Coys Ltd*, 24 below: *NMM*, 25: *M Decet*, 26: *NMM*, 28: *Alfa-Romeo*, 29: *AC Cars*, 30: *Bristol Cars*, 31: *Bristol Cars*, 32: *NMM*, 33: *NMM*, 33: *NMM*, 34: *M. Decet*, 37: *M. Decet*, 38: *NMM*, 39: *Rolls Royce*, 42: *M. Decet*, 42: *M. Decet*, 43: *M. Decet*, 44: *M. Decet*, 45: *Jaguar*, 45 below: *Ferrari*, 46: *BMW*, 48: *Citroen*, 50: *Renault*, 51: *M. Decet*, 52: *M. Decet*, 53: *Ford*, 56: *Citroen*, 57: *BMW*, 58: *BMW*, 59 below: *Fiat*, 60: *M. Decet*, 61: *Jaguar*, 62: *M. Decet*, 63: *Ford*, 64: *Ford*, 64 below: *Renault*, 65: *M. Decet*, 66: *Ford*, 67: *Ford US*, 68: *Ford US*, 69: *Julian McNamara*, 71: *LAT Photographic*, 72: *Ford*, 74: *Coys Ltd*, 76: *Tim Marlborough*, 77: *BMW*, 78: *Jaguar*, 78: *Jaguar*, 80: *Julian McNamara*, 82: *BMW*, 84: *BMW*, 86: *BMW*, 88: *Julian McNamara*, 90: *Mercedes Benz*: 91: *Mercedes Benz*, 93: *Julian McNamara*, 94: *VAG*, 96: *Tim Marlborough*, 96 below: *Ford*, 97: *Ford*, 98: *Tim Marlborough*, 99: *Fiat*, 100: *Opel*, 102: *VAG*, 104: *Julian McNamara*, 106: *Ford*, 108: *Opel*, 109: *Julian McNamara*, 110: *Renault*, 111: *Renault*, 112: *Citroen*, 113: *Peugeot*, 115: *Alfa Romeo*, 116: *British Leyland*, 116: *British Leyland*, 118: *M. Wood*, 120: *Lancia*, 123: *Julian McNamara*, 125: *Lancia*, 126: *Nissan*, 127: *Saab*, 127: *Julian McNamara*, 128: *Ford US*, 128: *Ford US*, 129: *Ford US*, 130: *Chrysler*, 131: *Chrysler*, 132: *Peugeot*, 134: *Toyota*, 134: *Honda*, 135: *Nissan*, 136: *Austin Rover*, 138: *Alfa Romeo*, 140: *Saab*, 140: *Alfa Romeo*, 141: *Alfa Romeo*, 143: *Alfa Romeo*, 144: *Lancia*, 145: *Lancia*, 146: *Mercedes Benz*, 148: *Citroen*, 149: *Julian McNamara*, 150: *VAG*, 152: *Saab*, 153: *Volvo*, 154: *Julian McNamara*, 156: *Rolls Royce*, 157: *Julian McNamara*, 158: *Bristol*, 160: *Bitter*, 160 below: *Ferrari*, 162 top: *Tatra*, 162 below: *Skoda*, 163: *Renault*, 164: *Renault*, 165: *Audi*, 166: *Audi*, 168 top: *BMW*, 168 middle: *Mercedes Benz*, 169 top: *Mercedes Benz*, 169 middle: *Opel*, 170: *Opel*, 171 top: *Aston-Martin*, 171 middle: *Rolls-Royce*, 172 top: *Jaguar*, 172 middle: *Austin-Rover*, 173: *Alfa-Romeo*, 174: *Ferraro*, 174/5: *Lancia*, 176: *Honda*, 177: *Isuzu*, 178: *Mitsubishi*, 179: *Nissan*, 180: *Toyota*, 181: *Volvo*, 182 top: *Chevrolet*, 182 below: *Chrysler*, 184: *Ford US*.